Simple Library Cataloging

by

Susan Grey Akers

Fifth Edition

The Scarecrow Press, Inc.

Metuchen, N.J.   1969

Contents

Introduction

The catalog. In making a catalog for a particular library one needs to consider the community or institution which is to be served. Is it growing or shrinking? What is the present size of the library? Its probable future size? Is it likely to be merged into a larger system in the near future? In deciding upon what materials to acquire, what records to keep, what methods to use, are there any legal restrictions that might affect them? For instance in a school or college library what courses are offered? Does the library have to submit reports to a central agency, such as a state library, the city or county superintendent of schools? What information is required for that report?

The use to be made of the materials and the best ways of serving the library's clientele are the first considerations in deciding upon the type of cataloging. Costs and time, however, must also be considered. It is not worthwhile to develop a plan which will require a larger staff and involve higher costs than are available or likely to become so. Adopt the simplest plan and method of control of material which will meet the needs of the library's clientele now and in the foreseeable future. Materials should be prepared and put out for use as soon as possible after they are received. For example, a book, pamphlet, map which would be of real use in a course if it is made available this week, if not may be of no value for another year. On the other hand a system which simplifies to the extent that it does not distinguish clearly between materials, as editions of the classics, and when the library grows the work has to be done over, is not a good system. Time and money saved in organizing materials that make it necessary to give much more personal service as in reference work is not really a saving. A good system for one library may not be a good one for another library because of different conditions. This is an age of cooperation and centralization, however, and insofar as it serves their purpose and clientele libraries should catalog and classify as other libraries do. Patrons use other libraries and it is an advantage if the libraries are alike.

A catalog is a record of the material in a library. It answers such questions as: What books have you by Robert

Nathan? Have you a copy of Some Enchanted Evenings? Have you material on interplanetary voyages? The catalog can also answer questions about the individual author or book, for instance: What is the most recent book in the library by A. J. Cronin? Does Schlesinger's Rise of Modern America include illustrations? Who published Anne Terry White's Prehistoric America? Besides showing what authors' works are represented in the library, whether or not the library has material on a given subject or contains a particular book, whether or not a certain book has illustrations, and so forth, the catalog may bring out portions of books; for example, there may be a card for High Tor in Barrett H. Clark's Nine Modern American Plays, and one for material on Christmas in J. Walker McSpadden's The Book of Holidays.

A given book is represented in the catalog under its author, title, and, if nonfiction--or, in some libraries, even if fiction--under the subject of which it treats. To illustrate: City Neighbor: the Story of Jane Addams would have cards under the title, City Neighbor; the author, Clara Ingram Judson; and under the subjects ADDAMS, JANE and HULL HOUSE, CHICAGO. Books may also be found under the name of the series, if it is an important subject series, e. g. , "American Guide Series. " In addition to the cards for specific books there are reference cards referring the reader from the form of the author's name under which he may look to the form used in that catalog:

Maxtone Graham, Joyce Anstruther

See

Struther, Jan, pseud.

There are also cards referring the reader from the term or terms under which he may look for material on a subject to the term or terms used in the catalog for that subject:

INTERSTELLAR VOYAGES

See

INTERPLANETARY VOYAGES.

Purpose of this manual. This book has a three-fold purpose: (1) to give to the librarian of the small public, school, college, or special library who lacks professional education and experience under expert guidance the necessary directions for classifying and cataloging a collection of printed and audiovisual materials, that they may be made accessible; (2) to serve as a textbook for short elementary courses in cataloging; and (3) to serve as collateral reading in the earlier parts of the basic cataloging courses. Fundamental rules for classifying and directions for using the Dewey Decimal Classification tables are given. An effort has been made to state the necessary cataloging rules as clearly, simply, and briefly as possible. No attempt has been made to suggest all of the possible ways of cataloging a small library.

Order of the chapters. There were three groups of users to be considered in deciding upon the order in which to arrange the chapters: (1) instructors of courses in cataloging; (2) inexperienced librarians with little or no training who study this book alone and follow it through in direct connection with their work; and (3) librarians using the book as a catalog code. The first group is the most diverse and thus was considered least. Cataloging instructors, like instructors in other subjects, vary widely in the order and the method they follow in presenting topics. It is expected, therefore, that they will use the material in whatever order best suits the requirements of their courses. The material has been arranged with reference to the convenience of the second group especially and to some extent to that of the third. It is logical in bringing together closely related topics; e. g. , Chapter I treats of classification and Chapter II of subject headings, two allied processes. Then follow the chapters which deal with the headings used as entries; and these chapters in turn are followed by the ones concerned with the actual description of the book in the catalog entry.

Scope. The following paragraphs summarize the contents of the chapters and indicate the changes made in this edition. It is based on and where necessary reference should be made to the Anglo-American Cataloging Rules, 1967; the ninth edition of the Sears List of Subject Headings, edited by Barbara M. Westby; and the seventeenth unabridged and the ninth abridged editions of the Dewey Decimal Classification system.

Recent books have been substituted in many of the examples. As in former editions there is an appendix of sample catalog cards; an appendix of abbreviations, revised to conform with the practice of the new rules for headings and the body of the entry; an appendix of definitions of technical terms, almost all of which are taken from the A. L. A. Glossary of Library Terms or the Anglo-American Cataloging Rules, 1967; and an appendix which gives a short bibliography of aids for author's names, subject headings, filing cards, etc.

Chapter I defines and describes classification and discusses book numbers. Illustrations are taken from the seventeenth unabridged and the ninth abridged editions of the Dewey Decimal Classification tables. Chapter II on subject headings has illustrations from the ninth edition of the Sears List. Chapters III-V, treating of personal names, anonymous classics and sacred books, and names of organizations have been rewritten to incorporate the changes made in the new edition of the catalog rules.

Chapters VI and VII deal respectively with main and added entries.

Chapter VIII on cataloging sets, serials, and independent works bound together is much the same as in earlier editions. Chapter IX on cataloging audio-visual materials has been revised to conform to the changes in the new rules for these types of materials.

Chapter X, as its changed title suggests, has been enlarged to include information on centralized and cooperative cataloging and processing. Centers and agencies are suggested which the reader might contact in order to ascertain what services would be available to and suitable for his library. The chapter also includes detailed directions for ordering and adapting to a given catalog the printed catalog cards of the H. W. Wilson Company and the Library of Congress, the oldest form of centralized cataloging.

If it is decided to take advantage of a centralized cataloging and processing agency, this manual may still prove useful. It contains basic information on the Dewey Decimal Classification and the Sears List of Subject Headings, both of which works are used in the majority of small libraries; and tells how to make catalog cards, useful information in the case of books not included in those cataloged by the agency selected and for which printed cards are not available from Wilson or the Library of Congress. Much of the other information given in this manual, for instance, the chapter on arranging cards in a catalog, is necessary for the librarian who subscribes for centralized cataloging but is responsible for filing the cards in his catalog, keeping classification numbers consistent, etc.

Chapter XI on arranging cards in a dictionary catalog has been rewritten to incorporate the new ALA filing rules, 1968. Chapter XII, ''Related Topics and Miscellaneous Information,'' has been revised to bring up-to-date the procedures described; and the information on cataloging supplies and equipment.

Throughout the manual significant--and in some cases insignificant--changes that will be made in libraries as an indirect effect of centralized cataloging and processing have been noted. The policies adopted by such centers, whether libraries or commercial firms, will influence libraries in such matters, for instance, as the use of book numbers.

Acknowledgments

The author wishes to acknowledge the courtesy of the American Library Association in granting permission to have this edition of her manual published. It contains not only material from the earlier editions to which they hold the copyright but also material from the Anglo-American Cataloging Rules, 1967 and the A L A Rules for Filing Catalog Cards, 2d ed. abr., 1968. All chapters and sections on cataloging rules are based on, hence are largely quotations from, the A. -A. rules, 1967, as indicated by quotation marks throughout. Many of the names illustrating these rules are also from this code, in this case quotation marks are not used as they would seem to complicate the text unnecessarily. The names so used were checked with the Standard Catalog Series of the H. W. Wilson Company as giving some indication of their suitability for this manual. Other illustrative names are from the fourth edition of this book or were selected by the author for this edition.

The author is under obligation to the Forest Press, Inc., owners of the copyright, for permission to reproduce parts of the Dewey Decimal Classification, Edition 17 and 9th Abridged Edition, copyrighted 1965; and to base certain rules for classifying on the Guide to Use of Dewey Decimal Classification; Based on the Practice of the Decimal Classification Office at the Library of Congress, copyrighted 1962.

The author wishes to express her appreciation of the kindness of the H. W. Wilson Company and the Library of Congress in granting permission to use their printed catalog cards freely as sample cards.

The author is also much indebted to Miss Pauline A. Seeley, Director, Technical Services, The Public Library, the City and County of Denver, Colorado, for her helpful criticism of the order of arrangement of the filing rules in Chapter XI; to Mr. Budd L. Gambee, Associate Professor, the School of Library Science, the University of North Carolina, Chapel Hill for his counsel regarding aids and the types of materials included in Chapter IX; and to Miss Ethel M. Fair, former Director, Library School, New Jersey College for Women, New Brunswick, N. J., for many valuable suggestions and for her encouragement throughout the task of this revision.

Chapel Hill, North Carolina
1969

S. G. A.

Chapter I
Classification

Definition. "To classify books is to place them in groups, each group including, as nearly as may be, all the books treating a given subject, for instance, geology; or all the books, on whatever subject, cast in a particular form, for instance poetry; or all the books having to do with a particular period of time, for instance, the Middle Ages,. . . . Its purpose is . . . to make. . . books more available. "[1]

Reasons for classifying. If a miscellaneous collection of books is to be used with ease, it should be arranged in some way. The books could be sorted and put on the shelves in alphabetical order according to their authors or titles. A collection arranged in that way would be many times more useful than a collection without any arrangement. Collections of books, however, are consulted more for material on a given subject than for any other purpose. Readers like to have the books on the same subject together, as they much prefer examining the books to searching a list or a catalog.

Dewey Decimal Classification scheme. If books are to be classified by subject, some scheme or system of classification should be adopted. Melvil Dewey's Decimal Classification is the one most widely used in the United States, especially in public and school libraries. It has also been adopted by many libraries in foreign countries. The Booklist and Subscription Books Bulletin, the H. W. Wilson Company's Standard Catalog Series, and many other library publications use this classification system. It is published in two forms, the unabridged[2] and the abridged. [2]

This system is called the decimal system because each class may be subdivided into ten divisions, each subdivision into ten further ones, the numbers being considered as decimals, not consecutive numbers. The ten main classes of the system are:

000 Generalities	200 Religion
100 Philosophy & related disciplines	300 The social sciences

400 Language   700 The arts

500 Pure sciences   800 Literature & rhetoric

600 Technology (Applied sci-   900 General geography,
    ences)   history, etc.

One hundred three-digit numbers are the notation used to
designate each class, e. g. , 500-599 for the pure sciences. The
first division of each class is used for general works on that
class, e. g. , 500-509 for general works on the sciences; the
subsequent divisions for the main divisions of the subject, e.g.,
510-519 for mathematics; 520-529 for astronomy and allied
sciences. In turn each subdivision is divided into ten sections,
e. g. , 510 for general works on the subject of mathematics;
511 for works on arithmetic; 512 for works on algebra. The
system can be further subdivided by adding a decimal point
after any set of three digits from 000 to 999. Adding as many
digits as are required, e. g. , 511. 4 for works on fractions and
decimal fractions, 523 descriptive astronomy; 523. 7 the sun;
523. 78 eclipses. The abridged edition of the Decimal Classification shortens or reduces the numbers, hence neither 511. 4
nor 523. 78 are in the 9th abridged edition tables. Similar
omissions will be found throughout the abridged edition.

Although as indicated above the classification is generally by subject, subarrangement is often desirable by the form
or presentation of a subject, e. g. , a dictionary of medicine,
a periodical of history, a work on how to teach mathematics.
These various forms or methods of treatment of a subject are
shown in the "Table of Standard Subdivisions. " Earlier editions of the Dewey Decimal Classification called them "form
divisions. " They are:

-01 Philosophy and theory   -06 Organizations

-02 Miscellany   -07 Study and teaching

-03 Dictionaries, encyclo-   -08 Collections and
    pedias, concordances   anthologies

-05 Serial publications   -09 Historical and geo-
                                         graphical treat-
                                         ment

A comparison of these standard subdivisions with the
form divisions in earlier editions shows that -02 Miscellany
replaces -02 Handbooks and outlines; in -03 Concordances have
been added to Dictionaries and encyclopedias; -04 is no longer
used for essays and lectures, collections of which have been
relocated in -08. A given library having used the old standard

subdivisions will probably have to continue their use, but can take advantage of the new ones under headings being used or being divided by standard subdivisions for the first time. The dash (-) preceding each number in this table emphasizes the fact that these standard subdivisions are never used alone but may be used with almost any number from the general tables, e. g., 511 arithmetic; 511. 07 study and teaching of arithmetic. Analyzing the number for mathematics 510; 5 indicates that it is in the general class of the pure sciences; 1 that it is in the division for mathematics; 0 that it is general mathematics, not limited to arithmetic, algebra, or any one of the other sections. In "synthesizing the notation, " "building the number" as it was formerly called, duplicate numbers are cancelled, thus 510 mathematics and -07 study and teaching become 510. 7. Although standard subdivisions are always preceded by a zero, if the zero is already there to round out the number to three digits, it is unnecessary to add another zero. 07 or 0. 7 may mean study and teaching when added to the number for a subject.

Standard subdivision -07 is for books on how to study, how to teach, not for textbooks on the subject, e. g., 507 would be for a work on how to teach science, not for a textbook on science, such a book would go in 500. In the first instance the content of the book is methods of teaching with illustrations; in the second, the content is science.

Examples of standard subdivisions in different classes are:

900   History

903   Dictionaries, encyclopedias, concordances

904   (Note that 904 is used as well as 704, although
          -04 is no longer used to indicate essays and
          lectures in all classes)

          Collected accounts of specific events
          Scope: adventure (formerly 910. 4)

    . 5   Events of natural origin
          Earthquakes, volcanic eruptions, tidal waves,
          floods, storms

    . 6   Events induced by man
          Battles, explosions, fires; mine, transportation,
          nuclear accidents

The 9th abridged edition does not have . 5 and . 6, one would put events of natural origin and events induced by man together in 904.

500   Pure sciences

.1 Natural sciences

.2 Physical sciences

.9 Natural history

505   Serial publications

508   Collections, anthologies, travels, surveys

.1 Collections and anthologies

.3 Travels and surveys

     Standard subdivisions are always preceded by a zero,
but zero and a figure do not always mean a standard subdivision, e. g. , under 759, .01-.06 signify periods of development,
not limited geographically, e. g. , 759.05 is used for painting
and paintings of the period, 1800-1900, as is true in the earlier editions of the Dewey Decimal Classification system.
Standard subdivisions under the numbers for European history
have two zeros, e. g. , 941.003 would be the number for an
encyclopedia of the history of Scotland; 944.005, for a serial
publication on French history. This is necessary since .01-
.08 are used for period divisions of history, e. g. , 941.03 is
the number for the Early period of independence, 1314-1424
of the history of Scotland; 944.05 for the First Empire, 1804-
1815 in the history of France. Standard subdivisions should be
used with great care, first making sure that the numbers have
not been used for some other purpose.

     In the 17th edition of the unabridged and the 9th edition
of the abridged Dewey Decimal Classification there is a new
table, the Area Table. Geographic detail is incorporated in
this new table, having been removed from the general history
schedules, 930-990. As in the case of the standard subdivisions the area notations are never used alone, hence are preceded by a dash, e. g. , -7, North America. A library having
many books on a subject, a number of which are on a given
continent, country, or locality may expand the number for that
subject by using the area notation. For instance the number
for coins is: 737.4; coins of specific countries, 737.49. This
latter number is followed in the tables by the instruction: Add
area notations 3-9 to 737.49. Turning to the Area Table one
finds -5 Asia, adding this, one has 737.495 for coins of Asia;
or, for Japanese, add -52, resulting number: 737.4952. Such
a number is rather long for a small library and would only be

used if the library had quite a large collection of books on coins, many on Japanese coins, and it was desirable to bring them together. A special library on coins would find it very useful to be able to group its books by country. This illustrates another device used in the 17th unabridged edition and 9th abridged edition--a space is left "between each successive set of three digits after the decimal point, " e. g. , -549 3 Ceylon. This space is used in the Dewey Decimal Classification tables for ease in reading and is not part of the notation and not to be used when assigning classification numbers to books, putting the number on the spine of the book or on the catalog cards.

If the library uses the printed catalog cards from the Library of Congress, described in Chapter X, it will find very helpful the suggested Decimal Classification numbers printed to the right of the hole. Beginning early in 1967 these numbers will be printed in from one to three segments. Segmentation will be shown by prime marks, for example, 301-29 ' 56 ' 073. 5-digit numbers are usually the maximum desirable length for small libraries. Where the numbers are printed in one segment the library would, in most cases, use the number as given. Where the numbers are printed in two or three segments it is recommended that small libraries or libraries having small collections in specific subjects use only the first segment of numbers in that subject.

The instruction "divide like" is another way of expanding numbers. The number for Human races (Ethnology) is: 572, for specific races 572. 8 with the instruction "Divide like 420-490, " e. g. , Semitic races 572. 892; as 492 is the number for Semitic languages; but this direction should be applied with care, otherwise one arrives at such absurd numbers as 572. 842, the English race. To take another illustration, the tables give 630. 21-. 29 for scientific aspects of Agriculture and agricultural industries and the instruction: "Divide like 510-590, " e. g. , agricultural physics 630. 23; agricultural chemistry 630. 24 for 530 is the number for physics; 540, the number for chemistry.

If a miscellaneous collection of books is to be classified according to the decimal system, the books will be grouped according to their subject matter, with, for instance, general books on all or many subjects, e. g. , encyclopedias in one group; books about philosophy in a second; books about religion in a third; and so on. A reader interested in literature will find all the material about literature and all the books of literature, poetry, drama, etc., together on the shelves.

The divisions of the social sciences, 300, given below
show the principle of subdivision:

300 The social sciences	350 Public administration
310 Statistical method & statistics	360 Welfare & association
320 Political science	370 Education
330 Economics	380 Commerce
340 Law	390 Customs & folklore

Economics is divided as follows:

330 Economics	335 Collectivist systems
331 Labor	336 Public finance
332 Lucrative capital	[337] Tariff,
333 Land (Natural resources)	Class comprehensive works in 382, government regulation and control of international trade in 350. 827 (350 in the 9th abridged edition)
334 Cooperative systems	
	338 Production
	339 Distribution & consumption

The third summary, giving the 1, 000 sections, simply omits
337. The full tables give the explanation regarding it.
Square brackets indicate that the number which they enclose is no longer used or no longer used with the meaning given.

In the social sciences (300) typical standard subdivisions
are: 300. 1-300. 9, i. e. , 300. 1 for material on the philosophy
and theory of the social sciences; 300. 6 for social organizations. This is done because 301-309 are used for general considerations of the social sciences, e. g. , 301, Sociology (The
science that deals comprehensively with social activities and
institutions); 302-308 have not yet been developed so are left
blank in these editions, but 309 is for "Social situations and
conditions. "

In classifying literature there are two groups of mater-

in classifying books on literature, first look for nationality of author

ial, those about literature, histories, criticism; and those of literature, a book of poems for instance. Books of literature consist of works of aesthetic value, belles-lettres; they are divided according to the literary form in which they are written, for instance drama, fiction; and the nationality of the author, e. g., the poems of an American poet would be put in American literature, the section for poetry; those of an English poet in the section for English poetry. Hence in classifying such books the first step is to look up the nationality of the author. If an author has changed his nationality a practical method is to put works by or about him in the number for his nationality at the time his first work is to be classified and to continue that number for both earlier and later works. If later there is a strong bias toward another country, the books can be reclassified.

In the class for Literature (Belles Lettres) and rhetoric the main divisions are by nationality; the next subdivision by literary form; and in the unabridged edition there is a third subdivision by specific periods.

800 Literature & rhetoric

810 American literature in English

820 English & Anglo-Saxon literature

880 Classical & modern Greek literature

811 American poetry

812 American drama

811 American poetry

.001-.007 Standard subdivisions, e. g., 811. 005 a periodical of and about American poetry

.009   History, description, critical appraisal, biographical treatment

811. 02-.08 Specific kinds of American poetry . . . . Divide like 808. 812-808. 818; 808. 814 is the number for Lyric and balladic poetry, hence 811. 04 is the number for American lyric poetry

811. 1-.5   Specific periods of American poetry, e. g., 811. 52 early 20th century United States poetry

In a classification system using Arabic numerals for the symbols of the classes and the decimal principle for subdivi-

sion of those classes, numbers grow in length as the classification is expanded to make a place for divisions of a subject.
The library which does not need these subdivisions, simply
uses the broad number, omitting any figures at the end which
it does not need, e. g. , 973 stands for United States history,
and if the collection is not large enough for period divisions
to be helpful, they are omitted. 973. 917 is the number for the
period of history when Franklin Delano Roosevelt was president; but the small library with a limited number of books on
United States history may use only 973. 9, Twentieth century
United States history, or 973. 91, Early twentieth century history.

The 17th unabridged and the 9th abridged editions of the
Dewey Decimal Classification each have a section in the Editor's Introduction on "Reduction, " read this carefully. As
stated there:

> "Do not cut notation to less than three digits. " (It
> is better to use the different second and third digits,
> rather than putting everything in the general number,
> e. g. , 510, 520, 511, etc. not 500 for all material.)

> "Do not cut a number so that it ends in a 0 to the
> right of the decimal point. "

> "Cut at a reasonable spot, i. e. , one that will bring
> about a useful grouping. "

> Cut but "do not change digits. "

Another important bit of advice in the Editor's Introduction,
"Record in the schedules all decisions for reduction. "

One of the important features of the Dewey Decimal
Classification system is its relative index. D. J. Haykin[3] defined a relative index as one "which will show under each entry the different senses in which the term is used and the
diverse aspects of the subject with their appropriate places
in the classification system. "

Below are given some sample entries from the indexes
to the 17th unabridged and the 9th abridged editions of the
Dewey Decimal Classification system; note the explanations of
the symbols used--†, +, boldface type--in the paragraph on
"Use of the Relative Index. "

Edition 17	Abridged . . . Edition 9
Astronautics	Astronautics

engineering
economics   338. 47+
technology
  gen. wks ┬629. 4
  mil.   623. 749
see also Celestial dynamics

. . .

Space (extraterrestrial)
  artillery pieces see
      Artillery (pieces)
  biology see Biophysics
  communication
    engineering
      economics   338. 47+
      technology
        radio   621.384 197
        television 621.388 97
  see also Telecommunication

  cosmology see Cosmology
  economics   333. 94
  flight see Astronautics
  flights
    engineering
      manned   629. 45
      unmanned 629. 43

. . .

stations
  engineering
    economics 338. 47+
    technology 629. 44

---

engineering
economics   338. 4
technology
  gen. wks   ┬629. 4
  mil.   623. 7
see also Celestial me-
    chanics

. . .

Space (extraterrestrial)
  artillery pieces see
      Artillery (pieces)
  biology see Biophysics
  communication
    engineering
      economics 338. 4
      technology
        radio   621.384 19
        television 621.388
  see also Telecommunica-
    tion

. . .

  economics   333. 9
  flight see Astronautics
  flights
    engineering
      manned   629. 45
      unmanned 629. 43

. . .

stations
  engineering
    economics 338. 4
    technology 629. 44

How to classify. The book which is to be classified should

be carefully examined to see what it is about, what the author's purpose was in writing it, what class of readers will
find it most useful. To do this, read the title page, preface,
all or part of the introduction, look over the table of contents (as this spreads out before the examiner the skeleton
of the book), and read parts of the book itself. Having determined to what class the book belongs, e. g., history, turn to
the table for that class--in this case 900. An examination of
the table shows that 900 is divided according to place and
time. Such questions arise as: What country or section of a
country is the book about? Does it cover the entire history
of that country or section or only a specific period? Of
course, if it covers the entire world from the creation to the
present time, it goes in the general number for history, 909.
But if the book is limited to United States history, it will go
in 973; the figure 9 indicating that it is history, 7 that it is
limited geographically to North America, and 3 that it is
further confined to the United States. The 900 class, which
includes history, geography, and biography, is a good one
with which to begin the study of classification. It is readily
determined whether or not a book treats of history, geography,
or biography; and, if it is history the country and period of
time covered are clearly indicated.

    If the book is one of pure literature, the first deciding
factor is the nationality of the author; the second, the literary
form. Thus Masefield's poems are put with other books of
English literature and in the section for poetry, 821. A book
on the theories of electricity and electronics would go in the
main class, science, the division for physics, and the section
on electricity and electronics, 537.

    The figures are the symbol of the class; e. g., 620 En-
gineering and allied operations and manufactures, and all general books on that subject would be so marked. If a book is
on a specific kind of engineering, the third figure changes to
show that fact, e. g., 621 Applied physics including mechanical,
electrical, etc., engineering. Having discovered what a book
is about and its place in the classification scheme, one puts
the number representing that subject in the system (the notation) in the book and on its cover, so that all books may be
kept together on the shelves in the order of their classes.

    Many books are on two or more subjects; or, two or
more aspects of the same subject. To give an illustration, a
book on farming may treat of both the economics and the
technology of farming; a work on wine, its commercial and

domestic manufacture and public health measures regarding it.

Having determined the subject and the aspect of which the book treats, the next step is to locate the classification number for it in the tables. As indicated in the second summary, 630 in Technology (Applied sciences) is the division for the technology of farming; 330, the division for economics, and under that 338, for production. Turning to the summary for 338, one finds 338.1, Agricultural economics; the summary under 631 gives: farm structures; farm tools, machinery, appliances; soil and soil conservation. Hence a book dealing with soil and soil conservation on the farm would be placed in 631.4; a book on food supply in 338.1 if using the 9th abridged edition of the Dewey Decimal Classification; 338.19 if using the 17th unabridged edition, provided that the library had or was likely to have so many books on the different phases of economics that it would need to separate them to the extent of using two figures beyond the decimal point. The smaller library, unless it is a special agricultural library, might not need to separate the books on agricultural economics beyond one point, and would use 338.1 for general books on the subject and also for books on machines in production (338.16) or food supply (338.19).

In all decisions regarding classification, cataloging, and processing of materials the library of today should consider centralized processing and cataloging centers and the effect their work would have if the library should decide to subscribe for such service. Note on page 27 of the 9th abridged edition the suggestion that the small library may wish to shorten the numbers recommended by central classification services for some specific titles. Chapter X of this manual discusses centralized processing and cataloging and its effects on all libraries, even the smallest. For instance Mrs. Barbara Westby[4] writing in the spring of 1964, says that most commercial cataloging firms use the abridged edition of the Dewey Decimal Classification system; this is also true of the library cataloging centers. Some commercial processing and cataloging centers use the Decimal Classification number suggested on the printed catalog cards of the Library of Congress or those of the H.W. Wilson Company.

The unabridged editions of the Dewey Decimal Classification system show broad general subjects and their subdivisions, so that a new subject can be fitted into its proper relationship with the older subjects. The abridged editions of the

Dewey Decimal Classification are for the use of smaller general libraries of all kinds, but particularly for public and school libraries. As shown on page 35 of this manual both the abridged and the unabridged editions have relative indexes but that for the unabridged edition has many, many more entries so it is especially helpful in locating the proper number for a subject, although in some entries there is little difference.

The lists of Dewey Decimal Classification numbers found in general books on school or other special libraries, which have a chapter on cataloging and classification, are often unsatisfactory as they offer no place for new subjects and no indication as to where they should go. The library, if it can possibly afford it, should obtain later editions of the Dewey Decimal Classification system as they are published, not limiting itself to the edition with which it began its classification.

General rules for classifying. The following rules are adapted from W. C. B. Sayers[5] and Lake Placid Club Education Foundation's Guide. [6] The classifier should also refer, as needed, to the various sections in the Editor's Introduction to the Dewey Decimal Classification under "How to use DC."

1. "Class a book first according to its subject, and then by the form in which the subject is presented, except in generalia and in pure literature where form is paramount." Sayers.

2. "In determining the subject consider the predominant tendency or obvious purpose of a book, and its author's intention in writing it." Sayers.

3. More than one subject:
   a. If a work deals with two subjects, (1) class with the one emphasized most, e. g. , class the effect of one subject on another with the subject affected; (2) if the emphasis is equal class with the one treated first; (3) if the emphasis is about equal and both subjects are treated concurrently, class with the subject coming first in the schedules, unless the schedules provide otherwise. Based on the Guide.

   b. If a work deals with three or more subjects, follow the preceding principles, modifying (2) and (3) as follows: if the emphasis is about equal but the subjects are subdivisions of one broader subject class with the broader subject. Based on the Guide.

4. Contrasting opinions or systems:
   If a work treats of two different opinions or systems,

with about equal treatment of each, but advocates one,
class with the one advocated; but if more attention to
one, class with it, regardless of advocacy. E. g., class
in 321. 8 a work dealing about equally with modern dictatorship and representative democracy but advocating
the latter; in 282 a work by a Protestant criticizing and em-
phasizing the Roman Catholic Church. Based on the Guide.

5. More than one aspect:

If a work deals with (1) the theory of or basic principles behind a process or procedure, (2) its technique,
and (3) its application to a specific subject, e. g. , electrodynamics 537. 64, dynamoelectric (generating) machinery 621. 313, electric locomotives 625. 263 and the
theory and technique are preliminary or introductory to
the application, and the author's purpose is to describe the
application, class with the application, but if the "application" is only an example (with much less space given to it)
and the author's purpose is to describe the theory or the
technique, class with the theory or technique. Based on
the Guide.

6. Subject not provided: ⋇

"Do not make up your own number for a new subject. "
A new edition may use that number for something else.
Follow the usual procedure in classifying and stop when
you locate the most specific number that will contain the
subject of the book, even though it is only a three digit
number. Later if the number for that subject is worked
out by the Decimal Classification editors you can add to
the number already assigned to the book. Based on the
Editor's Introduction to the Decimal Classification, 17th
unabridged and 9th abridged editions.

7. "Place in the most specific head that will contain it. "
Sayers. Class in the most specific number; if a subject is
limited geographically and there is a number for that specific subject, and if the schedules permit, add the subdivision for place; or, if the subject is in a certain form,
use the standard subdivision to show that form. Except in
the 800's class (1) by the most specific subject, (2) by
place and (3) by form. In the 800's, only, is authorship the
basis for classification. Based on the Guide.

8. Evaluations: The classifier is not a critic nor a judge, but
sometimes must be a judge so as to decide which of two
or more numbers will be best, e. g. , a collection of William Allen White's editorials would go in 814. 52 as he ranks

as an author of real literary merit; as a general rule,
however, a journalist's editorials would be classified in
040. Based on the Guide.

9. "Record in the schedules all decisions for reduction."
Editor's Introduction to the Dewey Decimal Classification,
17th unabridged edition, p. 33 and 9th abridged edition, p.
28.

10. "Finally (to repeat), place a book where you think it will
be most useful; and always have a reason for placing it
there." Sayers.

To illustrate the application of the first of these rules
for classifying: Grove's Dictionary of Music and Musicians
would be given the Dewey Decimal Classification number
780. 3; 78 shows that it treats of music, 0. 3 that it is in the
form of a dictionary. Masefield's poems would be given the
number 821, 8 showing that it is pure literature, 2 that it is
by an Englishman, and 1 that it is poetry. The literary form
here determines its symbol, not the subject matter. If the
period were to be shown, the number would be 821. 912, early
20th century.

Rule number 2 may be illustrated by John K. Cooley's
Baal, Christ, and Mohammed: Religion and Revolution in North
Africa. In the Introduction the author states that he has
"tried to set out some main themes in the relationship between religious faith, alien imperialism, and the native Ber-
ber revolutionary spirit." An examination of the table of contents and further reading in the Introduction show that the
book treats of the religion of North Africa, missions in North
Africa, and analyzes the reasons for the Islamic dominance in
North Africa. Hence Cooley's book would be classified in
209. 61, the history of religion in North Africa, or in the
small library simply in 209.

Some books deal with two distinct subjects or even three
or more. Rule 3A(1) covers material treating of two subjects
and the effect of one on the other. An illustration is M. S.
Stedman's Religion and Politics in America. To quote from
the Preface: "The purpose of this book is to advance an un-
derstanding of the relationships between religion and politics
on both the empirical and the theoretical level. . . ." Stedman would be classified in 261. 7, Christianity and civil government.

Skilling and Richardson's Sun, Moon and Stars deals with

the sun, moon, planets, stars, astronomers and observatories, with about equal space and emphasis on each. All sections are subdivisions of the broad subject descriptive astronomy, hence this book would be classified in 523. It illustrates rule 3B.

Rule number 4 regarding works on contrasting opinions or systems may be illustrated by Barrington Moore's Social Origins of Dictatorship and Democracy which would go in 321.09 or 321.

Rule number 5 shows what to do with a work that deals with more than one aspect of a subject. How to Fix Your Own TV, Radio, and Record Player, published in 1956 by Popular Science Publishing Company, illustrates this rule as it contains general information about TV, radio and record players, so that when repairing them the worker can understand and recognize the parts and their relations to one another. It also includes material on how to diagnose the trouble, and how to locate, remove, replace, or repair the part that is concerned. This book would be classified in 621.388. The theory of electrodynamics goes in 537, but its application, as for example, to electric trains would go in 625.26 and B. K. Cooper's Diesel and Electric Trains would go there also.

Rule number 6 may be illustrated by Kenneth Hamilton's God Is Dead; the Anatomy of a Slogan. This is one of the books on the "Death of God Movement," which subject has no specific place in the Decimal Classification. This book would go in 231, God, Trinity, Godhead. Do not create a new number, e. g. , 231.9 for the movement. Later if the number 231.9 should be assigned to the subject in the Decimal Classification tables, .9 could be readily added; on the other hand, .9 may later be used for another topic. Another illustration is Paul Griswold Macy's If It Be Of God: the Story of the World Council of Churches. Neither the World Council nor the National Council of Churches have a specific place in the Decimal Classification. 262.001, or simply 262 in the smaller library (formerly 280.1), would be the best place for this book. Do not try to make up a more specific number, even though the Classification table does not indicate that 262.001 includes either of these organizations. Add these names to the index of the Library's copy of the Decimal Classification with this number and one may also add these names in the table.

Applying rule number 7, one would give James Truslow Adams' Provincial Society, 1690-1763 the classification number

973. 2, the number for colonial history of the United States,
not 973, the general number for United States history; Maurice
Maeterlinck's The Life of the Bee, 595. 799, not 592. The
closeness of the classification, however, also depends upon the
amount of material the library has on the subject or is likely
to have in the future. Hence Maeterlinck's book in some libraries would go in 595. 7, Insects. C. G. Hart's Possums
would go in 599. 2, but in the very small library this book
would go in 599 with books on bears, etc. Formerly all books
on Southeast Asia in the average public or school library were
put in 959, but now with so much interest in that region closer
classification is necessary in order to bring together the books
on Vietnam, those on Malaya, etc.

Rule number 8 on evaluations may be illustrated by Sig-
mund Freud's The Future of an Illusion. This work may be
considered a philosophical analysis of religion, but it really is
an attack on Christianity and many think that it represents an
atheistic point of view. 201, Philosophy and theory of religion
would seem to be the best place for it, or 150. 19 Systems,
schools, viewpoints (150. 1952 Freudian in a library with a
large collection in this field) might be more useful. A critic
might class it in 211. 8 with material on atheism. Another illustration is Great Americans Speak; Short Speeches That Have
Shaped Our Destiny. The central theme of this work provides
a counteractive to Communism as a way of life. It might be
placed in 320. 52 or in 320. 532 as a polemic; or, it could go
in 815. 01, American speeches.

Rules 9 and 10 are so clear as not to need illustration.

When ready to classify a collection of books, first sort
them by general groups, then examine those in each group
carefully to see precisely what they are about. This is much
easier than taking books as they come and switching one's
thoughts from science to religion, to drama, to electronics, and
so forth. The rules for classifying quoted from Sayers, the
Guide, the Editor's Introduction to the Decimal Classification
will be found very helpful. But one learns to classify by classifying. Keep in mind the purpose of classifying, namely, "to
make books more available" to the readers for whose benefit
classification is used. Be as consistent as possible; in deciding
upon a certain class for a certain book, see what other books
are in that class. In her pamphlet, Classification, [7] Miss Corinne Bacon writes: "Concrete well-defined subjects should be
more closely classified than abstract ones. "

Changes in the Dewey Decimal Classification. The classifier will find some changes in the places assigned to a given subject in different editions of the Dewey Decimal Classification system. For instance in the 16th edition of the tables, 150. 13 is given as the number for Applied Psychology; in the 17th unabridged and the 9th abridged editions, the number is 158, followed by the explanation [formerly 150. 13]; 371. 895 the number for school plays in the 16th and earlier editions is changed to 800 in the 17th edition. In some places the basic number remains the same, but it has been expanded and some of the new numbers differ from the former number, e. g. , the 17th unabridged and the 9th abridged editions give 629. 4 Astronautics [formerly 629. 138 and 629. 138 8]. To give another illustration: the 17th edition gives 630 Agriculture and agricultural industries; 657. 863 Class accounting for agriculture, 658 Business management [both formerly 630].

Further examples of changes and how they are indicated in the tables:

658. 8 Management of distribution (Marketing)
        Of goods and services
        Scope: bookselling (book trade) [formerly
                655. 4-655. 5], Marketing of insurance
                [formerly 368]

331. 2 Wages
        . . .
        Including compensation of Christian clergymen
        [formerly also 254. 8], of teachers [formerly
        371. 16], of physicians [formerly also 614. 25],
        fees and commissions in building contracting
        [formerly also 692. 8]

324 Suffrage
        . . .

324. 24 Voting
        Including voting machines [formerly 324. 25]

328 Legislation

328. 1 Parliamentary rules and procedure [formerly also
        328. 37]

329 Practical politics
        . . .

329. 01 Political propaganda
        Class presidential campaign literature of specific parties of United States [formerly 329. 01]
        in 329. 1-329. 8

As a result of these changes in the numbers from one edition of the Decimal Classification to another, sometimes there are different numbers given for the same subject in different aids and on printed catalog cards. Beginning July 1, 1965 the Decimal Classification numbers assigned by the Library of Congress to the books for which they print cards, are from the 17th edition of the Dewey Decimal Classification, hence in a few instances they differ from those assigned to books on the same subject earlier. Likewise the Decimal Classification numbers on the Wilson printed cards vary, although not so often, as they use the shorter, broader numbers from the 9th abridged edition of the Decimal Classification.

The 17th unabridged and the 9th abridged editions give specific authority for certain choices in numbers, e. g., the first line under 813, 823, 833, etc., (the numbers for fiction in the different literatures) is: "If preferred, do not class works of fiction." Many public libraries and school libraries as well follow this suggestion. "If preferred" here and in other places in the tables means: If you, the librarian, prefer. Another illustration:

> 913-919 Geography of specific continents, countries,
> localities
> Scope: comprehensive works on geography and
> history of specific continents, coun-
> tries, localities
> If preferred, class in 930-990

but

> 930-990 Geographical treatment of general history
> History of specific continents, countries, lo-
> calities
> (Optional: geography of specific places; pre-
> fer 913-919)

"Optional" means that the editors of the Decimal Classification prefer 913-919 to 930-990 for this type of material.

The librarian must face these changes and choices and make the necessary decisions in order to keep the library's material consistently classified. The chief point to remember is that new material is being constantly added and could go in the number the library has not used. If the change is to be made the sooner it is done the better. Rule number 9 in the section, General rules for classifying, page 24 is particularly applicable here and should be broadened to include recording in the schedules all decisions regarding changes and choices as well as those for reduction. If the library has a very small amount of material on a subject the number for which has been changed in the tables, it would be well to change it immediately; if a great deal of material the amount of work involved may make it impossible. This is one reason for classifying a new subject broadly; later when the nature of the material is more apparent, the subject has been developed and the library has considerable material on the subject the material may be divided to better advantage. This is easily done by adding numbers after the decimal point. The number of new subjects unprovided for in the classification scheme increases as the scheme grows older. This is why it is so necessary for a library to get the new editions of the adopted classification scheme as they appear.

Classification aids and how to use them. The Booklist and Subscription Books Bulletin, Book Review Digest and the Wilson Standard Catalog Series and their supplements are aids which give the suggested classification number for each book listed. The Guidepost of the Public Library of Cincinnati; The North Carolina State Board of Education, Division of Textbooks', Library Book Catalogue, a Classified List for Elementary and High School Libraries; and the Oregon State Library's Books for High Schools are examples of bulletins which give the decimal classification numbers.

The use of these and other aids may show complete agreement or considerable variation as to the number for the book. The Book Review Digest, 1962, lists James Baar and W. E. Howard's Spacecraft and Missiles of the World and gives 629. 4 as the classification number. The Booklist and Subscription Books Bulletin, 1962, gives the classification number 623. 4519 for Baar and Howard. Which of these numbers should the library use? Is it a difference of opinion among the classifiers who assigned the numbers or variations in the editions of the Dewey Decimal Classification used by these two aids? A look at the tables and indexes of the 17th edition shows these two subjects and the numbers assigned to them:

Tables:

623. 4519 Guided missiles
(Strategic missiles)

629. 4 Astronautics [formerly 629. 138 8]

. 46 Unmanned vehicles

.47   Manned vehicles (The more general number,
         629. 4, would include ma-
         terial on both unmanned and
         manned vehicles)

Index:

    Guided missiles
        technology   623. 451 9

    Spacecraft (vehicles)
        . . .
        construction
        technology
        gen. wks.   629. 46-47

Obviously the Book Review Digest classified this book so
as to put it with other works on spacecraft; and the Booklist
and Subscription Books Bulletin classified it as a book on missiles. Both numbers are correct. Review rule 3, page 22 of
this manual. The questions for the individual library to consider are: which subject--spacecraft or missiles--is of most
interest to the Library's patrons; with which group of books--
those in 629. 4 or those in 623. 4519--will this book best fit?
The librarian may wish to shorten the number and use 623. 45
after reading section 3. 5 Reduction in the Editor's Introduction
to the 17th edition.

These aids and others will be found very useful as a
check on one's classification and may suggest more desirable
classification numbers when the specific topic is not included
in the index to the tables. If one is continually in agreement
with the aids, presumably one knows how to classify. In case
of doubt always consult the aids. But having consulted the aids,
be sure to consider the particular library's collection and see
that the number suggested is in accordance with its practice
and is the best place for the given book in that library.

An aid may change its policy as the Booklist and Subscription Books Bulletin has done in regard to the use of 810
and 820. At one time all literary works of American or English authors were put together, and 821 English poetry was
used for both American and English poetry. The eighth edition
of the Standard Catalog for High School Libraries puts books
on the Federal Bureau of Investigation in 353. 5; Secret Service
of the Treasury Department in 353. 2. Both were formerly
classified in 351. 74. If a library is to adopt such a change in
policy, all of the books and records involved should have the
classification numbers changed, while a bibliography such as

the Booklist and Subscription Books Bulletin may ignore earlier volumes and simply be consistent in present and future issues. It is a saving in time for the library to make the change when the aid first makes it. Otherwise the library using the Standard Catalog Series in its cataloging must assign different class numbers to all books issued after a change is made, and, if Wilson printed cards are used, must change the numbers on these cards.

Shelf arrangement of books within a class. The larger the number of books within any one class the more need there is for some symbol which can be used in arranging the books within that class. Another factor to consider besides the size of the collection is the actual need for keeping the books in exact order on the shelves. Many public and school libraries use no symbol whatever on the spines of the books of fiction, though fiction may comprise a rather large number of books even in the small library. A book with no symbol on its spine is fiction and is to be arranged alphabetically by author on the shelf. Even though occasionally a library may have two authors with the same surname, who write fiction, it does not usually matter if their books are mixed on the shelf. In this case no attempt is made to subarrange books by title.

Other public and school libraries use a symbol for fiction, F, or Fic, and many of these add the author's surname to the spine if it is not there originally or wears off. For instance, $\frac{F}{Milne}$, on the spine of Milne's Winnie the Pooh makes it easy to shelve and locate this book. The catalog cards would have the symbol, F or Fic on them. All fiction printed in English is shelved together, regardless of the language in which it was originally written. Some libraries use SC (Short Story Collection) to designate the books of short stories and shelve them immediately following the books of fiction. In public libraries juvenile fiction may be designated by a plus sign or a J. E is similarly used for Easy Books for children in the first to third grades. Easy books, because of their size and shape, may be kept on specially built shelves and are arranged alphabetically by author, but no attempt is made to subarrange them by title. Reference books are usually marked with an R above the classification number.

In the case of nonfiction library practice varies. Many libraries use book numbers as well as classification numbers; many do not. Book numbers make it possible to keep the books within a class--i. e. , those having the same content and therefore the same classification symbol--in exact order with

little difficulty. A. E. Markley[8] states that a general library
with up to 50,000 volumes can do without book numbers and
reminds the reader that book numbers can be added later to
any particular class or group of books that seem to require
them. It would, of course, involve considerable work to as-
semble the books and their catalog and shelf-list cards and
add book numbers, but this might never have to be done, and
certainly only for certain classes. A. R. Rowland[9] sent a
questionnaire to all junior college libraries and received re-
plies from 336 (50%) of them. The results were as follows:
238 (75.5%) used either Cutter or Cutter-Sanborn book numbers; 54 (17.2%) did not use any author notation. Margaret
Nicholsen[10] states that book numbers are not necessary in any
school library.

B. R. Barden[11] states that book numbers in addition to
class numbers are needed:

1. To arrange books in order on the shelves.
2. To provide a brief and accurate call number for each
   book.
3. To locate a particular book on the shelf.
4. To provide a symbol for charging books to borrowers.
5. To facilitate the return of books to the shelves.
6. To assist in quick identification of a book when in-
   ventories are taken.

Centralized cataloging has influenced local cataloging and
will continue to do so. Even though the library has not sub-
scribed to such a service it may later, hence its policies and
methods should not be too different. Centralized cataloging
and processing centers cannot provide book numbers for individual libraries, but they can and sometimes do provide such
special markings as SC (Short Story Collection). One such center states that they use the first initial of the author's surname
as a book number; give initial letter of surname of the person
written about for individual biography following B for individual biography.

Individual biography, whether or not book numbers are
used, is arranged by the name of the person written about,
the biographee, not the biographer, so that all of the biographies of one person will come together on the shelf. If book
numbers are not used, individual biographies should have the
biographee's name underscored on the spine of the book for
convenience in shelving. It should be added where it does not
appear; for example, Eaton's Leader by Destiny should have

"Washington" written on the spine and be shelved under Washington's name.

The name by which the book is to be shelved should be underscored on the back in the case of books with editors, translators, and joint authors when there may be doubt as to the choice of name. If fiction is published anonymously, but the author is known and his books are entered in the catalog under his name, the name should be added to the spine of the book. When a book is published under a pseudonym and is cataloged and consequently shelved under the real name, the name under which it is to be shelved should be underscored or added to the cover. Some libraries add the author's name on the spine of all books.

Book numbers. A book number is a combination of letters and figures taken from an alphabetic order table, e. g., the Cutter-Sanborn table.[12] The basic elements of the book number system now commonly used as stated by Barden[13] are:

1. An initial letter followed by figures to represent a name. This provides an alphabetic arrangement.
2. The figures arranged as decimals to make possible the insertion of a new name between any two combinations already used.

For example, Miles 645, Millikan 654, Mills 657; or better, if just two figures are used: Miles 64, Millikan 65, but Mills 657, since it must be distinguished from Millikan if the titles being cataloged have the same classification number. If the book by Millikan is classified in 530 and the one by Mills in 591. 5, however, M65 may be used for both, since the classification numbers differ.

If the books in the collection of individual biography are classified in 92 and arranged by the name of the subject of the biography, many book numbers may begin with the same initial letter or letters. To illustrate: Agassiz, A262; Allen, A425; Arliss, A724; or shortening them to two figures: A26, A42, and A72. Thus they may be distinguished with three symbols. By adding the initial letter of the biographer's name, one may readily differentiate several biographies of the same person and arrange them in alphabetical order by author: e. g., Goss' biography of Johann Sabastian Bach would have the book number 92 B11G and Wheeler and Deucher's 92 B11W ; Dan Beard's

autobiography 92   and Clemens and Sibley's biography of
            B36
Beard 92   . Note that the autobiography has no letter added
        B36C
after the number B36 and would stand before the biographies.

⁂   Many libraries have found the first letter of the author's
surname a satisfactory substitute for book numbers and use it
for both fiction and nonfiction. Thus Stevenson's Treasure Island might be marked F on the spine, this same symbol being
                      S
used on the catalog cards to show the location of the book.

    In the class of individual biography there are likely to
be some cases of persons with the same surname or surnames
beginning with the same letter or letters. To illustrate, Franklin D. Roosevelt's biographies would be marked 92, if the li-
                                                R
brary also has biographies of Eleanor Roosevelt and Theodore
Roosevelt, the simplest way to differentiate them is to add
a comma and the initial of the first name, e.g., 92   for
                                                 R, F
Franklin Roosevelt, if several; 92   for Ludwig's, etc.; 92
                                 R, F   R, E
                                 L
for Eleanor Roosevelt's biographies; 92   for biographies of
                                      R, T
Theodore Roosevelt. Another illustration may be drawn from
the Adams': Henry Adams' Letters (1892-1918); Mrs. Henry
Adams' Letters, 1865-1883; and J.C. Miller's Sam Adams,
Pioneer in Propaganda. They could all be assigned the number
92 with A, A1, and A2 as book numbers. If the Cutter-Sanborn
tables are used, the books present no problem if three figures
are used; the books would be marked, 92   , 92   , and 92
                                       A213   A215   A217
respectively. There are not likely to be many such cases in
the small general library. Cutter-Sanborn numbers may be
used for individual biography even though just the initial letter
is used in other classes.

⁂   To sum up this discussion: Adopt a policy regarding the
use of book numbers and adhere to it. If the library has used
book numbers, continue them at least for a time, observing
their advantages and disadvantages. If it does not have them,
continue without them unless certain that they would improve
the service to the public and that someone on the staff has
time to assign them. In the case of a new library or one pre-

viously uncataloged and unclassified, go over the arguments for and against book numbers in this and other manuals, make your decision and stand by it. Unless the book collection includes many different editions which may be difficult to distinguish without book numbers or many books by the same author in the same class and exact arrangement is important, follow Miss Markley's recommendation and do not use book numbers, remembering that they may be added to a class if it is found to require them. If it is decided to drop book numbers and use only the initial letter of the author's surname, books marked with book numbers and those with the initial letter can be shelved together without difficulty.

Book numbers from the Cutter-Sanborn alphabetic order table are given on the sample cards for nonfiction in this book as an aid to the libraries which use them; librarians who decide not to use book numbers have simply to omit them from their cards and follow the sample cards in all other respects.

References

1. J. C. Dana, A Library Primer (Boston, Library Bureau, 1920), p. 98.

2. Melvil Dewey, Dewey Decimal Classification and Relative Index (Ed. 17; Lake Placid Club, N.Y., Forest Press, Inc. of Lake Placid Club Education Foundation, c1965).

Dewey Decimal Classification and Relative Index: Devised by Melvil Dewey (Ed. 17 Vol. 2 (rev.); Lake Placid Club, N.Y., Forest Press, Inc., 1967). Available free of charge to all users of the original index.

Dewey Decimal Classification and Relative Index: Devised by Melvil Dewey (9th abr. ed.; Lake Placid Club, N.Y., Forest Press, Inc., c1965).

3. D. J. Haykin, Subject Headings: A Practical Guide (Washington, D.C., Govt. Print. Off., 1951), p. 2.

4. Library Journal, 89:1508, April 1, 1964.

5. W. C. B. Sayers, An Introduction to Library Classification (9th rev. ed.; London, Grafton, 1954), p. 179-180.

6. Lake Placid Club Education Foundation, Guide to Use of Dewey Decimal Classification; Based on the Practice of the Decimal Classification Office at the Library of Congress (Lake Placid Club, Essex Co., N.Y., Forest Press of Lake Placid Club Education Foundation, 1962).

7. Corinne Bacon, Classification (Rev. ed.; Chicago, American Library Association, 1925), p. 21.

8. A. E. Markley, "Cataloging Time-savers," School Library Association of California. Bulletin, 23:20-21 (January, 1952).

9. A. R. Rowland, "Cataloging and Classification in Junior College Libraries," Library Resources and Technical Services, 7:255 (Summer, 1963).

10. Margaret Nicholsen, "Streamlining Classification and Cataloging of Books," Library Journal, 79:107-115 (Jan. 15, 1954).

11. B. R. Barden, Book Numbers; a Manual for Students with a Basic Code of Rules (Chicago, American Library Association, 1937), p. 9.

12. C. A. Cutter, Alphabetic Order Table, Altered and Fitted with Three Figures by Kate E. Sanborn (Springfield, Mass., H. R. Huntting Co.).

13. Barden, op. cit., p. 7.

Chapter II
Choice of Subject Headings

Introduction. This chapter deals with the problem of determining of what subject a book treats and the topic or topics under which it should be listed in the catalog. The forms of the subject card and the subject analytical card[1] are discussed in a later chapter. Probably more library users want material on some subject, than want a specific book of which the reader knows the author or title or both, in which case the book is readily found. Entering material in the catalog under subjects involves a knowledge of the terms people use, and selection of as specific a term as the material warrants.

For geographic headings, e. g. , Formosa versus Taiwan, which term do the newspapers use? the radio and TV programs? the magazines? Differences in the vocabularies of people in different sections of the country are important in certain fields. With reference to geographic subdivisions, e. g., BIRDS - U. S. , consider these questions: does the library have anything on birds in countries other than the United States? is it likely to have? When the reader asks for a book on birds, though he does not say so, does he not mean birds in the United States. Then use the general subject heading, BIRDS. Use simple, modern subject headings; avoid cumbersome phrases and unnecessary subdivisions.

Some libraries find that subject entries for certain types of fiction serve a real purpose and improve the service of the library. If sea stories and mystery stories, to take two of the best known examples, are entered in the catalog under the headings SEA STORIES and MYSTERY AND DETECTIVE STORIES, respectively, as well as under author and title, time will be saved for both the readers and the library staff-- though the time saved by the staff in serving the public may possibly be counterbalanced by the time spent in assigning those subjects and in making those extra cards.

School libraries will find subject cards for fiction almost as useful as those for nonfiction. Both the Standard Catalog for High School Libraries and the Children's Catalog indicate subject headings for most of the books of fiction.

For example, Kate Douglas Wiggins' Rebecca of Sunnybrook
Farm has listed below the description of the book NEW ENG-
LAND - FICTION, Douglas Warner Gorsline's Farm Boy has:
FARM LIFE - FICTION. These are suggested subject headings
under which to list these books in the catalog. On the other
hand, it is not advisable to try to find subjects for all books
of fiction. The Standard Catalog for High School Libraries
does not suggest any subjects for Elizabeth Goudge's The
Dean's Watch; nor does the Children's Catalog give any for
Bunyan's Pilgrim's Progress. Make subject cards for the
catalog for fiction and nonfiction if the book gives definite information on a given subject.

Subject treated. To determine the subject of a book requires such a careful examination of its contents as is described on page 17 in discussing "How to classify." For this
reason the subject headings should be determined and assigned at the same time as the classification number; otherwise
examining the book and determining what it is about has to be
done twice. The two topics are separated in this manual because, since both subject headings and classification are difficult, it is better to take them up separately until each one
is clearly understood. Furthermore, in organizing or reorgan-
izing a library it is frequently best to classify the books,
make a shelf list, [2] and later catalog the collection.

Review directions given in Chapter I: Read the title page,
look over the table of contents carefully, read the preface,
read or look through the introduction, and dip into the book itself in several places. This scrutiny will show what the book
is about and what the author's purpose was in writing it. Such
an examination may bring out the fact that the book treats of
one subject, of several distinct phases of a subject, or of two
or more subjects. No matter of how many subjects a book
may treat, it can be classified in only one place and stand on
the shelves in only one place; but it may be entered in the
catalog under as many subject headings as are necessary. If
the book treats of one subject it requires only one subject entry: e. g., Landau and Rumer's What Is Relativity? deals with
the general subject and would be entered in the catalog only
under the heading RELATIVITY (PHYSICS).

On the other hand, Norman V. Carlisle's Your Career in
Chemistry needs to be brought out under two subjects, CHEM-
ISTRY, TECHNICAL and CHEMISTS. Similarly the Beards'
New Basic History of the United States treats of both the civ-
ilization of the United States and its history and should be rep-

resented in the catalog by two subject cards, one under U.S. -
CIVILIZATION and one under U. S. - HISTORY. Another type
of book has one general topic and includes a number of specific topics, W. Maxwell Reed and Wilfrid S. Bronson's The
Sea for Sam. The general subjects are marine biology and
ocean and cards will be made for the catalog with those words
as headings. But the book will be much more useful in the
children's library if it is also entered in the catalog under
the special topics with which it deals, e. g., pages 12-29 are
on sponges, pages 73-79 on the Gulf Stream, pages 84-93 on
icebergs, and pages 225-232 on whales. Subject analytical
cards should be made for each of these topics, or as many
of them as the library is likely to have calls for. This depends upon the other material available on the subject and
the special interests of the library's readers.

     Fenton and Fenton's Mountains illustrates another point
about added entries. The title of this book is Mountains and
the subject treated is mountains, so the subject heading would
be MOUNTAINS. It is unnecessary to have the same book entered in the catalog twice under the same word; but if only a
title card is made it will file at the end of all the cards for
the material about mountains even though the author's name
begins with F; hence the rule, if the first word or words of
the title and the subject are the same do not make a title
card.

     Thus the book is examined, the subject of which it
treats determined, and one or more subject cards are made
for the catalog. Whether these cards are general subject entries or subject analytical entries for a particular portion of
the book depends upon whether two or more subjects are discussed together throughout the book or each subject is discussed separately.

     Selecting subject headings. When deciding upon the head-
ing for a subject entry, choose that heading which most truly
represents the contents of the book or a certain part of the
book, that is, the most specific subject or subjects possible.
For example, if a book is about trees--how to identify them,
their uses for ornamentation--select the specific term TREES.
The subject heading BOTANY includes the subject heading
TREES, but it obviously includes a great deal more, and this
book tells of no other plant than the tree. The subject heading FORESTS AND FORESTRY would be used for a book which
treats of trees as they grow in forests, how to care for and
preserve forests, but not for a book which treats of trees as

individual varieties, trees as an ornament for lawns and
streets, and the like. It would not, therefore, be a suitable
heading for this book. Likewise, Fabre's The Life of the Fly
would have the specific heading FLIES, and not the general
one INSECTS. Of two equally correct and specific headings,
such as BIRDS and ORNITHOLOGY, the choice depends upon
the type of library, and a reference[3] may be made from the
one not chosen. In a public or a school library, choose the
heading BIRDS as the term commonly used by the readers. In
a special ornithological library, use the heading ORNITHOL-
OGY, for the users of such a library are quite familiar with
the scientific term.

Consider opposite terms such as tolerance and intoler-
ance. A book on one of these subjects necessarily includes
material on the other. Choose one, e. g. , TOLERATION, and
put all the material under it, referring from the other term.

Select as many subject headings as are necessary to
cover the contents of the book, but do not multiply them unnecessarily. Test each heading by asking whether or not a
patron would be glad to be given the book or books listed
under the given heading if he were looking for material on
the topic used as heading. It would be an unusual book which
would need more than three subject headings, and one or two
will cover most books. In the case of subject analytical entries, however, very many may be needed for certain kinds
of books. In the Children's Catalog, tenth edition, 1961, Sarah
R. Riedman's Shots Without Guns; the Story of Vaccination,
1960, has the general subject headings, MEDICINE - RE-
SEARCH, SCIENTISTS, and VACCINATION, and many subject
analytical entries, e. g. , SMALLPOX, pages 11-16; PASTEUR,
LOUIS, pages 42-65, 89-109. But, as is explained in more detail in a later chapter, it is not desirable to analyze books
already indexed in books available in the library. The usefulness of such books as Cutts' Scenes & Characters of the
Middle Ages, which is not analyzed in any of the Wilson
Standard Catalogs, would be greatly increased, however, by
having subject analytical entries made for each of the groups
described, e. g. , KNIGHTS AND KNIGHTHOOD, PILGRIMS AND
PILGRIMAGES.

Another example of the kind and number of subject headings may be illustrated by Percy Boynton's America in Con-
temporary Fiction, which is about American fiction and American authors. The Standard Catalog for High School Libraries,
1938-1941 Supplement, lists this book and suggests as subject

headings: AMERICAN FICTION - HISTORY AND CRITICISM and
AUTHORS, AMERICAN (10 biography anals). If the library
owns this catalog, the librarian will not need to make these
ten analytics, since the reader can refer to the printed book
catalog to find references on individual authors. The two subject cards, however, are necessary. First the suggested headings should be checked with the Sears List of Subject Headings, if it is the list adopted by the library, to see if they are
authorized. AMERICAN FICTION, as a subject heading, is
found in its alphabetical place; below it the heading AMERICAN
LITERATURE; the form subheading HISTORY AND CRITICISM
is included in the "List of Subdivisions" to be used in the
fields of literature and music. The form subheads used under
literature may also be used under the headings for the different types of literature, so for this book the heading AMER-
ICAN FICTION - HISTORY AND CRITICISM may be used. The
heading AUTHORS, AMERICAN is also found in the Sears List
and below it: AMERICAN AUTHORS. So a second subject card
should be made with the heading AUTHORS, AMERICAN, and
a reference card should be made, reading:

AMERICAN AUTHORS

See

AUTHORS, AMERICAN

Why use the terms AMERICAN FICTION, AMERICAN LITER-
ATURE, etc., but AUTHORS, AMERICAN? The aids and the
lists agree that it is important to bring all material in the
catalog together under AUTHORS, then separate it according
to nationality, e.g., AUTHORS, AMERICAN; AUTHORS, ENG-
LISH; while with the terms Literature, Poetry, Fiction, etc.,
it is more useful to put the national adjective first and bring
together everything on the literature of one country, as AMER-
ICAN DRAMA, AMERICAN FICTION, AMERICAN LITERATURE.
Among these headings in the catalog will be the reference from
AMERICAN AUTHORS.

　　Besides subject entries for books and parts of books,
subject cards may be made to call attention to an entire
group of books. One method is suggested in Mrs. Douglas'
Teacher-Librarian's Handbook[4] and is now in use in some
school libraries and children's departments of public libraries. By means of this scheme one subject card may serve for
all the general books on a given subject, by simply referring
the reader to the books on the shelves by classification number, and to the shelf list to find the books which may be tem-
porarily out of the library. This practice serves the reader
quite satisfactorily in a small library, where he makes his
choice from the books on the shelves and uses the catalog

only to see that there are books on the subject and where
they are. Also the librarian's time is saved and space is
saved in the catalog.

1. General subject entry for all of the books in a subject
   class

---

629. 13   AERONAUTICS

Books about aeronautics will be found
on the shelves under 629. 13.

For a complete author list of the books
in the library on aeronautics, consult the
shelf list under 629. 13.

If the library has books with chapters on a subject, e. g.,
volcanoes, not indexed in the Standard Catalog for High School
Libraries, Standard Catalog for Public Libraries, or Children's
Catalog and their supplements, or if the library does not have
these aids, subject analytical cards for the catalog should be
made for this material. Chapter VII (page 158-159) gives
details as to how to make these cards. Card 1 should be filed
in the catalog before these subject analytical cards and should
include as a third paragraph: "For parts of books on airplanes
see the cards following this one. "

Subdivisions of a subject. Some subjects need to be subdivided to be exact. Most subjects can be divided by either:
(1) phase, (2) form, (3) geographical area, or (4) period of
time. For instance, the subject heading BIRDS would be used
for a general book on that subject. But if a given book is
limited to the protection of birds or the migration of birds,
the general subject heading BIRDS can be limited by adding a
phase subdivision, e. g., BIRDS - PROTECTION; BIRDS - MI-
GRATION. If, however, the book is not a book about birds but
a list of books about birds, the form subdivision BIBLIOG-
RAPHY should be added and the heading becomes BIRDS -
BIBLIOGRAPHY. Or the book may be on birds of the United
States, and the heading may be limited by geographical area

to BIRDS - U. S.

For some subjects, notably history, next in importance
to the geographical area is the period of time covered. For
a general history in which there is no geographical limitation,
the period of time covered is the significant factor. For T. W.
Wallbank's Man's Story which covers all countries and all periods up to 1960, the subject headings would be GEOGRAPHY,
HISTORICAL and WORLD HISTORY. But a history which,
though including all lands, ends at the beginning of the Middle
Ages would have the subject heading HISTORY, ANCIENT. A
general history of the United States, however, would have the
subject heading U. S. - HISTORY. A time subhead may be
added, e. g. , U. S. - HISTORY - REVOLUTION, or U. S. - HIS-
TORY - 1898-1919. The use of subheads depends upon whether
or not the book is limited to one phase, period of time, etc. ,
and the amount of material on that subject which the library
has or expects to have.

If the collection contains only a few (e. g. , five) books
treating of United States history, they may as well all have
the same subject heading, namely, U. S. - HISTORY. The larger library may have a dozen books and expect to add more,
e. g. , six general works covering the history of the United
States from the Revolution to the present time; three books
dealing exclusively with the period of the Revolution; four
books on the Civil War period; five on the history of the period 1898 to 1919, etc. It would be well to group them in the
catalog under such headings as U. S. - HISTORY; U. S. - HIS-
TORY - REVOLUTION; U. S. - HISTORY - CIVIL WAR; U. S. -
HISTORY - 1898-1919.

To sum up this matter of the choice of subject headings:
use the term or terms which most clearly describe the contents of the book and are most likely to be familiar to the
users of the library, remembering that readers use different
libraries if not simultaneously at least over a period of time.
"In choosing between synonymous headings prefer the one
that (a) is most familiar to the class of people who consult
the library; (b) is most used in other catalogs; (c) has fewest
meanings other than the sense in which it is to be employed;
(d) brings the subject into the neighborhood of other related
subjects. "[5] But keep subject headings simple and do not sub-
divide unless the library has considerable material on each
subdivision.

Form headings. A subject heading, as noted before, is the

word or words used to describe the content of the book; thus
Peterson's How to Know the Birds will have the subject heading BIRDS. Novels do not usually have a definite subject and
are read for their style, characterizations, etc., rather than
for information. This is also true of poems and plays. They
have author and title entries in the catalog but seldom subject entries. The heading POETRY is not used for a book of
poems, but "for a work on the appreciation and philosophy
of poetry;"[6] the heading POETICS is "used for works on the
art and technique of poetry;"[6] e.g., Robert Hillyer's In Pur-
suit of Poetry requires two subject headings, POETICS and
POETRY. If the library has much material on poetry, a third
subject heading, POETRY - HISTORY AND CRITICISM, may be
added. The literary works of an individual are represented
in the catalog only under his name and under the title if distinctive. Whoever wishes to read Edwin Arlington Robinson's
Nicodemus will look under Robinson or Nicodemus; and his
collected poems will be found only under his name, not under
POETRY. It is, however, worthwhile and practical to bring together in the catalog collections of poems, essays, or dramas
of three or more authors. This is done by adding a form subdivision to the heading. The heading POETRY or AMERICAN
POETRY is used for books about poetry; while the headings
POETRY - COLLECTIONS or AMERICAN POETRY - COLLEC-
TIONS are used for such works as Untermeyer's Modern American Poetry. These latter headings, POETRY - COLLECTIONS
and AMERICAN POETRY - COLLECTIONS are called form headings, as they refer to the form in which the material is written, not to its content.

2. General subject entry for all of the books in one or more
    classes

AMERICAN POETRY - COLLECTIONS

Books of poetry by individual American poets will be found on the shelves under 811.

Collections of poetry by several American poets will be found on the shelves under 811.008.

For a complete list of books in the
library containing poetry by individual
(Continued on next card)

2a. Extension card

```
                              2

              AMERICAN POETRY - COLLECTIONS

         American poets, consult the shelf list under
         811; for collections by several American
         poets, 811. 008.




```

Form cards similar to card 2 might take the place of
the form heading POETRY - COLLECTIONS and AMERICAN
POETRY - COLLECTIONS and direct the reader to the books
on the shelves. If this practice is adopted, similar cards would
be made for ENGLISH POETRY - COLLECTIONS; AMERICAN
DRAMA - COLLECTIONS; ENGLISH DRAMA - COLLECTIONS,
etc.

Lists of subject headings. Next in importance to choosing the right subject heading for a given book is to use the
same wording for all the subject headings for books or parts
of books on the same subject, so that they may be brought together in the catalog. To do this it is essential to have a
carefully worked-out list of subject headings from which to
choose and to check it to show which headings have been used.

There are available two very good lists: for small public
and high school libraries, Sears List of Subject Headings[7] and
for elementary and junior high school libraries and for the
children's books of the public library, Rue and LaPlante's
Subject Headings for Children's Materials[8] Mrs. Wesby[9] states
that most of the commercial cataloging firms follow the Sears
List. If your state's processing center uses the Library of
Congress subject headings list as does the North Carolina
State Library Processing Center then your library should
adopt the Library of Congress list. Subject cards from cooper-
ating or regional processing centers must be consistent with
those in your catalog, changes being made if necessary to secure this.

Names of persons and of organizations are the subject
headings for material about the person or the organization.
The form of the name to be used for the subject heading is
determined from the rules in Chapter III for persons and the
rules in Chapter V for organizations. For instance, Hesketh
Pearson's Dizzy, the Life & Personality of Benjamin Disraeli
would have as its subject heading DISRAELI, BENJAMIN; and
a history of Yale University would have as its subject heading YALE UNIVERSITY. This type of heading is not found in
the printed lists of subject headings.

How to use lists of subject headings. Determine what
the book is about; then look in the list of subject headings
adopted by the library for a suitable heading which expresses
the content of the book. On examining the Sears List or the
accompanying reproduction of pages 52 and 186, one should
note that the headings are listed in alphabetical order and
that some are in boldface type. Those in boldface type, e. g.,
AIR DEFENSES are to be used as subject headings.

Note that just below the heading AIR DEFENSES is a
paragraph beginning "Use for...." This type of explanatory
note is given below some of the headings to explain for what
kind of material they are to be used. Following this note the
words see also introduce one or more suggested headings that
may be better for the book in hand than the first subject
heading looked up. If that is the case, turn to such headings
as AIR RAID SHELTERS or RADAR DEFENSE NETWORKS in
their alphabetical places in the list. But if AIR DEFENSES is
the better term, use it. Note that the next line begins with x;
this means that a see reference should probably be made from
the term AIR RAIDS - PROTECTIVE MEASURES, AIR WAR-
FARE, and DEFENSES, AIR to the one chosen, AIR DEFENSES.
A see reference is a reference from a heading which is not
used in the catalog to a heading that is used.

Below "x Air raids - Protective measures" is a line beginning "xx AERONAUTICS, MILITARY; CIVIL DEFENSE. " This
is to suggest related terms, which if also used as subject
headings in this catalog should have references made from
them to this heading, so that attention may be called to all
related subjects. Such a reference from one heading that is
used to another that is used is called a see also reference.
Sunset's Garden & Patio Building would have a subject entry
in the catalog under FENCES; GREENHOUSES; LANDSCAPE
GARDENING; and PATIOS. There would be see also references
from related headings, for instance, HEDGES, see also FENCES,

if there were other books in the catalog under HEDGES; FLOW-
ER GARDENING, see also GREENHOUSES, if there were other
books in the catalog under FLOWER GARDENING.

Sears List of Subject Headings, 9th ed., Pages 52 and 186

```
Air conditioning                     X = "see"
    See also Refrigeration and refrigerating   XX = "see also"
        machinery; Ventilation
    xx Refrigeration and refrigerating ma-
        chinery; Ventilation
Air crashes. See Aeronautics - Accidents
Air cushion vehicles. See Ground effect ma-
        chines
√Air defenses
    Use for works on civilian defense against
        air attack. Works on military defense
        against air raids are entered under
        Aeronautics, Military. General works
        on civilian defense are entered under
        Civil defense
    See also Air raid shelters; Ballistic missile
        early warning system; Radar defense
        networks
    x Air raids - Protective measures; Air
        warfare; Defenses, Air
    xx Aeronautics, Military; Civil defense
Air engines. See Heat engines
√Air freight. See √Aeronautics, Commercial
Air hostesses. See Air lines - Hostesses
Air lines
    Use for works dealing with systems of
        aerial transportation and with companies
        engaged in this business.
    Works dealing with the routes along
        which the planes are flown are entered
        under Airways
    See also Airways
    x Airlines
    xx Aeronautics, Commerical; Airways

√Courts and courtiers
    See also Kings and rulers; Queens
    x√Court life;√Courtiers
    xx Kings and rulers; Manners and cus-
        toms; Queens
Courts martial and courts of inquiry
```

See also Military law
x Court martial
xx Courts; Military law; Trials
Courtship. See Dating (Social customs)

x Bedspreads; Quilts
xx Interior decoration

Covered bridges
xx Bridges

The Sears List of Subject Headings contains a section, "Suggestions for the Beginner in Subject Heading Work, " by Bertha M. Frick, which will be found very helpful. The librarian who has a copy of this list may well pass over the directions given here.

The form of Rue and LaPlante's Subject Headings for Children's Materials is somewhat similar to that of the Sears List. It gives terms suitable for use as subject headings, sometimes with explanatory notes; includes suggested related headings and suggested see and see also references. Preceding the list of subject headings are some suggestions for the use of the list and four lists of subdivisions, which may be used as form subdivisions under the terms in the main alphabetical list of subject headings or as subdivisions under names of countries, states, and cities. This list does not include any personal names, but does include many geographic names not ordinarily found in a subject headings list, because they are names frequently used in children's catalogs.

Subject cross references. In deciding upon subject headings, as explained before (pages 39-41), sometimes it is found that there are two or more different terms that might be used for the same subject. For example, which is better, AVIATION or AERONAUTICS? MARIONETTES or PUPPETS AND PUPPET PLAYS? POTTERY or CERAMICS? COUNSELING or GUIDANCE? Pages 39-40 gives four criteria on which of two synonymous headings to choose. Unless there is some very good reason for not doing so, one should always use the heading given in the subject headings list adopted by the library. If one looks up these groups of terms, he will see that Sears gives AERO-NAUTICS, COUNSELING, PUPPETS AND PUPPET PLAYS, and POTTERY, but some persons who will use the catalog will undoubtedly look under the terms AVIATION, GUIDANCE, MARI-ONETTES, and CERAMICS. When they find nothing, will they think of the other terms? They may not. Therefore, adopt one of these terms and refer from the other; e. g. , use POTTERY and refer from CERAMICS. The lists of subject headings not only suggest headings to be used but list synonymous and related terms from which it is wise to refer.

Some librarians do not consider see also references necessary for the small library's catalog and do not make them. Other librarians feel that they are needed especially in the small catalog, since the collection is limited, and that all material on related subjects should be brought to the inquirer's attention.

Notice that the see also card is made precisely as the see card is except for the words see also. Card 11, at the end of this chapter, shows the indentions and spacing for subject reference cards, such as Cards 3-4, 9-10. Most see references are made at the time that the subject heading to which they refer is first used, since they are synonyms for the heading decided upon. One should avoid making too many references for the small catalog. It is not desirable to make see references from terms not in the vocabulary of the public; for example, one would not refer from CHASE, THE or GUNNING to HUNTING, or from HABITATIONS, HUMAN to HOUSES, even though they are suggested in the Sears List, unless the public using the library in question might be likely to look under the term chase or gunning or habitations. One need not make a card DUNGEONS see PRISONS if the book to be entered under PRISONS has nothing in it on dungeons.

3. See reference card

```
AVIATORS
See
AIR  PILOTS
```

4. See also reference card

```
                JUSTICE, ADMINISTRATION OF
                      See also
            COURTS.
            CRIME AND CRIMINALS.
```

Before making see also's one should consider the following questions:

Does the catalog have material under the term referred from?

Is the term suggested for a reference one which anyone is likely to use?

Is there material in the book on the topic that this reference term suggests? For example, does the book on pantomimes have anything on the ballet? If it has, make a reference from BALLET.

It is true that after a reference is once made from one subject to another, there is no way of telling which of the books treats of that phase of the subject except by examining the books in question. That does not matter, however. To revert to the example given above--if there is a card in the catalog which reads BALLET, see also PANTOMIMES the reader turns to PANTOMIMES and there among several books on the subject finds upon examination one or more which contains something on the ballet, and he is satisfied. But if, on the other hand, he turns to the subject PANTOMIMES and finds a few books, none of which has the slightest reference to the ballet, he may lose faith in the catalog.

Thus a catalog may be made much more useful by the wise and restricted used of the suggested see and see also references, since the first subject the reader thinks of may

not be exactly what he desires. References, especially see
also references, should be made sparingly, as nothing is more
annoying than to turn card after card and find only, see so
and so, or see also so and so.

   5. General reference card

```
                 MANNERS  AND  CUSTOMS
              See also names of  ethnic  groups,
        countries,  cities,  etc.  with the sub-
        division SOCIAL  LIFE  AND  CUSTOMS,  e. g.
        U.S.  -  SOCIAL  LIFE  AND  CUSTOMS
```

     Another and a slightly different kind of reference is the
so-called general reference card. In the Sears List, page 377,
in the list of see also's under MANNERS AND CUSTOMS is
found: ". . . also names of ethnic groups, countries, cities,
etc., with the subdivision Social life and customs, e. g., U. S. -
SOCIAL LIFE AND CUSTOMS. " This sort of reference is very
useful in a catalog and saves much duplication, as otherwise
it would be necessary to list on a reference card a heading
for each individual country with the subdivision SOCIAL LIFE
AND CUSTOMS.

     Keep down the number of cross references. Be absolutely
sure that no reference refers to a heading not in the catalog.
See the first restriction given above. Do not make a see also
reference from a subject on which there is no material, but
wait until there is material on that subject. On the other hand
one may make temporary see references. For example, in order that the reader may have the suggestion and find the small
amount of material on the ballet that is included in the book on
pantomime, one may make a temporary card, BALLET, see
PANTOMIMES. Later, if there is a card with the heading BAL-
LET, this reference card may be changed to read "see also. "

     Other aids for subject headings. Appendix IV contains in-

formation on where to find lists of subject headings for special subjects. Even small public libraries and school libraries will have books and parts of books treating of a subject
not included in the Sears List or Rue and LaPlante's list nor
authorized by them. This is especially true of the new subjects which are constantly developing, e. g. , nursing homes,
medicare, hovercraft. The subject headings used in general
and special periodical indexes, bibliographies of special subjects, and the terms in general and special encyclopedias
will be found very helpful in determining the wording for such
headings. First be sure that no term in the regular list meets
the need, then look in the authorities mentioned for the best
possible term.

Great care should be taken in the use of indexes coming
out at regular intervals, e. g. , the Booklist and Subscription
Books Bulletin, since these lists can best serve their purpose
by changing their headings to suit the latest development of
the subjects. If a heading in a catalog is changed, all the
cards with that heading should be changed.

To illustrate how the aids may vary, take the subject
airplanes. Since 1935 the Booklist and Subscription Books Bulletin, which follows Library of Congress practice, has used
the term AEROPLANES as a subject heading; the Standard
Catalog for Public Libraries, 1961, Supplement, on the other
hand, uses AEROPLANES as a see reference to the heading
AIRPLANES, as both the Cumulative Book Index, 1963 and the
Standard Catalog for High School Libraries in all of its editions do. Another example is the use of the terms aviators
and air pilots. The Cumulative Book Index since 1928 has
used AVIATORS with a see reference from AIR PILOTS. But
the Standard Catalog for High School Libraries, eighth edition,
Supplement, 1964, uses AIR PILOTS with a see reference from
AVIATORS.

Checking lists of subject headings for tracing. When a
heading is decided upon for the first time, it is checked in
the list of subject headings to show that it has been adopted
for entry. Note the check mark (√) before AIR DEFENSES
on the pages reproduced from Sears (page 47). In this way
the librarian can tell which subject headings have been used
without referring to the catalog. This is a great convenience,
and care should be taken that each subject heading is checked
the first time it is used. In cases where there is no suitable
heading in the adopted list and a heading is selected from some
other source, this heading is written in the printed list of sub-

ject headings in its alphabetical place. The sample page from
Sears shows the subject heading COVERED BRIDGES--used in
the Reader's Guide, March 1965-February 1966--written in.

As subject headings used for the catalog are checked in
the list, so also are subject references used in the catalog.
This shows the librarian which of the references have been
made. If it is decided to discontinue a heading in the catalog,
this checked list will be a guide in removing the references
to that heading.

The rule is: Mark with a check($\sqrt{}$) at the left the subject heading used and the references which have been made
to it; turn to each reference in its regular alphabetical place
and check it and the subject heading used. The checks on the
page reproduced from Sears indicate that there are entries in
the catalog under AIR DEFENSES and that a reference has
been made from AIR FREIGHT to AERONAUTICS, COMMER-
CIAL.

To summarize: In making subject entries for a catalog
use the headings and the references suggested in the list of
subject headings selected and keep it carefully checked for
all terms used.

Subject authority file. Instead of checking a printed list
of subject headings the special library for which there is no
suitable printed list or the general library may have a subject authority file on cards. In this file there is one card
for each subject heading used in the catalog and on this card
is a record of all references made to that subject. If the subject heading is not taken from the adopted list of subject headings, the source is given on this card. There is also a card
corresponding to each reference card in the catalog. Cards
6, 7, and 8 are sample subject authority cards.

The scope or explanatory note given just below some
headings in Sears, e. g. , on page 47, under AIR DEFENSES
the paragraph beginning: "Use for works . . ." may be copied
on the subject authority card. If this is done it will be unnecessary to look in the printed list for any heading that has
been selected; on the other hand the librarian may prefer to
do that rather than having scope notes copied on authority
cards. The paragraph beginning See also does not need to be
given on the authority card, as its use is in deciding whether
to use this heading or one of those suggested. When the question comes up again as to whether to use a certain heading

6. Subject authority card

```
Air defenses.

          Refer from
     x Air raids - Protective measures
     x Air warfare
     x Defenses, Air
     xx Aeronautics, Military
     xx Civil defense
```

7. Subject authority card with explanation of spacing

```
Air defenses.      2d line,  2d space from left
                   edge
          Refer from   4th line, 12th space
          from left edge
     x Air raids - Protective measures
     --- - 5th line, 6th space from left edge
      - - 5th line, 8th space from left edge
```

the printed list may be consulted. Likewise only the see and
see also references which are made for the catalog are listed
on the authority card. In other words in choosing a heading
the printed list is used with its scope notes, see also's and
its suggested references to that subject. The authority file is
used to show which headings have been used and which references have been made to them. If all suggested references
were put on the authority card it would be necessary to check
those which had been made.

8. Subject authority card showing source of heading

```
Covered bridges.        (R. G. 1965-66)

                Refer from
    xx Bridges
```

The reference cards in the subject authority file are made exactly as those for the catalog, except that the subject headings are not in full capitals. Subject headings in the catalog need to be distinguished in some way from other headings for the convenience of the readers. In some catalogs red ink is used for these headings; in other catalogs full capitals are used. As the subject authority file is only for the use of the librarian, the terms are given with only the first letter of each heading or subheading capitalized. Cards 9 and 10 are sample reference cards for the subject authority file.

9. See reference card for subject authority file

```
            Defenses,  Air
                See
        Air defenses
```

10. See also reference card for subject authority file

```
┌────────────────────────────────────────────────────┐
│                                                    │
│                                                    │
│              Aeronautics, Military                 │
│                  See also                          │
│          Air defenses                              │
│                                                    │
│                                                    │
│                                                    │
│                                                    │
│                                                    │
│                                                    │
│                                                    │
└────────────────────────────────────────────────────┘
```

     Card 11 shows the exact location on the card of the
heading referred from, in this example, DEFENSES, AIR, the
word See, and the heading referred to, AIR DEFENSES. If the
heading referred from cannot all be written on one line, it
would be continued on the line below, beginning on the fourteenth space from the left. See or See also begins on the line
below the heading referred from and on the fourteenth space.
Similarly the heading referred to, if very long, would be continued on the line below, beginning on the twelfth space from
the left. This arrangement makes the first word of each heading stand out.

11. See reference card with explanation of spacing

```
┌────────────────────────────────────────────────────┐
│                                                    │
│              ---------4th line,  12th space        │
│                     from left edge                 │
│                                                    │
│           Defenses, Air                            │
│               See--5th line,  14th space from      │
│                     left edge                      │
│           Air defenses. --6th line,  8th space     │
│                     from left edge                 │
│                                                    │
│                                                    │
│                                                    │
│                                                    │
└────────────────────────────────────────────────────┘
```

The advantages of a subject authority file on cards are:
(1) It avoids transferring checks when a new edition of the
adopted list comes out. (2) It is always up to date. (3) It
gives space in the proper alphabetical place for new subjects
to be added. (4) It saves adding to a printed list the headings
chosen from other sources.

References

1. An analytical entry is made for a portion of a book;
e. g. , a card with the heading AIRPLANES would be made for
pages 122-134 of Margaret and Edwin Hyde's Where Speed Is
King while a subject card under SPORTS would be made for
the entire book.

2. The shelf list, which will be discussed in detail in a
later chapter, is a brief record of the books in a library.

3. A reference directs the reader from one heading to
another.

4. M. P. Douglas, The Teacher-Librarian's Handbook
(2d ed. ; Chicago, American Library Association, 1949), p. 75.

5. C. A. Cutter, Rules for a Dictionary Catalog (4th ed.
rewritten; Washington, Govt. Print. Off. , 1904), sect. 169.

6. Sears List of Subject Headings (9th ed. , ed. by B. M.
Westby; New York, Wilson, 1965).

7. Loc. cit.

8. Eloise Rue and Effie LaPlante, Subject Headings for
Children's Materials (Chicago, American Library Association,
1952).

9. Library Journal 89:1508, April 1, 1964.

Chapter III
Choice of Personal Names

Introduction. This chapter is concerned with the names of persons as authors or subjects and the choice of the different forms for the headings in the catalog. The catalog presents a comprehensive display of the works of an author and the different editions of those works which are in the particular library. The form of the author's name used as the heading is very important as it determines its location in the catalog. As the majority of books are written by persons, one's first concern is with how to enter a personal author in a catalog. And in order that all of the material by or about one person may be brought together the first step in cataloging is to decide upon the name and its form. This is done by looking in printed catalogs and lists to see how the person's works are usually entered and consequently how they are known.

Even in cataloging the smallest collection, it will soon be discovered that all authors do not have simple names, such as George Bernard Shaw; and even if they have, they may publish one book as Bernard Shaw, another as George Bernard Shaw, and a third as G. Bernard Shaw. In that case the obvious thing to do in order that all entries for books by or about the same person may come together in the catalog is to find out how that person's name most frequently appears on the title pages of his works and use that form. If other forms of the name are rather well-known, a reference can be made from them, i. e. , a card or cards giving other forms can direct the reader to the form of the name used.

Many libraries--large, scholarly libraries, such as university libraries and the Library of Congress, as well as the smaller public and school libraries--have adopted the policy of using the form of name usually found on the title page of the author's works. Such cataloging aids as the H. W. Wilson Standard Catalog Series have done likewise.

Usage, as shown in biographical dictionaries, encyclopedias, publishers' catalogs, is important and should be considered when deciding upon the form of name. Printed aids, as, for instance, the Standard Catalog Series may change the

form of name used by changing it in the next published issue.
But if a library decides to change the form of a name already
used in its catalog, either a reference must be made from
the form formerly used to the form to be used, or all of the
entries for that name must be changed. Women authors marry
and may use their husbands' names for later works; some authors use pseudonyms.

Other questions to be considered in deciding upon the
form of name to be used are: does the library buy printed
catalog cards from such sources as The H. W. Wilson Company? does the library now or may it later participate in a
Catalog Center which supplies the catalog cards along with
the books? or does the library suscribe for such service from
a commercial firm? In these cases the library will want to
use the form of name used on the printed cards or those
from the central agency. Having considered these factors the
next question is what to do about the names for books to be
cataloged locally.

An investigation of any miscellaneous group of books
shows quite a variety of kinds of names and librarians have
sought to simplify the task of locating them in the catalog by
framing rules to cover the points most often met. To quote
from the Anglo-American Cataloging Rules[1] "The entry for a
work is normally based on the statements that appear on the
title page, or on any part of the work that is used as its substitute, . . . Outside sources are used to assist in determining the entry when the work is published anonymously or when
there is suspicion or evidence that the statements in the publication may be erroneous or fictitious. "

Basic rule (A. -A. 1967. 40)

"Enter a person under the name by which he is commonly identified, whether it is his real name, assumed name,
nickname, title of nobility, or other appellation. . . . The
form of name of an author, editor, translator, etc. , is ordinarily determined from the way it appears in his works. ..."

Choice among different names. General rule (A. -A. 1967.
41)

"Enter an author who is not commonly identified in his
works by one particular name according to the following order of preference: 1) under the name by which he is generally identified in reference sources; 2) under the name by which

he is most frequently identified in his works; 3) under the
latest name he has used. '' With a very few exceptions the
same form of the name is always to be used.

Personal names fall into the following groups: simple
surnames, compound surnames, surnames with prefixes, noblemen with both family name and title, given name or byname,
married women's names, pseudonyms.

Pseudonyms (A.-A. 1967. 42)

"A. If all the works of an author appear only under one
pseudonym, enter him under the pseudonym. ''

    Eliot, George
       Refer from: Cross, Marian Evans

    Dodgson, Charles Lutwidge
       Refer from: Carroll, Lewis

"B. If the works of an author appear under several
pseudonyms or under his real name and one or more pseudonyms, enter him under the name by which he is primarily
identified in modern editions of his works and in reference
sources. In case of doubt, prefer the real name. ''

    Creasy, John   His pseudonyms include: Gordon Ashe
                                  Michael Halliday

          No references seem necessary.

Joint pseudonyms (A.-A. 1967. 3C)

"1. If collaborating authors consistently use a joint
pseudonym instead of their individual names, enter under the
pseudonym and [if necessary] refer to it from their real
names. . . . ''

    Queen, Ellery
       Refer from: Dannay, Frederic
               Lee, Manfred

If more detailed guidance is necessary, make an explanatory reference, e. g. ,

    Dannay, Frederic
      For works of this author written in collaboration
    with Manfred Lee see entry under:
    Queen, Ellery

A similar reference may be made from Manfred Lee. Some small libraries may not find any references to Queen necessary.

"2. If for any reason the pseudonym cannot be used as a heading, enter the work under its title unless rule 3A[2] should be applied. Make added entries under the names of the authors and make an explanatory reference from the pseudonym to their names."

Title page:

Philip; the story of a boy violinist, by T. W. O.
(T. W. O. is the pseudonym of Mary O. Hungerford and Virginia C. Young)

Enter under title with added entries under Hungerford and Young and an explanatory reference from T. W. O. to Hungerford and Young.

Fullness (A. -A. 1967. 43)

"A. If the forms of name appearing in the works of an author vary in fullness, use the fullest form that has appeared on a . . . title page, half title, or cover, except that a rarely used initial . . . [or] an unused . . . forename . . . is normally ignored."

Belloc, Hilaire   Full name: Joseph Hilaire Pierre Belloc
Agar, Herbert   Full name: Herbert Sebastian Agar

Refer from the full name if anyone is likely to look under it, especially if the first name has been omitted.

"B. If the fullest form of the name . . . includes one or more forenames represented only by initials, spell out the forenames if necessary to distinguish two or more persons. Always spell out a first forename represented by an initial if the surname is a common one."

"C. If further differentiation is required, add the person's dates of birth and death" whether or not dates are usually used in name headings.

Entry under surname (A. -A. 1967. 46)

Basic Rule !

Simple surnames with one or more given names. "Enter a person whose name contains a surname and who is not known to be primarily identified by some other name, under

the surname followed by the other parts of his name in the
form and fullness he commonly uses . . . ."

    Adams, James Truslow
    Harris, Joel Chandler
    Milne, Alan Alexander
    Morgan, Alfred Powell

    Compound surnames. "B. 1. . . . Enter a person with
a compound surname under the element of his surname by
which he prefers to be entered, or, if this is unknown, under
the element by which he is listed in reference sources, . . ."

    Lloyd George, David
        Refer from: George, David Lloyd

    Hyphenated surnames. "B. 2. . . . If the elements of the
surname are hyphenated, either regularly or occasionally, enter under the first."

    Mendelssohn-Bartholdy, Felix
        Refer from: Bartholdy, Felix Mendelssohn

". . . In other cases of names known to be compound surnames
the entry element is determined by normal usage in the language of the person involved, . . ."

    Johnson Smith, Geoffrey
        Refer from: Smith, Geoffrey Johnson

References should be made from the other part if it is at all
likely that anyone would look under it.

    Married women's names. "B. 3b. . . .Names of married
women that include both the maiden surname and the husband's
surname are entered under the husband's surname. . ."

    Stowe, Harriet Beecher

    "Different names (A.-A. 1967. 121. 1a) Refer from a
name used by the author or found in reference sources that is
different from the one used in the heading."

    Boissevain, Edna St. Vincent Millay
    see Millay, Edna St. Vincent

    Surnames with prefixes (A.-A. 1967. 46) "E. 1. . . . Enter

a surname that includes a separately written prefix consisting of an article, a preposition, or a combination of the two, under the element most commonly used as entry element in alphabetical listings in the person's language,. . . . ''

a. ''Dutch and Flemish. . . enter under the part of the name following the prefix except that if the prefix is ver, enter under the prefix. If the name is not of Dutch or Flemish origin, 1) enter a person from the Netherlands under the part of the name following the prefix, 2) enter a person from Belgium according to the rules for the language of the name. ''

> Hoff, Jacobus Hendricus van't
> Du Barry, Jeanne Bécu, comtesse

b. ''English. Enter under the prefix''

> De Quincey, Thomas
> De Voto, Bernard
> La Farge, Oliver
> Du Maurier, Daphne
> Van Buren, Martin

c. ''French. If the prefix consists of an article or of a contraction of an article and a preposition, enter under the prefix. ''

> Du Chaillu, Paul
> Le Rouge, Gustave

''If it consists of a preposition or of a preposition followed by an article, enter under the part of the name following the preposition. ''

> La Fontaine, Jean de
> Muset, Alfred de

d. ''German. If the prefix consists of an article or of a contraction of a preposition and an article, enter under the prefix. ''

> Vom Ende, Erich

''If it consists of a preposition or a preposition followed by an article, enter under the part of the name following the prefix. ''

> Goethe, Wolfgang von

Mühll, Peter von der

e. "Italian. In general, enter under the prefix. "

La Guardia, Fiorello Henry

"The following forms in particular are rarely construed as prefixes: <u>de</u>, <u>de</u>', <u>degli</u>, <u>dei</u>, and <u>de</u> <u>li</u>. "

Medici, Lorenzo de'

f. "Scandinavian. . . . Enter under the part of the name following the prefix when the prefix is of Scandinavian or Germanic origin . . . " otherwise enter under the prefix.

Linné, Carl von
La Cour, Jens Lassen

g. "Spanish. Enter under the part of the name following the prefix, except that if the prefix consists of an article only, enter under the article. "

Cervantes Saavédra, Miguel de
Gama, Vasco da

"2. Other prefixes. In general, if the prefix is other than an article, preposition, or combination of the two enter under the prefix. "

Fitzgerald, David
MacDonald, William
O'Connor, Denis
St. John, Francis R.

"F. Prefixes hyphenated or combined with surnames. If the prefix of a person's surname is regularly or occasionally hyphenated or combined with the surname, enter the name under the prefix. If necessary, refer from the other form. "

De Bure, Guillaume
    Refer from: Bure, Guillaume de

Explanatory references (A. -A. 1967. 121)

"B. 2. . . . Make explanatory references under the various separately written prefixes to surnames explaining how names with such prefixes are entered in the catalog. "

"De la

When this prefix, written as separate words, occurs at the beginning of the surname of a person whose language is English or Swedish, or whose nationality is South African, the surname is entered

under the prefix. The prefix and the remainder of
the name are filed as though they were written as
one word. If the person's language is French, the
surname is entered under the prefix La. In other
cases the surname is entered under the part of the
name following the prefix. ''

Titles of nobility, honor, address, etc., added to the
name (A.-A. 1967. 46)

"G. 1. Titles of nobility. Add the title of nobility in the
vernacular to the name of a nobleman who is not entered under his title and make appropriate references. . . . In the
case of the wife of a nobleman, the title corresponding to
that of her husband is used. ''

Bacon, Francis, Viscount St. Albans
Byron, George Gordon, Baron Byron

"2. British titles of honor. Add before the forenames
the terms of honor, Sir, Dame, Lord, or Lady used in conjunction with the names of British baronets and knights; dames
of the Order of the British Empire and the Royal Victorian
Order; younger sons of dukes and marquesses; and the daugh-
ters of dukes, marquesses, and earls, respectively. ''

Landseer, Sir Edwin
Sitwell, Dame Edith
Gordon, Lord George
Stanhope, Lady Hester

"Add after the forenames the titles of rank, bart. or
Lady, in the cases of a baronet and of the wife of a baronet
or knight who is not entitled to the prefixed title of 'Lady'
by virtue of her father's rank, respectively. ''

Beecham, Sir Thomas, bart.
Duff-Gordon, Lucie, Lady

"4. . . . Other titles borne by persons entered under
surname are added only when required to distinguish persons
with identical names. . . .''

Entry under title of nobility (A.-A. 1967. 47)

"A. Enter under the proper name in the title of nobility
(including a courtesy title) 1) an author who uses his title

rather than his surname in his works and 2) any other person who is generally so listed in those reference sources that do not list noblemen either all under title or all under surname. The entry word is followed by the personal names in direct order, except for forenames that are not used, and by the term of rank in the vernacular. . . . ''

> Beaverbrook, Maxwell Aitken, Baron
>   Refer from: Aitken, Max, Baron Beaverbrook
>   Aitken, William Maxwell, Baron Beav-
>   erbrook

''B. If the proper name in the title is the same as the surname, however, or if it is uncertain how the name is, or will be, generally listed in reference sources, enter under the surname followed by the forenames and title. . . . ''

> Macaulay, Thomas Babington, Baron Macaulay

''C. If the bearers of a title of nobility are sequentially numbered, include the English abbreviation of the ordinal number when two or more of the bearers also have the same personal name and are represented in the catalog. ''

> Buckingham and Chandos, Richard Grenville, 1st Duke of
> Buckingham and Chandos, Richard Grenville, 2d Duke of

Entry under given name or byname (A. -A. 1967. 49)

''A. General rules

   ''1. Enter a person whose name does not include a surname and who is not primarily identified by a title of nobility under the part of his name by which he is primarily identified in reference sources, normally the first of the names that he uses. Include any . . . (secondary name acquired informally, such as a nickname, epithet, sobriquet--Footnote 17, p. 90). ''

> John the Baptist

   ''3. Add after the name any identifying word or phrase (title of honor, rank or position, place of origin or residence, etc.) that is commonly associated with the name (but cannot be regarded as an integral part of it) as it appears in publications by the person and in reference sources. ''

> Joseph, Nez Percé chief

"4. Treat a word or phrase associated with the name and denoting place of origin or residence as part of the name if no preposition is involved or if a foreign-language preposition is found in English language sources."

Giovanni da Ravenna

If the preposition is given in English in English language sources, however, treat the phrase as an identifying phrase unless the name is English or established in an English form. In the latter case treat the phrase as part of the name.

Moses ben Jacob, of Coucy

but

John of Gaunt, Duke of Lancaster

Royalty:

Alfred the Great, King of England
Richard I, King of England
Richard II, King of England
Gustav I Vasa, King of Sweden
Mary, consort of George V, King of Great Britain

Saints:

Constantine I, Emperor of Rome
    Refer from: Constantine, Saint
Francis of Assisi, Saint
Augustine, Saint, Bp

Popes:

Gregory I, Pope
    Refer from: Gregory, Saint, Pope Gregory I
            Gregory the Great, Pope

Bishops, cardinals, etc.:

Bessarion, Cardinal
Newman, John Henry, Cardinal
Dositheos, Patriarch of Jerusalem
Gregorius, Abp of Corinth

Entry of Roman names (A.-A. 1967. 50)

"Enter a Roman of classical times under the part of his name most commonly used as entry element in reference sources. In case of doubt, enter under the first of his names."

Cicero, Marcus Tullius

Adapter or original author (A. -A. 1967. 7)

"A. Enter an adaptation or other rewriting of a work in a different literary style (e. g. , a paraphrase, epitome, version for children) or in a different literary form (e. g. , a dramatization, novelization, versification) under the person who did the adapting or rewriting, if known; otherwise under its title. Make the appropriate added entry for the original work. In the case of paraphrases of Biblical texts, however, the added entry is omitted; a form subject heading is provided instead. . . . "

Title page:

> Sinclair Lewis' Dodsworth, dramatized by Sidney Howard.

Enter under Howard, with an added entry under Lewis.

Title page:

> The boys' King Arthur, Sir Thomas Malory's History of King Arthur and his knights of the Round Table; edited for boys by Sidney Lanier.

Close examination of this book and its title page shows that it is Malory's book, edited and with an explanatory introduction to make it clear to readers. It would be entered in the catalog under Malory with an added entry under Lanier.

Title page:

> The book of King Arthur and his noble knights; stories from Sir Thomas Malory's Morte Darthur by Mary Macleod.

This work is similar to the one edited by Sidney Lanier. Miss Macleod has selected certain stories from Malory and reworded them to suit her young readers. It is neither Malory's language nor his selection, hence it would be entered in the catalog under Macleod with an added entry under Malory. Lamb's Tales from Shakespeare is cataloged in the same way, the main entry under Lamb, the adapter, with an added entry under Shakespeare.

Another type of book which is sometimes puzzling is selections from an individual work of an author. Hill's translation of a selection of The Canterbury Tales is an example.

In some titles, the term selected is used in the sense that the selections included are taken from all the works of an author rather than from a single work. In either case the treatment is the same. The main entry is made under the author's name and the translator's or editor's name is included in the entry. An added entry would be made for the editor or the translator; for this book, Frank Ernest Hill.

Collections. (A. -A. 1967. 5)

"A. With collective title. If a collection of independent works by different authors, not written specifically for the same occasion or for the publication in hand, or of extracts from such works, has a collective title, enter it under the person who compiled it when he is named on the title page as compiler or editor, or is known to have been so named in another edition of the collection; otherwise enter it under its title. Add the designation comp. to the heading. Use this designation also if the compiler translated the collection. Make an added entry under the compiler, editor, or title that is not used as main entry. Make author-title added entries for the works included if there are not more than three. . . ."

Title page:
    . . . Regency poets; Byron, Shelley, Keats. Compiled by C. R. Bull.

Enter under Bull with added entries under Byron, Shelley, Keats, and under title.

"B. Without collective title. If a collection of previously existing works by different authors, or of extracts from such works, lacks a collective title, enter it under the heading appropriate to the work listed first on the title page, or, if there is no collective title page, under the heading appropriate to the first work in the collection. Make an added entry under the compiler or editor if he is named on the title page as compiler or editor. Make added entries under the works or authors included if appropriate under the criteria given in A above . . . ."

Title page:
    The vision of Sir Launfal, by James Russell Lowell; the Courtship of Miles Standish, by Henry Wadsworth Longfellow; Snowbound, by John Greenleaf Whittier; edited with an introduction and notes by Charles Robert Gaston.

For this work the main entry would be under the first
author, Lowell; there would be added entries under the other
two authors and under the editor.

Conclusions regarding choice of personal names. It will
be seen from these rules that nearly all authors' names will
fall into one of the preceding groups. Sometimes the rule is
not absolutely definite. Many rules include the phrase "commonly identified," or "primarily identified," and many include the phrase "refer from the part...," "References
should be made from the other part," "make appropriate references." It is believed that the illustrations will make the
meaning clear, as in most instances the form of the reference
is indicated. The form of the name by which the person is
commonly identified would be the one used on the title pages
of the author's books, the one given in most biographical dictionaries, encyclopedias, the Booklist and Subscription Books
Bulletin, and other standard authorities. It is necessary to
consult only one reliable aid for each name provided that aid
gives the full name and does not suggest other forms. If
other forms are indicated, the librarian should consult several aids before deciding on the form for the catalog.

Where one form is as well known as the other, choose
one and always use it. A few authors use their real names
for one type of writing and a pseudonym or pseudonyms for
other types. Ray Stannard Baker wrote under his own name
except when writing his popular essays, Adventures in Con-
tentment, Adventures in Friendship, etc., for which he used
the pseudonym David Grayson. In some libraries his books
are entered in the catalog under both his real name and his
pseudonym, his essays under Grayson, his other works under
Baker, with see also references connecting the two. For the
small library it would seem better to put all his works under
his own name and refer from Grayson, David, pseud. Consider, however, what the printed cards use or the Cataloging
Center from which the library gets its catalog cards.

There may be cases where the librarian does not know
whether the name is real or a pseudonym. Consider it a real
name. If later it proves to be a pseudonym, add the abbreviation pseud. to the name as given in the catalog and make a
reference from the real name, unless it is decided to change
the entry to the real name.

Some libraries find it very useful to have authors' dates
of birth and death included in the heading on the catalog card:

     Cather, Willa Sibert, 1876-1947.
     Bennett, Arnold, 1867-1931.

In a number of schools the pupils are required to know the
dates of birth and death of the authors on whose works they
report. Where bibliographical tools are few, it is convenient
for both pupils and librarians to have these dates on the catalog cards. The librarian, in looking up the forms of the name
for the heading in the catalog, may note the dates if they are
given and include them in the heading. If the dates are not
readily found, they may be omitted and added later. Dates
are essential for the identification of different authors whose
names are the same.

     Authority file for names. Many librarians find it conven-
ient to have an authority file for the names used in their catalogs. The librarian may decide to enter all of Elizabeth Janet
Gray's books under Vining, Elizabeth Gray. A card would then
be made using the adopted form as heading. It would be followed by the title of one of her books to identify the author,
by a list of the authorities consulted in deciding on that form,
and by a note indicating a reference from Gray. After an author's name has been established, all that is necessary when
a book is added is to look in the authority file for names,
note the form adopted, be sure it is the same person, and use
that form for the new title.

     The items and form for the cards in this file may be
described as follows: (1) The heading on the name authority
card is the one adopted for the catalog. (2) The title is that
of the first book by that author cataloged for that library and
serves to identify him. (3) The date is the copyright date (if
no copyright date, the imprint or some other date) of that
book, as found on the back of the title page, preceded by the
word "copyright" and given on the card as [c1952]. (4) The
abbreviations are for the bibliographical and biographical aids
in which the librarian looked. (5) An n to the left of the abbreviation for the name of an aid means that the author's
name was found in that aid; a t means that the title was found.
(6) If the author's dates of birth and death are included in the
heading, a d may be added to indicate that the date or dates
were found. (7) If the form of the name in the aid differs
from that given in the heading on this card, or if the date
differs, the variant form is put in parentheses after the abbreviation for the aid. (8) If references are made from other
forms of the name, they are indicated on the line or lines
directly above the hole in the card, preceded by an x, the

symbol for a see reference.

12. Name authority card for person as author

```
        Vining, Elizabeth (Gray) 1902-
            Windows for the Crown Prince.
        [c1952]

    ntd C. B. I. 1943-1948 (Gray, Elizabeth
        Janet (Mrs. Morgan Vining))
    nt Bklist v. 48



                            x Gray, Elizabeth Janet
```

If the name is not that of the author of the book, but the subject or the illustrator, for example, it is given above the author's name and is indented farther to the right. To the left of the author's name is given an abbreviation which stands for the relation of the name in the heading to the book. The form is shown in Card 13, the authority card for Henry Hudson, subject of James Maurice Scott's biography. The abbreviation subj. indicates that Hudson is the subject of this book. The remainder of the card would have exactly the same form as the card for Vining. The aids would be those con-

13. Name authority card for person as added entry

```
            Hudson, Henry, d. 1611.
    subj. Scott, James Maurice, 1906-
            Hudson of Hudson's Bay.        1951.

        n Amer. ency. 1951 ed.
        ntd Std. cat. for h. s. libs. 6th ed.
        nd Webster's dict. (? - 1611)
```

sulted for Hudson. There would be another authority card for the heading Scott, James Maurice, the same form as Card 12.

The name authority file may have an authority card for every name used as a heading in the catalog whether as author, subject, illustrator, or in any other capacity, or only for those names requiring cross references.

When to have authority files for names. If the library uses printed cards, which are discussed in Chapter X, and is able to get them for practically all of its books, it is best to use the form of the name given on the printed card; thus an authority file for names would be unnecessary. If a special library's collection, however, is of such a nature as to include many works by authors with complicated names--foreign names, for instance--and there are no printed cards for many of them, a name authority file will be found to save time. It records, once for all, the form of name to be used, the information obtained in establishing the form of name, and the references to it which have been filed in the catalog.

If the library is small and the catalog is near the desk, a name authority file is not necessary; the catalog itself may be the authority file. If this plan is followed, when references are made from other forms of the name than that adopted, either a special file of name references must be maintained or these references must be noted on the first main card for that author; when that card is withdrawn, the tracing of the references must be transferred to another main card, and so on.

The value of an authority file for names depends upon: (1) whether or not printed cards are used; (2) whether or not the names to be entered are so complicated that any one of a number of different forms might be used; (3) whether there are one or more references from other forms to be recorded; (4) the distance from the desk of the librarian to the catalog.

References

1. Anglo-American Cataloging Rules. North American Text (Chicago, American Library Association, 1967), Chapter I, Entry, p. 9, cited in this manual as A.-A. 1967, with the number of the rule.

2. ''Enter a work of shared authorship under the person or corporate body, if any, to whom principal responsibility is attributed, e. g. , by wording or typography. ''

Chapter IV
Anonymous Classics and Other Title Entries

Anonymous Classics

An anonymous classic is "A work of unknown or doubtful authorship, commonly designated by title, which may have appeared in the course of time in many editions, versions, and/or translations. "[1] Uniform titles enable the cataloger to bring together in the catalog all entries for a given work, be it a poem, epic, romance, tale, play, chronicles or sacred literature if it has appeared under various titles in different editions, translations, etc. The use of uniform titles has been widespread and of long standing for sacred scriptures, anonymous works without titles, early anonymous chronicles and literary works, peace treaties and international conventions, etc.

General rule. (A. -A. 1967. 100)

"A. When the editions . . . translations, etc. , of a work appear under various titles, select one title as the uniform title under which all will be cataloged. "

"B. In the case of works entered under title, treat the uniform title as a heading. Make references from variants of the title but prefer added entries for titles that apply to the particular edition rather than to the work itself. "

The title page of The Arabian Nights as reproduced and the main card for an anonymous classic illustrate this rule.

The
Arabian Nights
Based on the Translation
From the Arabic By
Edward William Lane
Selected, Edited, and Arranged
For Young People By
Frances Jenkins Olcott
Illustrations and
Decorations By
Monro S. Orr
New York
Henry Holt and Company

14. Anonymous classic--main entry

Arabian nights.
    The Arabian nights, based on the trans-
lation from the Arabic by Edward William
Lane; selected, . . .

    <u>Arabian nights</u> is the form given in the list of common-
ly used headings for anonymous classics on page 76 and is
in accordance with the rule given there. These headings take
the place of an author and are in the position of the author's
name on the card.

Works written before 1501. (A. -A. 1967. 102)

    "A. . . . Prefer the title, in the original language, by
which a work written before 1501 has become identified in reference sources," e. g. , Beowulf, Chanson de Roland, Nibe-
lungenlied.

    "B. . . . Prefer a well established English title, when
there is one, for a work in classical Greek. . . . "

Homer.
    The Iliad
Plato.
    The Republic

Uniform titles. (A. -A. 1967. 124)

    "A. . . . Refer to the uniform title from the different
titles or variants of the title under which a work has been
published or cited in reference sources. . . . "

Song of the Nibelungs
    <u>see</u> Nibelungenlied

"B. . . . When separately published parts of a work are cataloged under their own titles, make an explanatory reference from the uniform title of the main work to any such parts."

"Arabian nights.
            For separately published stories from this work see:
Ali Baba
Sindbad the sailor
[etc.]"

The following list, based on various codes and aids, gives some headings commonly used:

Arabian nights.	Cuchulain.	Nibelungenlied.
Arthur, King.	Grail.	Njals saga.
Beowulf.	Kalevala.	Reynard the Fox.
Chanson de Roland.	Mabinogion.	Robin Hood.
Cid Campeador.	Mother Goose.	Seven sages.

The entering of anonymous classics under the name of the person who retells the story is explained in Chapter III. For instance, James Baldwin's Story of Roland has the main entry under Baldwin, but has an added entry under "Chanson de Roland." Likewise Eleanor Hull's Boys' Cuchulain; Heroic Legends of Ireland may be entered under Hull as in the Children's Catalog, but with an added entry under Cuchulain.

Sacred Scriptures

Bible. (A. -A. 1967. 108)

"Use the uniform title Bible for the Bible and any of its parts. Add to this heading the designation of a part, . . ."

Parts of the Bible. (A. -A. 1967. 109)

"A. . . . Designate the Old Testament . . . and the New Testament . . . . Treat the titles of individual books . . . as subheadings under the appropriate testament. . . . Use Arabic numerals for books, . . ."

Bible. New Testament.
Bible. New Testament. Luke.
Bible. Old Testament. Ezra.

"B. . . . Enter editions . . . of books of the Bible commonly identified by a group name, under that name in the form of a subheading under the appropriate testament. . . . ''

      Bible. New Testament. Epistles.
      Bible. Old Testament. Pentateuch.

"D. Make appropriate references from the titles of individual books, from variant forms of these titles, and from
the names of groups of books. Refer from these also in the
form of direct subheadings under <u>Bible</u> and, in the case of
variants, in the form of indirect subheadings under the testament. ''

     "Bible. Old Testament. Ezra. ''
       Refer from: Ezra.
               Bible. Ezra.

     "Bible. Old Testament. Pentateuch. ''
       Refer from: Pentateuch.
               Bible. Pentateuch.

     Version. (A. -A. 1967. 111)

"A. Give a brief form of the name of the version as a
subheading. . . . ''

      Bible. Authorized. (In the small library it is unneces-
                 sary to give the language, e. g.,
        Bible. English. Authorized.)
but   Bible. Latin. Vulgate.

Other Sacred Scriptures.

The sacred literature of any other religion is entered in
a similar way under a uniform heading, e. g., <u>Koran</u>, <u>Talmud</u>.

A special library of religious literature although small,
would need to consult the <u>Anglo-American Cataloging Rules</u> for
the rules governing headings for religious literature.

Anonymous Works

Anonymous works are those whose authors are not known,
or, at least, are not given in the book. There may be: (1) no
indication of authorship; (2) a descriptive or generic word or
phrase preceded by an article, e. g., "by 'the soldier' ''; (3)
the title of another of the author's works, e. g., "by the author of . . .''; or (4) initials, which may or may not be those

of the author's name.

Works of unknown or uncertain authorship, or by unnamed groups. (A.-A. 1967. 2)

"A. Enter under title a work that is of unknown or uncertain authorship, or that is by a group that lacks a name. Make added entries [when necessary] under as many as three persons to whom authorship has been attributed, . . ."

Title page:

> The secret expedition; a farce (in two acts) as it has been represented upon the political theatre of Europe.
>
> (Author unknown)
>
> Enter under title.

Title page:

> A memorial to Congress against an increase of duties on importations, by citizens of Boston and vicinity.
>
> Enter under title.

"C. If the only clue to authorship is in the appearance on the title page of initials, some other alphabetical device, a characterizing word or phrase preceded by the indefinite article, or a phrase naming another work that the author wrote, make an added entry under this clue. . . ."

Title page:

> Indiscretions of Dr. Carstairs, by A. De O.
>
> (Author unidentified)
>
> Enter under title and make added entries under initials.

Works of shared authorship. (A.-A. 1967. 3)

"B. 1c. If the authors are not named in any edition of the work, enter it under its title and make added entries under the authors if they can be determined from reference sources. If reference sources make $3A^2$ applicable, however, follow its provisions."

"2. If no one is represented as principal author and there are more than three authors, enter the work under its title unless the work is produced under the direction of an

editor named on the title page. In this case apply rule 4A.[3]
Make an added entry under the author named first on the
title page. "

Title page:

> The United Nations and economic and social cooper-
> ation, by Robert E. Asher, Walter M. Kotschnig,
> William Adams Brown, Jr., and associates.

Enter under title with an added entry under Asher.

Serials. (A. -A. 1967. 6)

"A. . . . Enter a serial that is not issued by or under
the authority of a corporate body and is not of personal authorship under its title. "

Title page:

> The Atlantic

> Who's who in America

"B. . . . 1. Enter a periodical, monographic series, or
a serially published bibliography, index, directory, biographical dictionary, almanac, or yearbook, issued by or under the
authority of a corporate body, under its title with an added
entry under the corporate body. "

Title page:

> Law library journal . . . American Association of
> Law Libraries

> Statistical abstract of the United States
> (Yearbook issued successively by various agencies
> of the U. S. Government)

Name authority cards. Name authority cards are made for
anonymous classics and sacred books. They are similar in
form to those for personal names, but omit title and date,
used for personal authors for identification of the author.

In the smaller, general libraries name authority cards
are not necessary for individual books, periodicals, almanacs,
encyclopedias, etc. entered under title.

15. Name authority card for anonymous classic

```
        Chanson de Roland.

        n Children's cat. 11th ed.
        n Americana, 1965 ed.   (Roland Song, The)




            x Roland
            x Song of Roland
```

References

1. A. L. A. Glossary of Library Terms (Chicago, American Library Association, 1943), p. 5.

2. A. -A. 1967. 3A. Enter a work of shared authorship under the person or corporate body, if any, to whom principal responsibility is attributed, e. g. , by wording or typography.

3. A. -A. 1967. 4A. Enter a work produced under editorial direction under its editor providing: 1) he is named on the title page of the work, 2) the publisher is not named in the title, and 3) the editor appears to be primarily responsible for the existence of the work. In all other cases enter under the title and make an added entry under the editor if he is named on the title page. If authors are named on the title page, make an added entry under the one named first.

Chapter V
Names of Organizations

Introduction. In Chapter III the authors' names considered are those of persons. There is a kind of publication for
whose contents no person is primarily responsible, namely,
the publications of societies and institutions, and the official
publications of countries, states, cities, and towns. Examples
of such publications are: Annual Report of the Board of Re-
gents of the Smithsonian Institution; Journal of the National
Education Association of the United States; Annual Report of the
Los Angeles Public Library; Collections of the State Historical
Society of Wisconsin; Official Guide, New York World's Fair,
1964/1965; Handbook of the Layton Art Gallery. Are not the
Smithsonian Institution; National Education Association of the
United States; Los Angeles Public Library; State Historical
Society of Wisconsin; New York World's Fair, 1964/1965; and
the Layton Art Gallery the authors of these publications? Since
this is so, the works are cataloged under their authors' names
just as are other works.

As personal authors upon closer observation group themselves into certain classes--simple surnames, compound surnames, names with prefixes, etc., so the rules for corporate
authors may be grouped as rules for subordinate and related
bodies; geographic names; governments; government bodies and
officials; conferences, congresses, meetings, etc.; religious
bodies and officials; radio and television stations.

The collections on a special subject, even in a library
whose collection as a whole is small, are frequently quite extensive; hence a library practically limited to legal publications; or, one containing chiefly religious publications would
need to use the Anglo-American Cataloging Rules. This manual attempts only to include those rules likely to be needed
for a general collection such as is found in a school or smaller public library.

This chapter gives the general rules for entry for corporate bodies; then the rules for particular types of publications. For instance, is the work of a subordinate unit to be
entered directly under the specific unit or under the parent
body? What is the proper entry for legislative decrees of the

chief executive issued instead of a legislative enactment; a
constitution of a state, province, etc.; texts of a religious observance? This section is followed by the basic rules for the
headings for corporate bodies; then the detailed rules regarding the choice and form of the name; for instance, variant
forms; additions to names; changes of names; subordinate and
related bodies; governments; etc.

Corporate author or personal author (A.-A. 1967. 17)

". . . This rule applies to works issued by or bearing
the authority of a corporate body, but with authorship or edi-
torship specifically and prominently attributed to one or more
persons, either by name or by official title.

"A. Works of corporate authorship.

"1. Enter under the corporate body, with an added entry under the personal author or the one named first, a work
that is by its nature necessarily the expression of the corporate thought or activity of the body. Such works include official
records and reports, and statements, studies, and other communications dealing with the policies, operations, or management of the body made by officers or other employees of the
body. Single reports, however, that are made by officers or
other employees and that embody the results of scholarly investigation or scientific research are excluded unless written
by more than three persons, none of whom is represented as
the principal author. All reports and studies prepared by con-
sultants engaged for the particular purpose are excluded. "

Title page:

Public water supplies of Colorado, 1959-60, by Dean
O. Gregg, Eric L. Meyer, Margaret M. Targy, and
Edward A. Moulder, U. S. Geological Survey. Prepar-
ed by the U. S. Geological Survey . . .

Enter under: U. S. Geological Survey with an added entry
under Gregg.

"2. Enter under the corporate body a work, other than
a formal history, describing the body, its functions, procedures, facilities, resources, etc., or an inventory, catalog,
directory of personnel, list of members, etc. "

Title page:

The Metropolitan Museum of Art A guide to an exhibition of Islamic miniature painting and book illumination, by M. S. Dimand

Enter under: New York. Metropolitan Museum of Art with an added entry under Dimand.

"B. Works not of corporate authorship.

If the work would not be entered under corporate body under the provisions of A above or if there is doubt as to whether it would, enter it under the heading under which it would be entered if no corporate body were involved. Make an added entry under the body unless it functions solely as publisher. "

Title page:

The Library of Congress subject headings; a practical guide, by David Judson Haykin, Chief, Subject Cataloging Division

Enter under: Haykin and make an added entry under U. S. Library of Congress. This is a general guide, not just for the Library of Congress.

"C. Works by chiefs of state, heads of governments, etc.

"1. Official communications

"a. Enter an official communication (e. g., a message to a legislature . . .) issued by a chief of state, a head of a government, or a head of an international intergovernmental body under the corporate heading for the office which he holds. . . . "

"c. Enter a collection of official communications of more than one chief of state, etc., under the heading for the office held.

Title page:

. . . Congress . . . session. House document no
. . . . Economic report of the President transmitted
to the Congress (Annual)

Enter under the heading for the President.

"2. Other speeches and writings

"a. Treat any other speech or writing of such a person as a work of personal authorship. "

Title page:

The second inaugural address of Abraham Lincoln

Enter under: Lincoln.

"c. Enter a collection containing both official communications and other works of such persons as a work of personal authorship, if by one person; as a collection, if by several persons and monographic in character; or as a serial, if by several persons and serial in character. In each case make an added entry under the heading for the office held, with or without specifying the name of an incumbent, . . ."

Title page:

A compilation of the messages and papers of the Presidents . . . by James D. Richardson

Enter under: Richardson as compiler with an added entry under the heading for the President.

Corporate body or subordinate unit (A. -A. 1967. 18)

"A. Enter a work specifically and prominently attributed to a subordinate unit of a corporate body under the heading for the subordinate unit unless the unit simply acts as the information or publication agent for the parent body. In this case enter under the parent body and make an explanatory reference from the heading for the subordinate unit. "

Title page:

A. L. A. cataloging rules for author and title entries, prepared by the Division of Cataloging and Classification of the American Library Association. 2d ed. Edited by Clara Beetle

Enter under the heading for the association's division.

"B. If the responsibility of the subordinate unit for preparing the work is not stated prominently, or if the subordinate unit cannot be identified, enter the work under the parent body.

"C. If two or three subordinate units are prominently represented as sharing responsibility for the work, enter it under the one indicated as principally responsible; otherwise under the one first named. Make added entries under the other subordinate units, " if such entries would be useful.

"D. If authorship is prominently represented as being divided among more than three subordinate bodies, none of which is indicated as principally responsible, enter the work under its title unless all of the bodies would be entered as subheadings under the same parent body. . . . In this case enter the work under the parent body. In either case make an added entry under the first-named subordinate body. "

Laws, etc. (A.-A. 1967. 20)

"A. Laws governing one jurisdiction. Enter legislative enactments and the decrees, etc., of the chief executive issued in lieu of legislative enactments under a heading consisting of the name of the jurisdiction governed by the law followed by one of the subheadings indicated below. " If needed added entries may be made "under the names of persons and corporate bodies, exclusive of legislative bodies, responsible for compiling or issuing the laws. If the jurisdiction is a country, state, city-state, province, or equivalent jurisdiction, use the subheading Laws, statutes, etc. If it is a local jurisdiction (e.g., a county or a municipal jurisdiction), use the subheading Ordinances, local laws, etc. . . . . "

Title page:

The school law of Illinois . . . Prepared by T.A. Reynolds, Assistant Superintendent. Issued by John A. Wieland, Superintendent of Public Instruction. Amended by the Fifty-ninth General Assembly

Enter under: Illinois. Laws, statutes, etc., with an added entry under the heading for the Department of Public Instruction.

"B. Laws governing more than one jurisdiction.

"1. Enter compilations of laws governing each of two or three jurisdictions under the one first named with added entries under the others [if likely to be used]; each followed by the appropriate subheading. . . . "

Cover-title:

> Traffic laws, city and state
> (Foreword signed: Ray Scruggs. Contains ordinances
> of the City of Houston and laws of the State of Texas)

Enter under: Houston. Ordinances, local laws, etc., with an added entry under the heading: Texas. Laws, statutes, etc. May also need, especially in the locality, Houston in this case, an added entry under Scruggs.

"2. Enter compilations of laws governing more than three jurisdictions under the personal or corporate compiler if named on the title page; otherwise under title. "

Title page:

> Motor bus laws and regulations; a complete
> code of all motor bus regulatory laws . . .
> Compiled and edited by John M. Meighan

Enter under: Meighan as compiler.

Administrative regulations (A.-A. 1967. 21)

"A. Enter under the promulgating agency the regulations, rules, etc., it has adopted under authority granted by legislative enactment. . . ."

Title page:

> Regulations under the Destructive insect
> and pest act as they apply to the importa-
> tion of plants and plant products. Depart-
> ment of Agriculture, Ottawa

Enter under the heading for the department with an added entry under the heading:

Canada. Laws, statutes, etc.
Destructive insect and pest act.

Constitutions and charters (A.-A. 1967. 22)

"A. Political jurisdictions.

"1. Enter a constitution or charter of a political jurisdiction under that jurisdiction, followed by the subheading Con-

stitution or Charter, as appropriate. "

Title page:
  Pocket edition of the Constitution of the United States

Enter under U. S. Constitution and make a see also reference from U. S. Laws, statutes, etc.

Court rules (A. -A. 1967. 23)

"A. Enter court rules under the name of the jurisdiction from which the court derives its authority followed by the
subheading Court rules and the name of the court governed by
the rules. . . . "

Title page:
  Rules of the Supreme Court of Canada

Enter under: Canada. Court rules. Supreme Court and
make a see also reference from Canada. Supreme Court.

Treaties, Intergovernmental agreements, etc. (A. -A.
1967. 25)

"A. International treaties, etc.

"1. . . . Enter a bilateral or trilateral treaty, other
than a peace treaty . . . or any other bilateral or trilateral
instrument embodying a formal agreement between two or
more countries according to the following order of preference:
a) under the home country if it is a signatory; b) under the
party on one side of a bilateral treaty if it is the only party
on that side and there are two or more parties on the other
side; c) under the party whose catalog heading is first in alphabetical order. Add the subheading Treaties, etc., after the
name of the country. If the treaty is bilateral and there is
only one party on the other side, add also the name of that
party. Add the date of signing as the final element in all
cases. If there is more than one date of signing, use the
earliest. Make added entries . . . under the other parties to
the treaty. . . . "

Title page:
  Special economic assistance. Agreement between the
  United States of America and Burma, effected by ex-
  change of notes signed at Rangoon, June 24, 1959.

Enter under: U. S. Treaties, etc. Burma, June 24, 1959
and make a general reference: Burma. Treaties, etc. U. S.
see U. S. Treaties, etc. Burma.

"B. Agreements contracted by intergovernmental bodies.

"1. . . . Enter a formal agreement contracted between
an intergovernmental body and a country or between two intergovernmental bodies according to the provisions for bilateral
treaties . . . except that the main entry for agreements between either the League of Nations or the United Nations and
another intergovernmental body is always under the League
of Nations or the United Nations. "

Title page:

Loan agreement between the United States of America
and the European Coal and Steel Community, signed
April 23, 1954

Enter under: U. S. Treaties, etc. European Coal and
Steel Community, Apr. 23, 1954 and make a see reference
from: European Coal and Steel Community. Treaties, etc.
U. S.

"2. . . . Enter a formal agreement contracted between
an intergovernmental body and a jurisdiction or corporate
body, other than a country or another intergovernmental body,
under the intergovernmental body and make an added entry under the other party. . . . "

Liturgical works (A. -A. 1967. 29)

"A. General rule.

"1. Enter an officially sanctioned or traditionally accepted text of a religious observance, book of obligatory
prayers to be offered at stated times, or calendar or manual
of performance of religious observances under the specific
denominational church to which the work pertains, followed by
the subheading Liturgy and ritual. If the work is special to
the use of a particular corporate body within the church, such
as a diocese, cathedral, monastery, or religious order, make
an added entry under that body. "

Title page:

Common service book of the Lutheran Church, authorized by the United Lutheran Church in America

Enter under: United Lutheran Church in America. Liturgy and ritual.

Serials (A. -A. 1967. 6)

"B. Serials issued by a corporate body

"1. . . . Exception: if the title (exclusive of the subtitle) includes the name or the abbreviation of the name of the corporate body, or consists solely of a generic term that requires the name of the body for adequate identification of the serial, enter it under the body. "

Title page:

ALA bulletin. American Library Assocation

Enter under: American Library Association.

"2. Enter any other serial issued by or under the authority of a corporate body under the body. . . . "

Title page:

Annual report of the Librarian of Congress for the fiscal year . . . Library of Congress

Enter under: U. S. Library of Congress.

Headings for Corporate Bodies

Basic rule (A. -A. 1967. 60)

"Enter a corporate body directly under its name except when the rules . . . provide for entering it under a higher body of which it is a part, under the name of the government of which it is an agency, or under the name of the place in which it is located. "

General rule (A. -A. 1967. 61)

"When the name of a corporate body found in reference sources varies from that used by the body on the publications of which it is author, publisher, or sponsor, the latter form is preferred. . . . "

Variant forms in the publications (A. -A. 1967. 62)

"If variant forms of the name are found in the body's
own publications, use the name as it appears in formal presentations (as at the head of the title, in the imprint, and in
formal author statements). . . .

"A. . . . If one of the variant forms found in formal
presentations is a brief form that provides adequate identification for cataloging purposes, use the brief form. "

> Huntington Library and Art Gallery
>   Refer from: Henry E. Huntington Library and Art Gallery

In the locality or even in the region, reference from the
full name may be unnecessary, e. g., in California or on the
West Coast, no reference may be necessary from Henry E.
Huntington Library and Art Gallery.

"1. Initial letters of the name. If the body has used a
brief form consisting of the initial letters of the words or
principal words of its name, use this form only if it has been
written in capital and lower case letters. . . .

> Unesco
>   Refer from: United Nations Educational, Scientific
>   and Cultural Organization

but

> American Federation of Labor and Congress of Industrial
> Organizations
>   Refer from: A. F. L. -C. I. O.

"B. . . . [Otherwise] prefer the official form of the name
wherever found. "

"D. . . . In case of doubt as to the predominant form,
prefer the form most recently used at the time of establishing the heading. . . . "

Conventional name (A. -A. 1967. 63)

"A. When a body is frequently identified by a conventional form of name in the reference sources . . . prefer this
conventional name to the official name and other forms of
name used in its publications. "

Westminster Abbey

"B. When the name of a body of ancient origin or one that is international in character has become firmly established in English language usage under an English form, enter it under this form, regardless of the forms that may appear on its publications. Instances of conventional names of this type are especially prevalent among religious bodies, fraternal and knightly orders, and diplomatic conferences."

>Catholic Church
>Benedictines
>   Refer from: Order of St. Benedict
>Freemasons
>Yalta Conference

Language (A. -A. 1967. 64)

"A. . . . If the name of an international body appears in English on its own publications use this form. . . ."

European Economic Community

Additions to names (A. -A. 1967. 65)

"A. . . . Add the name of the place in which the body is located if the same name has been used by another body in a different location."

>Union College, Lincoln, Neb.
>Union College, Schenectady, N. Y.

"5. Prefer the name of an institution to the name of the place in which a body is located when it provides better identification."

Quadrangle Club, University of Chicago

"B. . . . 1. Add the name of the country, state, province, etc., in parentheses, instead of the local name if the name has been used by different bodies that have a character that is national, state, provincial, etc."

>Labour Party (Gt. Brit.)
>Labour Party (New Zealand)

"2. If a local place name that is part of a corporate name is insufficient to differentiate two or more bodies, add in parentheses the name of the state, province, or country. ''

      Washington County Historical Society (Ark.)
      Washington County Historical Society (Md.)

    ''D. 2. If the name alone does not convey the idea of a corporate body, add in parentheses a suitable general designation to clarify the meaning of the heading. ''

      Bounty (Ship)

      Omissions from names (A. -A. 1967. 66)

    ''A. . . . Omit initial articles unless required for reasons of clarity or grammar. ''

      Library Association
but   The Club, London

    ''E. . . . 1. Omit adjectival terms indicating incorporation (such as 'incorporated, ' 'limited, ' etc. ,) or state ownership of a commercial enterprise . . . providing 1) they are not regarded as integral parts of the name and 2) they are not needed to make clear that the name is that of a corporate body (as when there is no such word as 'company' in the name.)''

      Bell Telephone Laboratories
but
      Films Incorporated

      Modifications of names (A. -A. 1967. 67)

    ''A. . . . When the corporate name begins with one or more initials or abbreviations of forenames followed by a surname, place them in parentheses after the surname in the heading. ''

      Schirmer (G.), inc.
      Smiley (A. K.) Public Library

      Changes of name (A. -A. 1967. 68)

    'If the name of a corporate body has changed . . . establish a new heading under the new name for cataloging publications appearing under this name. Make appropriate cross references between the headings under which publications of the body appear in the catalog. ''

Pennsylvania State University

The name of the Farmers' High School was changed in 1862 to Agricultural College of Pennsylvania; in 1874 to Pennsylvania State College; in 1953 to Pennsylvania State University.
Works by this body are entered under the name used at the time of publication.

Make the same explanatory reference under the other names.

Subordinate and Related Bodies

Bodies with names implying subordination (A. -A. 1967. 69)

"Enter a subordinate body as a subheading under a higher body if its name . . ."

1) "includes the entire name of the higher body . . ."

British Museum. Trustees (Name: Trustees of the British Museum)

2) "contains a term that by definition implies that the body is a component part of something else, e. g. , 'department,' 'division,' 'section,' 'branch.'"

New York University. Division of Education

3) "contains a word ordinarily implying administrative subordination, e. g. , 'committee.'"

Catholic Library Association. Michigan Unit. Booklist Committee

4) [is that] "of a university school or college that simply indicates a particular field of study."

Columbia University. Teachers College
Syracuse University. College of Medicine

5) "is entirely descriptive of the body's functions and . . . has a character that is common to the names of both subordinate bodies and independent bodies, e. g. , many 'institutes,' 'centers,' 'laboratories,' etc. of universities."

Indiana University. Audio-Visual Center

6) "is so general that the name of a higher body is required for its identification."

Bell Telephone Laboratories. Technical Information
Library
(Name: Technical Information Library)

"A. Direct or indirect subheading. Enter a body treated
subordinately as a subheading of the lowest element in the
hierarchy above it that may be independently entered. Omit
intervening elements in the hierarchy that are not essential to
clarify the function of the smaller body as an element of the
larger one.

"C. Additions to names.

"1. . . . Add to the heading for a particular meeting of
a governing congress, council, convention, etc., of an association or other corporate body, its number, place, and date
. . . ."

Congress of Industrial Organizations. Constitutional
Convention 3d, Atlantic City, 1940

"2. . . . If the locale of activity or jurisdiction is not
indicated in the name of a chapter, branch, or other subordinate unit that carries out the activities of a body in a particular locality, add the local place name in the case of local
units. In the case of units with borader jurisdiction, add in
parentheses the name of the jurisdiction. "

Freemasons. Concordia Lodge, No. 13, Baltimore
Knights Templar (Masonic Order) Grand Commandery
(Me.)

If the locale of activity or jurisdiction is an institution, use
the name of the institution instead of a geographic name.

Chi Omega. Epsilon Beta Chapter. University of North
Carolina, Chapel Hill

Other subordinate bodies (A. -A. 1967. 70)

"A. Enter a subordinate body directly under its own
name if its name does not belong to one of the types described in 69. . . ."

Ansco
Refer from: General Aniline and Film Corporation. Ansco

Related bodies (A. -A. 1967. 71)

"A. General rule. Enter a society, association, or other

body that is auxiliary or otherwise closely related to another
body as a subheading under the heading for the body to which
it is related if its name 1) contains the entire name of the
body to which it is related . . . 2) is insufficient for identification without the addition of that body's name, or 3) is normally used only in association with that name. . . ."

      Smith College. Alumnae Association
          (Name: Alumnae Association of Smith College)
but
      Harvard Alumni Association
          Refer from: Harvard University. Alumni Association

      "B. Joint committees, commissions, etc.

      "1. Enter a joint committee, commission, or other unit
made up of representatives of two or more corporate bodies
under its own name. "

      Joint Commission on Mental Illness and Health

"Omit names of parent bodies when these occur at the end
of the name if the name of the joint unit is intelligible without them. "

      "2. If the parent bodies are themselves subordinate to
a common parent body and if they would be entered as subheadings under the name of that body, enter the joint unit as
a subordinate body according to the provisions of 69. "

      American Library Association. Joint Committee to
      Compile a List of International Subscription Agents
      Refer from: American Library Association. Acquisitions
              Section. Joint Committee to Compile a
              List of International Subscription Agents
          American Library Association. Serials Sec-
              tion. Joint Committee to Compile a List
              of International Subscription Agents
          American Library Association. Resources
              and Technical Services Division. Joint
              Committee to Compile a List of Inter-
              national Subscription Agents

      "C. Bodies requiring conventionalized names. . . . In
certain cases . . . it is desirable to conventionalize the names
of similar subordinate or related bodies that are entered as
subheadings under another body when their names exhibit minor
variations as to form.

"1. . . . Enter a graduating class organization of an educational institution under the institution with a conventionalized subheading in the form of Class of [year]. . . . "

Dartmouth College. Class of 1880

"2. . . . Enter an element of an American political party that is below the national level under the name of the party followed in parentheses by the name of the jurisdiction within which the element functions. . . . [add] the name of the element, omitting any proper nouns or adjectives that are part of the name of the party or the jurisdiction. "

Democratic Party (Texas) State Convention, Waco, 1857
(Name: State Convention of the Democratic
Party of the State of Texas)

Geographic Names. . . .

"Geographic names frequently constitute essential elements in headings for corporate bodies. They may be required to differentiate bodies with identical names . . . they may be used arbitrarily, as the entry element of headings . . . and they are normally the names conventionally used for governments. . . . "

Additions (A. -A. 1967. 73)

"If the name of a given place is insufficient to differentiate two or more places with the same name . . . add the name of a larger geographic entity in which it is located. "

"A. Normally the addition is the name of the country, or, when appropriate, the name of the colony or other dependent territory. "

Victoria, Australia

"B. In the following cases of local place names (i. e. , cities, towns, boroughs, communities, etc. , and such larger areas of limited size as counties, etc.), the addition is as specified below:

"1) if in a state, province or territory of the United States or Canada, add the name of the state, province, or territory":

Kingsport, Tenn.
Winnipeg, Manitoba

"2) if in the British Isles, add <u>Eng.</u>, <u>Ire.</u>, <u>Scot.</u>, or <u>Wales</u>, as appropriate . . . "

    Dublin, Ire.
    Conway, Wales

"3) if in a constituent state of the Soviet Union, the Yugoslav Republic, the United Arab Republic, or Malaysia, add the name of the state":

    Luxor, Egypt
    Krahkov, Ukraine

"4) if on an island, add the name of the island or island group when either of these is predominantly used to identify the place":

    Palma, Majorca
    St. Aubin, Jersey

"5) if in a city, add the name of the city, and make a reference from the heading for the city followed by the name of the part as a subheading":

    Richmond, New York
    Refer from: New York (City) Richmond

Omissions and alterations (A. -A. 1967. 74)

"If a geographic name begins with a term indicating a type of governmental administration . . . . "

"A. Omit the term if usage permits and if the term is not required to distinguish the place from another place of the same name. "

    Meath
    <u>not</u> County Meath

If the term is needed to distinguish the place from another place of the same name, [see] 77A, page 98.

"C. Enter the name in the form in which it is found. "

    District of Columbia

Governments

General rule (A. -A. 1967. 75)

"Use the conventional name . . . of a country, province,

state, county, municipality, or other political jurisdiction as
the heading for its government, unless the official name of
the government is in more common use.

> Massachusetts (not Commonwealth of Massachusetts)

Distinguishing governments with the same name (A. -A.
1967. 77)

"A. Distinguish governments that are identified by the
same conventional name and that cannot be satisfactorily distinguished by" applying the following rules instead of, or if
necessary, in addition to, the provisions of 73.

"1. Add in parentheses the type of jurisdiction [if they
differ] unless one is so much better known that it would be
correctly understood by users of the catalog without such
designation. . . . "

> New York (City)
> New York (State)

"2. If the type of jurisdiction does not provide a satisfactory distinction, add whatever words or phrases are most
appropriate in the particular state. "

> Berlin (West)
> Germany (Democratic Republic, 1949-)
>   Refer from: Germany (East)
> Germany (Federal Republic, 1949-)
>   Refer from: Germany (West)
> Russia (U. S. S. R.)
>   Refer from: Union of Soviet Socialist Republics

"B. Distinguish the legitimate government of a country
from the government of an occupying power or that of an insurgent group by adding in parentheses after the name of the
country a suitable designation for the occupying or insurgent
government, followed by the inclusive years of its existence
as such. "

> France
> France (Territory under German occupation, 1940-1944)

"C. Distinguish the former colonies and territories that
became states of the same name of the United States of America by adding the designation (Colony) or (Ter.). "

> Rhode Island (Colony)
> Alaska (Ter.)

Government Bodies or Officials

". . . The general principle underlying the following
rule is that agencies through which the basic legislative,
judicial, and executive functions of government are exercised
should be entered as subheadings under the heading for the
government; other bodies created and controlled by the government should be entered, if possible, under their own names. .
. . "

General rule (A. -A. 1967. 78)

"A. Enter a corporate body created or controlled by a
government under the general rules for corporate bodies, i. e.,
60-61, 63-68, pages 89-92, as qualified by 98-99, pages 110-
112, regardless of its official nature (except for necessary references) or of whether or not it is subordinate to an
agency of government, if it is one of the following types. "

"1. Organizations engaged in commercial, cultural, or
scientific activities, or the promotion of such activities. "

National Science Foundation

"2. Institutions (typically with their own physical plant). "

National Agricultural Library
Veterans Administration Hospital, Durham, N. C.

"3. Installations and parks. "

Mather Air Force Base
Grand Teton National Park

"4. Bodies created by intergovernmental agreement. "

Houston Independent School District
Minneapolis-St. Paul Sanitary District

"5. Authorities and trusts for the operation of utilities
and industries. "

National Coal Board
Tennessee Valley Authority

"6. Banks, corporations, manufacturing plants, farms,
and similar specific enterprises. "

Canadian National Railways
Federal Reserve Bank of Richmond

"7. Established churches."

Church of England

A body that is subordinate to one that is entered under
the provisions of this rule is treated according to the provisions of rules 69-70.

"Exceptions: The following are excluded from this rule
and are treated under the provisions of B below: 1) bodies
that are designated as ministries . . . or by terms that by
definition denote that the body is a component part of something else (e. g. , 'department,' 'division,' 'section,' 'branch')"
. . . If the parent body would be entered independently under this
rule, however, apply the provisions of rule 69. 2) Libraries,
archives, and other government bodies that normally function
primarily as service units of a particular agency of government if their names contain the name of the agency as the
sole identifying element or require the addition of the agency's
name for their identification."

Gt. Brit. Air Ministry. Library
Name: Air Ministry Library

"B. If the body is not one of the types listed in A above,
or if there is doubt that it is one, enter it as a subheading
under the heading for the government and in accordance with
the provisions of rules 79-86 below.

U. S. Copyright Office
Virginia. Governor

"Omit the name of the country, state, etc., or an adjective derived from its name when either occurs at the beginning or the
end of the body's name unless objectionable distortion would
result."

North Carolina. Supreme Court
Name: Supreme Court of North Carolina

but   Gt. Brit. British Caribbean Federation Judicial
                                        Commission
           A commission preparing a plan for a British Carib-
           bean Federation

Subordinate agencies and units (A. -A. 1967. 79)

"A. Direct subheading. If a government body that is to be
entered under the name of the government according to rule 78B

above is subordinate to another such body, treat it as a direct subheading under the name of the government if its name has not been or is not likely to be used by another body in the same jurisdiction. ''

U. S. Bureau of the <u>Census</u>[1]

''B. Indirect subheading. If the name of the body does not meet the above conditions or if there is doubt that it does, treat it as a subheading under the lowest element of the hierarchy that can be entered directly under the name of the government, omitting any intervening unit in the hierarchy that is not or is not likely to be essential to distinguish bodies with the same name or to identify the body. ''

U. S. Food and Drug Administration. Bureau of Enforcement
Hierarchy: Dept. of Health, Education, and Welfare
Food and Drug Administration
Bureau of Enforcement

Government officials (A. -A. 1967. 80)

''A. Chiefs of state, etc.

''1. The heading for a sovereign, president, other chief of state, or governor, in his official capacity (see 17C1, page 83), consists of the title of his office in English unless there is no proper equivalent for the vernacular term, followed by the inclusive years of his reign or incumbency and, in parentheses, by his name in brief form in the language used for the heading for the person--all as subheading under the name of the government. If the title varies with the incumbent (e. g., 'King' and 'Queen') use a common designation of the office (e. g., 'Sovereign'). ''

Gt. Brit. Sovereign, 1936-1952 (George VI)
U. S. President, 1946-1952 (Truman)

If, in addition to the heading for a chief of state, a heading is established for him as a person, make explanatory references under each heading.

George VI, King of Great Britain, 1936-1952

''Here are entered private communications, public speeches, and collections that include both private and official communications. For publications constituting official acts of the sovereign

(e. g. , messages to Parliament, proclama-
tions, etc.) see entries under'' (A. -A. 1967.
121B1)

Gt. Brit. Sovereign, 1936-1952 (George VI)

''2. When the heading applies to more than one incumbent, omit dates and names from the heading. ''

North Carolina. Governor

''B. Heads of governments. The heading for a head of
government who is not also a chief of state in his official
capacity consists either of his title as office-holder or of the
title of his office, according to the usage found on publications, as a subheading under the government. Dates and names
are not included in the subheading. ''

Gt. Brit. Prime Minister
Detroit. Mayor

''C. Governors and governing bodies of dependent or
occupied territories. The heading for a governor or governing
body of a colony, protectorate, or other dependent territory,
or for a territory under military occupation, takes the form
of a subheading under the entry for the territory governed. .
. .''

District of Columbia. Board of Commissioners
Germany (Territory under Allied occupation, 1945-
1955. U. S. Zone) Military Governor

''D. Other officials. The heading for any other government official is that of the ministry or agency which he represents.

U. S. General Accounting Office
Refer from: U. S. Comptroller General

''If, however, the official is not a part of a ministry or other
agency or if he is part of one that has no name but that of
the official, the heading consists of his title as subheading under the government. ''

Legislative bodies (A. -A. 1967. 81)

''A. If a legislature has more than one chamber, enter
each as a subheading under the legislature. ''

U. S. Congress. Senate
Refer from: U. S. Senate

"B. Enter committees and other subordinate units as subheadings under the legislature or of a particular chamber, as appropriate. "

> U. S. Congress. Joint Committee on the Library
> U. S. Congress. House. Select Committee on Government organization

"C. If successive legislatures are numbered consecutively, include the number and the year or years whenever the heading is for a particular legislature as a whole or for one of its chambers as a whole. If in such cases numbered sessions are also involved, give the session and its number, following the name and number of the legislature, and add the year or years of the session. "

> U. S. 89th Congress, 2d session, 1966.

Constitutional conventions (A. -A. 1967. 82)

"A. Enter a constitutional convention directly under the name of the jurisdiction for which the constitution was prepared, and add the year or years of convocation.

"B. If there is variation in the forms of name of constitutional conventions of the same jurisdiction . . . prefer the conventionalized form Constitutional Convention. "

Courts (A. -A. 1967. 83)

"A. Enter a court under its name as a subheading under the name of the country, state, or other jurisdiction whose authority it exercises. "

> North Carolina. Supreme Court
> Vermont. Court of Chancery

"C. In the case of courts having jurisdiction over particular districts within the area of the jurisdiction from which they derive their authority, omit the statement of the area of jurisdiction from the name of the court, if the grammatical construction permits, and give it at the end of the heading within parentheses. . . . "

> U. S. District Court (North Carolina, Eastern District)
> Name: United States District Court for the Eastern District of North Carolina

Armed forces (A. - A. 1967. 84)

"Enter each of the principal services . . . as a direct
subheading under the name of the government. Enter a component branch, command, district or military unit . . . as a
direct subheading under the heading for the service unless its
name begins with the name of the service or with an adjective
derived from that name; in either of the latter cases enter it
as a direct subheading under the name of the government.
Note that military installations and institutions are treated under 78A, page 99. "

>U. S. Army. General Staff
>U. S. Marine Corps
>U. S. Navy. 7th Fleet

but
>U. S. Naval Air Transport Service

"If the name contains internally the name or part of the name
of the service, this part is omitted [whenever feasible]. "

>U. S. Marine Corps. 2d Division
>   (Name: 2d Marine Division)

but
>Canada. Army. Royal Canadian Army Medical Corps

"In the case of numbered units, follow the style of expressing
the numbering that is found in the names, . . . "

>U. S. Army. Fifth Army
>U. S. Army. II Corps
>U. S. Army. 2d Engineer Combat Battalion

"A. Military forces below the national level

"1. Enter military forces that are under the control or
partial control of governments below the national level . . .
as subheadings under the names of such governments. "

>New York (State) Militia
>New York (State) National Guard

"2. Enter a unit of such a force as a subheading under
the heading for the force. . . . "

>New York (State) Militia. 9th Regiment Artillery
>   (Name: 9th Regiment, New York State Artillery. . .)

"3. Enter a unit of a force below the national level

that has been absorbed into the national military forces under
its designation as part of the national forces (for the period
of absorption) in the form of a subheading under the heading
for the appropriate military service. . . . "

> U. S.   Army.   83d New York Volunteers
> U. S.   Army.   9th Regiment Infantry, New York Volun-
>   teers

"4. Make see also references between the different
headings used in the catalog for the same military unit. . . . "

Embassies, legations, etc. (A. -A.   1967.   85)

"Enter an embassy, legation, consulate, or other con-
tinuing office representing the government of one country in
another, as a subheading under the name of the country represented. . . . If the heading is for an embassy or legation,
add, within parentheses, the name of the country to which it
is accredited; if it is for a consulate or other local office,
add the name of the city in which it is located. "

> U. S.   Legation (Bulgaria)
> Gt. Brit.   Consulate, Cairo

"If the name itself would be distorted by following the above
pattern, however, it is used in the form that is found. "

> Australia.   High Commissioner in London

Delegations to international and intergovernmental bodies (A. -A.   1967.   86)

"Enter a delegation, commission, etc., representing the
government of a country in an international or intergovernmental body, conference, undertaking, etc. , as a subheading
under the country represented . . . . If the name of the delegation is uncertain, the subheading is formed in the language
of the country represented by using the terms found in the
work being cataloged . . . i. e. , Delegation [Mission, etc.] to
_____ . If it is uncertain that the body represents the government of the country, enter directly under its name. "

> U. S.   Mission to the United Nations

Conferences, Congresses, Meetings, Etc.

General rule (A. -A.   1967.   87)

"Enter a conference, congress, or other meeting under

its name, followed in many instances by one or more of the following elements: number, place, date. . . . "

Name (A. -A. 1967. 88)

"A. If the formal presentations of the name vary and one form includes the name . . . of a sponsoring body, prefer this form. "

> University of Illinois Symposium on Self-Organization,
> Robert Allerton Park, 1961

"B. If a conference has both a specific name of its own and a more general name as one of a series of conferences, enter it under its specific name. "

> Symposium on Endocrines and Nutrition, University of
> Michigan, 1956
> Refer from: Nutrition Symposium, University of
> Michigan, 1956

"C. Omit words in the name of a conference that denote its number, frequency, or year of convocation. "

> Louisiana Cancer Conference
> not Biennial Louisiana Cancer Conference

Number (A. -A. 1967. 89)

"If a conference is one of a series of numbered conferences of the same name, follow its name by the abbreviation of the ordinal number in English. If the numbering is only inferred from the numbering of other conferences in the series, use the implied number, but do not enclose it in brackets. If the numbering is irregular, it may be omitted from the heading. . . . "

Place (A. -A. 1967. 90)

"A. The name of the place in which a conference was held follows the name or the number. For forms of geographic names see rules 73-74. "

> Catholic Social Life Conference, Vatican (City)

"B. Prefer the name of the institution at which the conference was held to the geographic name of the place if it provides a better identification. . . . "

> Arden House Conference on Medicine and Anthropology, 1961

"C. If the sessions of one conference were held in two places, use both names. If there are more than two, use only the principal or first-named one followed by etc. "

> Institute on Diagnostic Problems in Mental Retardation, Long Beach State College and San Francisco State College, 1957

Date (A. -A. 1967. 91)

"Add the year in which the conference was held if the heading is for a single conference. Specific dates are used if necessary to identify the meeting or distinguish it from another. "

Religious Bodies and Officials

"Religious bodies are entered according to the general rules for corporate bodies except as these are modified by the special provisions given below or, in the case of local religious institutions, in rule 98. "

Church councils (A. -A. 1967. 92)

"Enter church councils as provided by A-C below and indicate the number, place, and date of the council in the same style as prescribed in rules 89-91.

"A. Enter under their names, according to the general rules . . . 1) the general, ecumenical and local councils of the early Christian Church, prior to its divisions; 2) the general and ecumenical councils of the Catholic Church subsequent to the divisions of the Christian Church; 3) interdenominational and intradenominational councils. "

> Vatican Council, 2d

"B. Enter a general council, etc., of a corporate denominational body as a subheading under the heading for the body unless the name of the council would qualify it for independent entry under the provisions of rule 70. In case of doubt, prefer entry under the heading for the denominational body. "

> Methodist Church (United States) General Conference

"C. Enter other councils, etc., of the national, regional,

provincial, state, or local clergy or membership of a denomination as a subheading under the corporate heading for the denomination. . . . ''

> Society of Friends. Philadelphia Yearly Meeting

''If, however, such a council is subordinate to a particular corporate district of the denomination, enter it under the heading for the district (see 93B). ''

> Catholic Church. Province of Baltimore. Provincial Council, 10th, 1869

Patriarchates, dioceses, etc. (A. -A. 1967. 93)

"A. 2. Enter autonomous Orthodox archdioceses, etc., which have been established in modern times, directly under their names. ''

> Greek Archdiocese of North and South America

"B. 1. General rule . . . enter dioceses, provinces, and other subordinate units of religious bodies having jurisdiction within geographical districts as subheadings under the name of the body. ''

> Protestant Episcopal Church in the U. S. A. Diocese of Southern Virginia

"2. Catholic patriarchates, dioceses, etc. Use an English form of name for a patriarchate, diocese, province, etc., of the Catholic Church. Give the name of the see according to the provisions for geographic names. ''

> Catholic Church. Archdiocese of Santiago de Cuba

Bishops, patriarchs, etc., as ecclesiastical officials (A. -A. 1967. 94)

"The heading for a bishop, patriarch, etc., in his capacity as ecclesiastical head of a diocese, patriarchate, etc., or for the head of a monastic order consists of his title as a subheading under the heading for his diocese, patriarchate, order, etc., followed by the inclusive years of his incumbency and, in parentheses, by his name in brief form. . . . ''

> Winchester, Eng. (Diocese) Bishop, 1367-1404
> (William of Wykeham)
> Dominicans. Master General, 1486 (Barnabas Sassone)

Administrative Offices of the Catholic Church (A. -A. 1967. 95)

"Enter the congregations, tribunals, and offices of the Roman Curia, the office of Pope, the College of Cardinals, and nunciatures, etc., as subheadings under the heading for the church. Use the Latin form of name except for the office of Pope and for the nunciatures, etc. . . ."

"A. . . . The heading for a Pope in his capacity as Supreme Pontiff consists of the word Pope as subheading under the heading for the church, followed first by the inclusive years of his reign and then, in parentheses, by his pontifical name in its catalog entry form. Correlate such headings with the corresponding personal name headings by suitable references. . . ."

Catholic Church. Pope, 1958-63 (John XXIII)

Religious orders and societies (A. -A. 1967. 96)

"A. Enter a religious order or society under the name by which it is best known, according to the following order of preference: 1) the conventional name by which its members are known, when such a name is well established in English language usage; 2) the English form of name used by units of the order located in English-speaking countries; or 3) the name of the order or society in the vernacular of the country of its origin. "

Franciscans
Refer from: Order of St. Francis
Jesuits
Refer from: Society of Jesus

"B. Treat a congregation of members of a religious order as a related body under the provisions of 71A and, if required, under the provisions of the other general rules, 60-68. "

Servants of Relief for Incurable Cancer
Refer from: Dominican Sisters. Servants of Relief
for Incurable Cancer

Radio and television stations (A. -A. 1967. 97)

"Enter a radio or television station under its call letters followed by the words Radio [Television] station (within

parentheses) and the place with which the station is identified,
providing the call letters constitute the primary or sole identifying element of the name. Otherwise, the heading is formulated according to the general rules 60-71 with the exception that
if the name of the place with which the station is identified
does not appear in the name, it is added at the end. Make an
explanatory reference under the words 'Radio [Television] station. ' "

WFMY-TV (Television station) Greensboro, N.C.

Exceptions for Entry Under Place

The following rules (98-99) can be fully applied only after the form of the name of any corporate body coming under
their provisions has been determined in accordance with general rules 61-64. "

Local churches, etc. (A. -A. 1967. 98)

"A. General rule. Enter a local church, cathedral, monastery, convent, abbey, temple, mosque, or the like, under
the name of the place (i. e., city, town, village, etc., whether
incorporated or not) in which it is located unless the first
word of its name is the name of that place in its catalog entry form. . . . In this case enter it directly under its name.

> Baltimore. Third English Lutheran Church
> London. St. Paul's Cathedral

but
> Tenafly Presbyterian Church
> San Gabriel Mission

"B. . . . When there is a choice between the name of a
formerly independent municipality and the name of a larger
local jurisdiction in which it has been absorbed, prefer the
name of the more specific jurisdiction if it continues to function under the same name as a corporate element of the larger jurisdiction. "

> Brooklyn. St. George's Episcopal Church
> Westminster Cathedral

"C. . . . If a church, etc., is located in the open country and if its name is not associated with a local place, enter
it under its name. Add the name of the district or county in
which it is located, whichever is most appropriate, if its
name does not appear to be unique. "

> Mount Pisgah Church, Woodford County, Ky.
> Tintern Abbey

"D. . . . Enter a church, chapel, etc., that is a subordinate unit of a larger institution and that serves primarily the community of the larger body rather than the local community, as a subheading under the heading for the larger body."

> Yale University. Church of Christ

A chapel that is actually a local church, however, or that serves as such (e. g., a chapel that is a mission of another church) is treated as a local church.

> London. Wesley's Chapel

"F. . . . If the headings for two or more churches, etc., are identical or so similar that they are likely to be confused, distinguish them by adding in each case one of the following: 1) the type of institution . . .; 2) the name of the denomination, in parentheses . . . 3) the name of the district or community or the street address, whichever is more appropriate; or, if necessary, both."

> New York (City) St. James Church (Catholic)
> New York (City) St. James Episcopal Church, Bronx
> New York (City) St. James Episcopal Church, Manhattan

"G. . . . Enter a congregation, parish, church society, or other group that is the corporate body holding worship in a church, according to the rules for local churches, A-F above."

> English River Congregation of the Church of the Brethren

"In some instances, however, a parish or society may be a corporate body distinct from but related to that of the church. Relate such bodies by see also references."

> New Haven. First Church
>   Refer from (see also): New Haven. First Ecclesiastical Society
> New Haven. First Ecclesiastical Society
>   Refer from (see also): New Haven. First Church

Certain other corporate bodies (A. -A. 1967. 99)

". . . The rules below have application only to corporate bodies of the following types:

agricultural experiment stations   galleries
airports   hospitals
botanical and zoological gardens   libraries
educational institutions   museums

"A. If the name of such a body consists solely of 1) a
common word or phrase followed by the name, in noun or ad-
jectival form, of the municipality or other larger jurisdiction
below the national level in which it is located, or 2) such a
word or phrase modified by an adjective indicating one of
these jurisdictions by its type (e. g., 'city,' 'municipal,' 'county,' 'state,' 'provincial'), enter the body under the jurisdiction that is named or implied, followed by the name of the
body. . . ."

> London. University
> Name: University of London
> Pittsburgh. Carnegie Library
> Name: Carnegie Library of Pittsburgh

"B. If the name of the body consists of a common word
or phrase followed by the names, or words implying the
names, of more than one such jurisdiction, enter it under the
one that is named or implied first. Make references from the
names of other places or jurisdictions that are named or implied, followed by the name of the body."

> Cincinnati. Public Library of Cincinnati and
> Hamilton County
> Refer from: Hamilton County, Ohio. Public Li-
> brary of Cincinnati and Hamilton
> County

"C. If the name of the body consists solely of a common word or phrase, enter it under the municipality in which
it is located, except that American agricultural experiment
stations with such names are entered under the state in which
they function. . . ."

> Fort Lauderdale. Memorial Hospital
> Name: Memorial Hospital
> New Hampshire. Agricultural Experiment Station
> Name: Agricultural Experiment Station

Names of corporate bodies (A. -A. 1967. 122)

"A. See references

"1. . . . Refer from a name used by the body or found

in reference sources when it is different from the one used
in the heading. . . . ''

Persia	Quakers
see Iran.	see Society of Friends

"2. . . . Refer from a form of the name used by the
body or found in reference sources when it differs significantly from the one used in the heading. . . . ''

American Red Cross
   see American National Red Cross.

"3. . . . Refer from different forms of entry under
which the name might reasonably be sought, '' e. g., ''when entry is under the place in which it is located or under the government that controls it. ''

National Shrine of the Immaculate Conception
   see Washington, D. C. National Shrine of the
      Immaculate Conception
State Teachers College, Bridgewater, Mass.
   see Massachusetts. State Teachers College,
      Bridgewater.

"The name and its variants in the form of subheadings
under a parent body or controlling government when the subordinate body has been entered independently. ''

American Library Association. American Association
   of School Librarians
   see American Association of School Librarians.
U. S. Tennessee Valley Authority
   see Tennessee Valley Authority.

"The name and its variants in the form of subheadings
under the immediately superior body when the subordinate
body has been entered directly under the main body or under
some other unit in the hierarchy that is higher than the immediately superior unit. ''

American Library Association. Resources and Technical Services Division. Cataloging and Classification Section
   see American Library Association. Cataloging and
      Classification Section
General Motors Corporation. Fisher Body Division.
   Production Engineering Dept. Engineering Pictorial
   Section
   see General Motors Corporation. Fisher Body Divi-

sion.   Engineering Pictorial Section.

"The name of the place where a body is located if the user may reasonably expect the body to be so entered. "

> Paris.   Bibliothèque nationale
> see Bibliothèque nationale (France)

"Arbitrarily inverted or shortened forms beginning with the principal identifying noun or adjective when the latter is not the first word in the heading, as deemed necessary. "

> William and Mary, College of
> see College of William and Mary

"B. See also references. Make see also references from the names of international and diplomatic conferences to the uniform titles of international conventions and peace treaties that they produce and vice versa. "

> International American Conference, 6th Havana, 1928
>   see also Convention regarding the status of aliens.
> Convention regarding the status of aliens
>   see also International American Conference, 6th,
>   Havana, 1928.
> Paris Peace Conference, 1919
>   see also Treaty of Versailles, 1919
> Treaty of Versailles, 1919
>   see also Paris Peace Conference, 1919

"C. Explanatory references. " When more detailed guidance is required, "make explanatory references giving the information necessary for the effective use of the headings involved. Explanatory references for corporate headings most commonly deal with: . . . scope of heading, . . . method of entry, . . . changes of name and relationships to other bodies . . . ''

> "Freemasons.
>
>> "Under subdivisions of this heading will be found publications of the lodges, grand lodges, etc., of the basic order of Freemasonry, sometimes called 'craft' Masonry, in which are conferred the first three Masonic degrees, culminating with that of Master Mason. "
>
> "Church of . . .
>
>> "Local churches are entered under the name of the city or other community in which they are located. "

"University of . . .

"Universities with names beginning as indicated above and identified by the name of a city, state, province, or the like are entered under the name of the city, state, or province. "

Special headings for legal publications (A. -A. 1967. 123)

"A. . . . When the jurisdiction promulgating a law is not the one under which the law is entered, refer from the promulgating jurisdiction, followed by the appropriate legal subheading and the title of the publication, to the jurisdiction under which the law is entered, followed by the appropriate legal subheading and, where necessary, the title. "

Maryland. Laws, statutes, etc.
Code of the public local laws of Worcester County
see
Worcester County, Md. Ordinances, local laws, etc. ,
Code of the public local laws of Worcester County.

"B. . . . 1. In the case of bipartite treaties entered under the home country, make a reference from the name of the other country, followed by Treaties, etc. and the name of the home country, to the name of the home country, followed by Treaties, etc. and the name of the other country, to serve for all instances of bipartite treaties with that country. "

France. Treaties, etc. U. S.
see U. S. Treaties, etc. France.

"2. As required refer from the names of countries involved in a peace treaty, followed by Treaties, etc. and the date, to the title under which the treaty is entered. "

Germany. Treaties, etc. June 28, 1919
see Treaty of Versailles, 1919.

"C. . . . 1. Refer in author-title form from the conventional name of a constitution or charter to the jurisdiction and special subheading that is prescribed for entering such works. "

United States
Constitution
see
U. S. Constitution

"3. When the title of the constitution or charter includes the word 'act' or some other word or phrase indicating that it is a law, make a reference from the name of the
jurisdiction, followed by the subheading Laws, statutes, etc.,
and the title of the law, to the special heading."

    Norway. Laws, statutes, etc.
    Grundlov
    see
    Norway. Constitution

    Conclusions regarding choice of name of organization.
As indicated on page 81 and in the preceding rules, corporate authors may be divided into groups, such as subordinate
and related bodies, geographic names. Note that these authors consist of the name of a country, city, etc., with subheadings such as Laws, statutes, etc.; Supreme court; Ordinances, local laws, etc.; the name of an association, American Economic Association; commercial firm, Hagstrom Company, Inc., New York; joint committees, commissions, etc.,
Joint Commission on Mental Illness and Health; government bodies or officials, Tennessee Valley Authority; legislative bodies,
U. S. Congress. Senate; religious bodies and officials, Vatican
Council, 2d; Radio and television stations, WFMY-TV (Television) station.

    In deciding upon the form of the entry for an organiza-
tion it is necessary to consider what type it is. Take for example: Tax and Trade Guide, Venezuela of Arthur Anderson
and Company; Anderson is the author and this organization
would come under Rule 17A1, page 82, "Enter under the
corporate body . . . a work that is by its nature necessarily
the expression of the corporate thought or activity of the body.
Such works include official records and reports . . . studies
and other communications dealing with the policies, operations,
or management of the body made by officers or other employees of the body." Rule 67A, page 92, states that "When
the corporate name begins with one or more initials or abbreviations of forenames, followed by a surname, place them in
parentheses after the surname. . . ." By analogy forenames
given in full, likewise would follow the surname in parentheses,
e. g., Anderson (Arthur) and Company.

    Another example is Cars in Housing, Design Bulletin, 10
of the Ministry of Housing and Local Government of Great
Britain. The Ministry is the author and rule 78B, page 100:
". . . enter it as a subheading under the heading for the gov-

ernment . . . '' hence the heading would be: Gt. Brit. Ministry
of Housing and Local Government. Rule 75, page 97: ''Use
the conventional name . . . of a country, province, state,
county, municipality, or other political jurisdiction as the
heading for its government, . . . '' The examples given in the
Anglo-American Cataloging Rules and on the printed Library
of Congress catalog cards always give the abbreviations for
Great Britain and United States, Gt. Brit., U.S.

A different type of corporate body is the conference,
congress, meeting, etc. Rule 87, page 105: ''Enter a conference, congress, or other meeting under its name, followed
in many instances by one or more of the following elements:
number, place, date. . . . '' Rule 90, page 106: ''The name of
the place in which a conference was held follows the name
or the number. . . . '' Rule 91, page 107: ''Add the year in
which the conference was held if the heading is for a single
conference. '' Hence the Proceedings of the National Conference on Law and Poverty would be entered under: National
Conference on Law and Poverty, Washington, D.C., 1965.

Another illustration is: ''Weeds of California, by W.W.
Robbins, Margaret K. Bellue, Walter S. Ball. For sale by
Printing Division (Documents Section) Sacramento. '' Printed
at the top of the page bearing the Foreword is ''State of California, Department of Agriculture, '' and on the spine of the
book, ''1951. '' Should this book be entered in the catalog under Robbins, the first author on the title page, or under: California. State Department of Agriculture, with an added entry
under Robbins? The title page states that Robbins is Professor
of Botany and Botanist in the Experiment Station, University of
California, and this information is confirmed in his biographical sketch in Who's Who in America, 1952-1953. The Cumulative Book Index, April, 1953, lists under Robbins, Wilfred
William: Weed Control; a Textbook and Manual, a 1952 publication of McGraw-Hill. Mr. Robbins is of sufficient importance to be listed in Who's Who in America and has had published a book on weed control.

Rule 17A1, page 82, ''Enter under the corporate body
. . . a work that is by its nature necessarily the expression
of the corporate thought or activity of the body. . . . Single
reports, however, that are made by officers or other employees and that embody the results of scholarly investigation
or scientific research are excluded . . . unless written by more
than three persons, none of whom is represented as the principal author. . . . B. . . . If the work would not be entered

under corporate body under the provisions of A above or if
there is doubt as to whether it would, enter it under the
heading under which it would be entered if no corporate body
were involved. Make an added entry under the body unless it
functions solely as publisher. " This publication fits nicely under this rule and should be entered in the catalog under: Robbins, Wilfred William, 1884-1952; with an added entry under:
California. State Department of Agriculture. The California
Blue Book, 1950, lists the State Department of Agriculture as
one of the executive departments of the state, and the form
given here would come under rule 75 quoted on page 97,
"Use the conventional name . . . of a country, province, state,
county, municipality, or other political jurisdiction as the
heading for its government, . . . " Rule 79, page 100, "If a
government body that is to be entered under the name of the
government according to 78B . . . is subordinate to another
such body, treat it as a direct subheading under the name of
the government . . . . "

16. Name authority card for an organization

```
+--------------------------------------------------------+
|                                                        |
|          Carnegie Corporation of New York.             |
|                                                        |
|               Established 1911.                        |
|                                                        |
|      n Americana, 1965                                 |
|      n World almanac, 1967 (Carnegie Corpora-          |
|           tion of N. Y. )                              |
|                                                        |
|                                                        |
+--------------------------------------------------------+
```

In determining the headings to be used for the publication of an organization one consults the cataloging rules and
library aids. An authority card may be made if it is considered desirable to have a permanent record of the form adopted
and the aids consulted (see Card 16).

References

1. For convenience in locating cards in the catalog the
distinctive word in the subdivision under the name of a country,
state, city or other government district; or of a society, institution, or other body may be underscored.

Chapter VI
Main Catalog Entries

Introduction. Up to this point the reader has been concerned with the contents of the book and how books of similar content may be grouped together; the forms of personal names and names of organizations, with reference to the choice of proper headings for catalog entries; and how to present books which have neither a personal nor a corporate author. This chapter discusses the description of the book which is to be put on the unit catalog card. This description should include such information as is necessary to distinguish the book from all other books, even different editions of the same work, and should include its scope, contents, and bibliographic relationships. This data should be presented as simply and concisely as possible and in the same form and order for all books. The basis for this description is the title page of the book and what can be gained from an examination of the book itself. Stated more simply the purpose of cataloging is to identify the book and to distinguish it from all other books and even other editions of the same work.

The catalog is expected to answer such questions as: What books by Archibald MacLeish are in the library? Has the library a copy of Treasure Island? What material has the library on space craft? These questions can be answered by consulting the catalog for the author's name, the title, or the subject heading and noting the call numbers in order to locate the books on the shelves.

Besides these types, however, such questions are asked as: What is the latest book in the library by André Maurois? Has the library the "Young Readers Edition" of Profiles in Courage by John F. Kennedy? What books has the library with illustrations by Brian Wildsmith? When and by whom was the first edition of Robinson's Collected Poems published? In deciding upon what to include in the description of the book in the catalog entry consider the items given for books in such aids as the Standard Catalog Series of the H. W. Wilson Company. Remember that where the shelves are open to the readers, little time is spent at the catalog looking at the cards. On the other hand, even in the smallest library the catalog may be called upon to answer some question about a book

which is out in circulation; and in looking for material on a
subject the reader will sometimes examine all the cards before going to the shelves, considering the author, publisher,
date and size of the book as indicated by the number of pages.

⋇ Cataloging a book. The first step in cataloging a book
is to examine the title page, the official page from which the
librarian gets most of the information for the catalog entry.
Besides the author and the title, the title page may give the
author's degrees and other information, yet this information
on the catalog card would not be of sufficient value to warrant the space it would take. The title page may also give a
statement about the edition--as second edition or revised edi-
tion--and may specify how the book is illustrated. Then there
is the imprint, that is, place of publication, publisher, and
date of publication, given at the bottom of the title page. The
librarian should examine not only the title page for the items
mentioned but also the pages preceding the title page and the
cover to see if the book belongs to a series, e. g., "The
Rivers of America"; the back of the title page for the copyright date; the preface for further information regarding the
edition; the table of contents for the list of works if the book
includes a number of separate works, e. g., plays; the book
itself: (1) for the collation--that is, the number of pages or
volumes and illustrations and (2) for bibliographies, appendixes containing material of special value and other special features which should be brought out in notes.

Take, for instance, Foster Rhea Dulles' Yankees and
Samurai:

YANKEES

AND SAMURAI

America's Role in the Emergence
of Modern Japan: 1791-1900

Foster Rhea Dulles

Harper & Row, Publishers

New York

On the back of the title page is found:

YANKEES AND SAMURAI. Copyright [c] 1965 by
Foster Rhea Dulles. Printed in the United
States of America. . . .

FIRST EDITION

17. Main entry for nonfiction with person as author

---

327. 73
D88   Dulles, Foster Rhea, 1900-
            Yankees and samurai; America's
        role in the emergence of modern Japan:
        1791-1900.   Harper [c1965]
            275 p.   illus. , map, ports.

        Bibliography, notes: p. 255-268.

            1. Japan - Relations (general) with the
        U. S. 2. U. S. - Relations (general) with
        Japan. I. Title.

     Examination of the book shows that it has 275 pages and
is illustrated, including portraits and a map. After the cataloger has examined the book, the next step is to assign the
classification number and the subject headings. Chapter I describes the process of classifying and gives directions for doing it. Chapter II does the same for subject headings. The
classification number, 327. 73, should be written in pencil in
the upper left-hand corner of the page following the title page
about an inch from the top of the page and from the hinge.
Here it will be easy to locate, and if the book is rebound it
will not be cut off in the trimming nor hidden by the sewing.

     The author card for the book would include: the classi-
fication number, book number if the book numbers are used
in the library, author's name and his dates (if dates are
used), title, publisher, copyright date, [1] the total number of
pages, information about the illustrations.

     In some books part of the title of the book, of the au-
thor's name, or the place of publication or publisher's name
spreads over two pages, facing each other. This is called a
"double title page" or a "double-spread title page. " The
necessary information for the catalog entry is taken from
both pages. No mention of this type of title page is needed
in the catalog entry. An example of a double title page is
given.

A Girl   Grows Up
BY RUTH FEDDER
NEW EDITION   Psychologist, Bucks County Schools
Completely Re-   Bucks County, Pennsylvania
vised and En-
larged

Drawings by Roberta
Paflin

(PICTURE)
Whittlesey House, NEW YORK: TO-
RONTO
McGRAW-HILL BOOK COMPANY, INC.

Indention and spacing on cards. Before discussing the
place and the order of the items given in the catalog entry it
is necessary to explain the indentions and spacing commonly
used on catalog cards. The purpose of indention and spacing
is to emphasize the different groups of information and to
give special prominence to certain words, e. g., the author's
surname.

Cards 7 and 11 in Chapter II show the indentions and
spacing used on subject authority and cross reference cards.
The sample name authority cards, numbers 12-16 in Chapters
III-V, show the indention and the spacing recommended for
these types of cards, but do not indicate the specific lines
and spaces. They are, in general, the same as for the catalog cards given in this and subsequent chapters. Card 18 is a

18. Skeleton card showing location of the different items

Call
no.   Author ------------------------------
                 ----------------------.
           Title ----------------------------

------------. Edition --.   Imprint
        Collation ----.   (Series note)

           Notes ----------------------------.

           Tracing -------------------------
-------------------------------------.

skeleton card with indentions and spacing indicated to make clear the use in this manual of the terms first, second, and third indention. This card also shows the relative location on the card of the call number, author, title, imprint, collation, series note, and other notes.

Call number	Classification number, 3rd line, 2nd space from left edge of card. Book number 4th line, 2nd space from left edge of card.
Author	4th line, 1st indention (8th space from left edge of card). If author's name runs over, the succeeding line begins at 3rd indention (14th space from left edge of card).
Title	Line below author, 2nd indention (12th space from left edge of card). If title runs over, the succeeding line begins at 1st indention.
Edition	3rd space after period following title.
Imprint	5th space after period following title or edition statement, if there is space; if not, at 1st indention. If the imprint runs over, the succeeding line begins at 1st indention.
Collation	Line below imprint, 2nd indention; if it runs over, the succeeding line begins at 1st indention. There are two spaces between the subgroups giving the pages and the illustrations.
Series note	5th space after collation if there is space; if not on the next line at 1st indention. If the series note runs over, the succeeding line begins at 1st indention.
Notes	One line is skipped before the first note. Notes begin at 2nd indention, the succeeding line at 1st indention. Each note forms a separate paragraph.
Contents	In paragraph form beginning at 2nd indention, the succeeding line at 1st indention.
Tracing[2]	In paragraph form beginning at 2nd indention, the succeeding line at 1st indention. This paragraph is on the front of the main card just above the hole. If necessary part of the tracing can go on the back of the card--in which case put the word over on the front of the card just below the hole.

Rules for Cataloging

The elements describing the book are given in the entry in the order that will best serve the user of the catalog. For

instance, the price of the book, usually omitted from a library catalog as the reader is borrowing the book not purchasing it, is always included in a book dealer or publisher's
catalog and is in a conspicuous place. All entries in the catalog should be uniform in style, i.e., in spelling, capitalization, punctuation, abbreviations, use of numerals, and location of the items in the entry.

Organization of the description (A. -A. 1967. 130)

"A. The basic part of the description, commonly called
the 'body of the entry,' is presented in the first paragraph after the heading. It consists of the following elements in this
order: title, subtitle, author statement, edition statement, and
imprint. "

"C. The second paragraph consists of the collation and
series statement. "

Source of the description (A. -A. 1967. 131)

"In general, the items in the body of the entry and the
series statement represent the information presented by the
work itself. The collation is the cataloger's description of
the physical work and is limited to standard bibliographical
terminology. "

Relationship of the title page to the description of a
work (A. -A. 1967. 132)

"A. 1. The title page serves as the basis of the description to be presented in the body of the entry. If an element. . . is supplied from another source, it is enclosed
within brackets. . . ."

"B. 1. A work that is published without a title page, or
without a title page applying to the whole work . . . is cataloged from some other part of the work if possible and that
part specified as the source of the data, . . . this [may] be
cover title, half title, caption title . . . or other part. "

Another kind of book it may be well to mention here is
the book with more than one title page. In some instances
there is an added title page for the series to which the book
belongs, a special title page for a second volume, or a fac-
simile of the title page of an earlier edition. Catalog the book
from the title page for the volume rather than the series, for
the set rather than the volume; catalog from the printed title
page if there is also an engraved one. If such information

would be useful in the particular library give information in
a note about the other title page or title pages.

Call number. The call number is the classification symbol and the book number or initial of the author's surname,
e. g., 327. 73 is the call number for Foster Rhea Dulles' book.
     D88
Other illustrations of call numbers are: 92   973 or if the
                                          C87   B31
author's initial letter only is used: 92 973. This combination
                                        C   B
of figures and letters, which is necessary to direct the reader to the shelves, is given on the catalog cards, on the spine
of the book, and on the book card. Some librarians put this
number on the catalog cards in red to make it more conspicuous.

Author. Chapters III-V explain how to determine the
form of the name to be used, and show name authority cards
with the name properly written for a catalog entry. Whether
or not the librarian makes name authority cards, each new
name must be searched and the form to be used in the catalog decided upon. For example, in the Booklist, volume 48,
the heading for Windows for the Crown Prince is Vining,
Elizabeth (Gray), the form used on Card 12.

The author's surname is followed by a comma, one
space, the forenames, comma, one space, dates of birth and
death, period. If only initials for forenames appear on the
title page and the forenames cannot be found, eight spaces
are left after each initial so that the names may be filled in,
if found later. The name of an organization as author, i. e.,
a corporate author, is given on the same line and in the
same position as that of a personal author. There are periods
at the end of the main heading and each subheading and each
subheading is preceded by two spaces, e. g., Texas. History.

"The official designations of countries, national domains,
and their principal administrative divisions are capitalized
only if used as parts of proper names, as proper names, or
as proper adjectives. "[3]

          U. S. Maritime Commission.
          Virginia. Conservation Commission.

"The full names of existing or proposed organized bodies and their shortened names are capitalized; other substi-
tutes, which are most often regarded as common nouns, are

capitalized only in certain specified instances to indicate pre-
eminence or distinction."[4]

> Minneapolis. Public Library.
> National Conference on City Planning.

Capitalize: proper names, derivatives of proper
names, common nouns and adjectives forming an essential
part of a proper name. [5]

> Child Study Association of America.
> Association of American Geographers.

Title (A.-A. 1967. 133)

"A. General rule. The title proper . . . is transcribed exactly as to order, wording, spelling, accentuation, and
other diacritical marks . . . but not necessarily as to punctuation and capitalization. If accents, umlauts, and other diacritical marks are omitted from the title page, they are added in conformity with the usage in the text."

"B. Abridgment. Long titles are abridged if this can be
done without loss of essential information. The first words of
the title are always included.

"The first word of the title may be the name of the author; in the possessive form it is generally considered the author statement and is included or omitted according to the provisions of 134. Parts of the title more intelligibly presented in
a contents paragraph are omitted from the transcription of the
title."

"E. Additions. 1. Additions may be made to the title in
the language of the title if it needs explanation and if brief
statements to clarify it can be taken from the work itself."

> Longfellow. [Selections]

"G. Alternative title. An alternative title is always
transcribed in the catalog entry because the book may be referred to by it and because another edition may be published
with the alternative title as the title."

"H. Subtitle. The subtitle is considered a part of the
title and transcribed in the entry in the same manner as the
title proper, except that a long subtitle which is separable
from the title may be omitted. . . ."

Author statement (A. -A. 1967. 134)

"A. The statement of authorship appearing in a work is
. . . omitted . . . in the following cases unless it appears as
an integral part of the title (e. g., if it is the antecedent of
a pronoun)": when the form of the name in the heading: 1)
"is the same as that in the author statement"; 2) "varies
from that in the heading only in fullness"; 3) "is the same
as that in the author statement except for the addition to the
heading of some specification such as date, place, or distinguishing term"; or 4) "is in the possessive or other in-
flected form. When the form of the name in the heading for
a corporate body is the same as that in the author statement
except for the fact that the body is entered under place. . .
[or] is the same as that in the author statement except that
the latter includes the names of one or more bodies to which
the body named in the heading is subordinate and these names
are omitted from the heading; e. g.,

> "Heading: U. S. Agricultural Research Service
> Author statement omitted: Agricultural Research
> Service, U. S. Department of Agriculture. "

"When the form of the name . . . for a government body entered under country, state, city, or other jurisdiction is the
same as that in the author statement except for the form of
name of the jurisdiction; e. g.,

> "Heading: Pennsylvania. Dept. of Revenue
> Author statement omitted: Commonwealth of Pennsyl-
> vania, Department of Revenue. "

Works of shared authorship (A. -A. 1967. 3)

"Preliminary note. The rules below apply to 1) works
produced by the joint collaboration of two or more authors,
2) works for which different authors have prepared separate
contributions (e. g., composite works, symposia, series of ad-
dresses, lectures, etc., written specifically for a particular
occasion or for the publication in hand) providing the authors
are not acting as members of a corporate body" (see
rule 17, page 82), 3) "works consisting of an exchange between different persons (e. g., correspondence, debates). They
apply equally to cases of shared responsibility among compil-
ers, editors, translators, adapters, etc., when the applicable
rule requires main entry under such a person. "

"For collections of previously existing works by different authors apply rule 5, page 69. "

"A. Principal author indicated. Enter a work of shared authorship under the person or corporate body, if any, to whom principal responsibility is attributed, e. g., by wording or typography. Make added entries under the other authors involved if there are not more than two [if such entries would be useful]. Always make an added entry under an author, other than the principal author, . . . whose name appears first on the title page. "

Title page:

>The humanities and the library . . . by Lester Asheim and associates

Enter under Asheim

Title page:

>Animal motivation; experimental studies on the albino rat, by C. J. Warden with the collaboration of T. N. Jenkins, L. H. Warner, E. L. Hamilton and H. W. Nissen

Enter under Warden

"B. Principal author not indicated

"1. If no one is represented as principal author and if there are not more than three authors, enter under the one that is named first. . . . "

Title page:

>Health for effective living; a basic health education text for college students, by Edward B. Johns, Wilfred C. Sutton, Lloyd E. Webster

Enter under Johns

Title page:

>The correspondence between Benjamin Harrison and James G. Blaine, 1882-1893 . . .

Enter under Harrison

"a. If such a work is in more than one volume and the names of the authors appear in a different order on the title pages of the different volumes, enter under the author named first on the title page of the first volume. "

Title page, book 1:

>Child-life arithmetics. . . Three book series, by

Clifford
Woody, Frederick S. Breed [and] James R. Overman

Title page, book 2:

. . . by Frederick S. Breed, James R. Overman
[and] Clifford Woody

Title page, book 3:

. . . by James R. Overman, Clifford Woody [and]
Frederick S. Breed

Enter under Woody and make added entries under
Breed and Overman

"b. If the names of the authors appear in a different
order on the title page of a later edition of the work, enter
it under the author named first in the first edition unless the
later edition is revised or updated. In this case enter the
later edition under the one named first on its title page. ''

Title page:

Outlines of sociology, by John Lewis Gillin and
Frank W. Blackmar. 3d ed.

("A somewhat thorough rewriting. '') In earlier
editions Blackmar's name appeared first on
the title page)

Enter under Gillin with added entry under Blackmar

"3 B. 2. If no one is represented as principal author and
there are more than three authors, enter the work under its
title unless the work is produced under the direction of an editor named on the title page. Make an added entry under the
author named first on the title page.

Title page:

The United Nations and economic and social cooperation, by Robert E. Asher, Walter M. Kotsch-
nig, William Adams Brown, Jr. , and associates

Enter under title and make an added entry under Asher

Joint authors (A. -A. 1967. 134)

D. "If there are more than three joint authors, collabo-
rators, or contributors named in the author statement, all after the first named are omitted. The omission is indicated as
follows: 1) By the phrase "and others" if the title page is in
English. "

E. 1. "Titles and abbreviations of titles of address,
honor and distinction (but not of nobility), initials of societies,
etc., are generally omitted from the author statement. Exception is made as follows: . . . c) If the title explains the relationship of a personal author to the corporate author used as
the heading for the work. "

"By Luther H. Evans, Librarian of Congress. "

F. 1. "If necessary for intelligibility, a word or phrase
in the language of the title is added to express what is shown
on the title page by arrangement, or to clarify an ambiguous
or misleading statement. "

Edition (A. -A. 1967. 135)

Barb says to include even the first edition

"A. An edition statement in a work [other than that of
a first edition] is always included in its catalog entry, the
impression or printing only in the case of items having particular bibliographical importance. This makes it necessary
for the cataloger to be aware of the lack of uniformity among
publishers in the use of the terms 'edition' and 'impression'
or 'printing' and their equivalents in other languages, and to
interpret them according to the accepted definitions. "

"B. If the volumes in a set are of different editions, the
edition statement is generally omitted from the body of the
entry and the various editions are specified in a supplementary
note or in the list of contents. . . . "

Statement of the number of volumes (A. -A. 1967. 136)

"A. A statement of the number of volumes in a work is
specified in its catalog entry, between the title and the imprint, only if such a statement appearing on the work is at
variance with the information shown in the collation of the
work. "

Illustration statement (A. -A. 1967. 137)

"The statement of the illustrative matter appearing on

the title page of a work is included in the catalog entry only
if it adds an important characterization of the material that
cannot be shown in the collation; e. g., the number of illustrations in a work containing many unnumbered plates or test illustrations, the kind of illustrations (such as photographs or
engravings), or the name of the artist. "

Imprint (A. -A. 1967. 138)

"Preliminary note. The place of publication, of printing, or of copyright, name of the publisher and date of publication, which constitute the imprint of a work, serve both to
identify and to characterize the work and sometimes to indicate where it is available. Different editions are most commonly distinguished by the differences in their imprints. . . .
The date generally indicates the timeliness of the subject matter. "

When publishers are well known the place of publication
may be omitted and the publishers' names abbreviated. Appendix II gives a list of well-known publishers, with abbreviations,
to be used without place. If the publisher of a given book is
not included in this list its name is to be given in the entry
with such abbreviations as are authorized in this appendix.
When a publisher's name becomes more common in catalog
entries, it may be used in abbreviation and without place if
it is added to the list in the appendix.

"A. Order of elements. The imprint is recorded in the
catalog entry in the conventional order of place, publisher,
date. "

"B. Works with more than one place and publisher.

"1. A work that gives indication of being published in
several places by one publisher or by several publishers, is
generally described in the catalog entry by an imprint consisting of the first named place of publication and the corresponding publisher. If, however, a place or publisher that is not
the first named is distinguishable by type or position, or
otherwise, as the actual or principal place or publisher, it
is given in the catalog entry; in this case the first named
place or publisher is omitted. "

"3. If a city in the United States, with . . . an American publisher, is named in a secondary position in a work
containing a foreign imprint, it is . . . [substituted for] the
foreign imprint. "

London, New York, Longmans, Green.
Paris, Gauthier-Villars; Chicago, University of
    Chicago Press.

"C. Printer's imprint as a substitute for publisher's imprint.

"If neither the place of publication nor the publisher is named in the work and the place of printing and the name of the printer are, the latter are used in the imprint. . . ."

Place of publication (A. -A. 1967. 139)

"A. Place unknown. If the place of publication is unknown, the location of the editorial office, or the seat of the institution, or headquarters of the society publishing the work, is to be given in the imprint of the catalog entry. . . . If neither the place of publication nor the place of printing is known, the place is represented by the abbreviation 'n. p. ' for 'no place, ' enclosed in brackets. "

"C. Additions to place name. The place of publication is followed by its country, state or similar designation if it is necessary to identify the place or to distinguish it from another place of the same name. Abbreviations are used for most such designations. " *Example: Birmingham England or Alabama.*

Abbreviated place name   "D. Abbreviated place names. The name of a city which is abbreviated in the imprint on the title page is abbreviated in the catalog entry. If required for clarity, the abbreviated form is completed or followed by the full form. "

Rio [de Janeiro]
Mpls [i. e., Minneapolis]

Publisher (A. -A. 1967. 140)

"A. General rule. The publisher statement appearing on a work is abridged as much as possible without loss of intelligibility or identification of the publisher. Unnecessary parts of the statement are omitted, abbreviations are employed [see Appendix II] . . . and names known to be forenames are represented by initials or, in the case of well-known publishers, omitted. . . . [Forenames of persons in whose honor a firm is named are spelled in full.] Lack of a publisher is not shown. " *Ex. Charles C. Thomas could be C. C. Thomas or Thomas*

"B. Essential parts of the publisher statement. Data that are considered necessary for the intelligibility of the publisher statement include the following:

"1) Words or phrases indicating that the name in the imprint is not that of the publisher.

> Printed by the G. Banta Pub. Co.
> Planographed by Edwards Bros.

5) Phrases indicating the official status of a government printer, or the official authorization of a commercial printer. 6) The statement that a work is privately printed, if a publisher or press is named in the imprint. 7) Phrases showing that the publisher is also the author of the work, if an author statement is needed. . . . "

"C. Unnecessary parts of the publisher statement:
. . .

"a) The phrases 'published by, ' 'published for, ' and the word 'publisher, ' and their equivalents in other languages; b) words showing that the publisher is also the printer or bookseller; c) the initial article, except when necessary for clarity; d) the phrases, 'and company, ' 'and sons, ' etc., and their foreign equivalents; e) terms meaning 'incorporated' or 'limited' and their abbreviations; f) either the name of the press or the name of the publisher if both are used, the second name generally being omitted; g) either the initialism (or abbreviation) of a corporate name or the name it represents if they are used together, the full form being omitted if it appears in any other place in the catalog entry; h) the name of the publishing firm if it is used with the name of a branch or division which is adequately identified by its own name; e. g., McGraw-Hill and its branch, Whittlesey House. "

"D. Omission of publisher. The publisher statement is omitted from the imprint when the work is entered under the publisher's name, unless the responsibility for authorship is implied by the publisher statement and not otherwise shown; in this case the provisions of 134 (author statement) are applicable. "

Date

The date of publication is the date given at the foot of the title page. This date is usually changed when the book is reprinted. The important point is not when the book was printed, but when it was written and when the latest changes in it

were made. The latest copyright date shows this, for books
can be recopyrighted only when important changes are made
in them; therefore, the latest copyright date is used, e.g.,
"Copyright, 1914, 1942"--choose the latter. The person or
firm copyrighting an average volume is of no importance in
the catalog, so variation in this fact is not noted. The letter
c before a date, c1952, shows that it is the copyright date.
If there is no copyright date, give the date of publication; i.e.,
the date at the foot of the title page; if no publication date,
give the date in or at the end of the preface or introduction,
preceded by the abbreviation pref. or introd. or the appropriate word written out; if no date is given anywhere, write n. d.
Some librarians may prefer to use no date instead of the abbreviation n. d. Use arabic figures for dates even though the
book uses roman numerals.

"B. . . . If the work is in more than one volume and
the imprint dates [or the copyright dates] of the individual
volumes vary, the inclusive dates are given... . . Inclusive
dates in the same century are given in the form 1923-30
[c1905-25]. . . . If the date of the first or the last volume
or of both does not correspond with the respective year given
in the imprint, the irregularity is shown in the form 1923-30
[v. 1, 1930]. "

Place, publisher, and date, if not found on the title
page, are enclosed in brackets.

Ann Arbor, The University of Michigan Press [c1963]
Harper [c1965]
Morrow, 1953
New York, The Modern Library [pref. 1880]
[New York] Fordham University, n. d.

Hudson Strode's Jefferson Davis, a work in three volumes, came out over a period of years.

Imprints and copyright dates from versos of title pages
are:

Harcourt, Brace and Company   v. 1
New York
[c1955]

Harcourt, Brace and Company   v. 2
New York
[c1959]

Harcourt, Brace & World, Inc.   v. 3
New York
[c1964]

Using the abbreviations given in Appendix II, the catalog entry for this three volume work would give the imprint
as: Harcourt [c1955-64].

Collation. This term is used to include the number of
pages of a one-volume work, or the number of volumes of a
work in more than one volume, and information about the illustrations.

The title page may include a statement as to the number
of volumes and the number of and type of the illustrations, or
this information, like the paging, may be discovered only
through an examination of the book. In giving the number of
pages the preliminary paging is to be ignored and the last
numbered page in the book is to be recorded, whether it is
the last page of the text, the next to the last, or the last
page of the index. If a work is in two or more volumes and
the library does not have them all, give what it has in pencil so that the changes may be made easily if other volumes
are added, e. g., v. 1, 3. When a book does not have its
pages numbered, write "unpaged." If the paging is irregular
or complicated simply give: 1 v. (various pagings). If the number of bibliographical volumes or parts of a work differ from
the number of physical volumes, give both, e. g., 2 v. in 1.

Illustrative matter (A. -A. 1967. 142)

C. 1. a. "Brief mention of the illustrative matter in a
work comprises the second part of the collation statement.
The abbreviation 'illus.,' for illustrations, is used to describe all types of illustrative matter unless particular types
in the work are considered important enough to be specifically designated." When they are designated use the following
terms: genealogical tables, maps, plates, portraits. (See Appendix II, Abbreviations.)

"6. . . . The location of a map or other illustrative
matter printed on the lining paper or papers is specified in
the collation if it is the only map or other illustrative matter
of its type in the work."

"E. . . . 1. Volumes or portfolios consisting of plates
and not numbered consecutively with the other volumes of a

set are specified separately in the collation." E. g., "3 v. and atlas . . ."; "169 p. and atlas. . . ."

"2. If, however, the title of the atlas or portfolio differs from that of the main work, if there is a special compiler, or if some other feature requires further description, the form of entry adopted for supplements is preferred (see 155, page 142-43).

Series note. Many books belong to a series and it is sometimes important to include this information in the catalog entry. A series is "A number of separate works, usually related to one another in subject or otherwise, issued in succession, normally by the same publisher and in uniform style, with a collective title. . . ."[6] There are three kinds of series: author, subject, and publisher's. Pilgrimage, parts I-XII, by Dorothy M. Richardson, which includes Dawn's Left Hand and Clear Horizon, is an example of an author's series; "American Guide Series" and "Rivers of America" are examples of subject series; "Everyman's Library," an example of a publisher's series.

The name of the series is found at the top of the title page, on the cover of the book, or on one of the pages preceding the title page.

Series statement (A.-A. 1967. 143)

A. . . . 1) "The series statement gives the information that a work is part of a series of publications issued under a collective title. 2) The series statement on the work may include, in addition to the title of the series . . . the name of an editor or editors, and the number of the volume, if the series consists of consecutively numbered volumes or parts. . . ."

"D. . . . A series title occurring in combination with the monograph title is separated, if possible, from the latter and given in the regular series position."

"From morality to religion, being the Gifford lectures delivered at the University of St. Andrews, 1938.

Title: From morality to religion.
Series: (Gifford lectures, 1938)."

"E. 1. If the author of the series is the same as the

author of the individual part being cataloged, the appropriate possessive pronoun is substituted for the author's name, unless the name is integrated with the series title. "

>(Its Publications in research and records)
>(His Wild world tales)

"2. If the author of the series is not the author of the individual part being cataloged, the former's name is included in the series statement as specified below.

"a. The author of the series is included if author and title are integrated in the statement of the work. "

>(Historical publications of the Society of Colonial Wars in the Commonwealth of Pennsylvania)

"b. The name of the author is included if the series statement would not be intelligible without it. The series statement, in such a case, begins with the name of the author in catalog entry form, 1) if it can be given without supplying any part and without breaking up an integrated author statement, or 2) if the entire author statement needs to be supplied. In other cases, which will be the most common, the series statement will be given in the form provided by the work with the omission of any unessential part. "

>[U. S. Dept. of the Army] Educational manual, EM 509. 2)

"F. 1. If a work is a part of more than one series, [7] the second series statement is placed, without parentheses but with brackets if necessary, in the position of the first supplementary note. The series that is chosen for the first (regular) position is the one that is more specialized and less extensive, if such a comparison is possible. . . .

"2. If the second series is a subordinate part of the first, the series and the subseries are specified in the same statement. . . . "

>(U. S. Dept. of State. Publication 1564. Executive agreement series, 94)

A series note states the name of the series to which the book belongs. If the name of the series begins with an article, the second word as well as the article begins with a capital letter. The series note is enclosed in parentheses and begins on the fifth space after the collation; if there is not space on that line, it begins at the first indention on the following line. If the series is not of sufficient importance for an added entry, it is unnecessary to make a series note.

Notes. Notes may be added to catalog entries when needed to explain the title or to correct any misapprehension to which it might lead; to supply essential information; to give important bibliographical details not included in the title, imprint, or collation. They should be brief and clear. The safest rule is not to add a note if there is doubt as to its value.

(A. -A. 1967. 144)

"A. . . . Notes amplify or qualify the formalized description, either when the rules do not permit the inclusion of the needed information in any form other than a note or when the incorporation of the information in the formalized description would be misleading, cumbersome, or inappropriate. . .

"B. . . . Notes to provide the following types of information are generally indispensable: 1) To identify the work or edition and distinguish it from others; e. g., an edition statement that cannot be presented in the body of the entry because of its length, complexity, or other consideration (see 135, page 130). . . . A note may be essential also to explain the source of the title used in the entry (e. g., title from cover), to show a variation from the title page title appearing elsewhere in the work (a variant cover title, caption title, or running title), to show variations in the title in a work of several volumes. . . . 2) To clarify the relationship of the heading or of an added entry to the work. . . . 6) To describe accompanying material; e. g., a separate index or supplement (see 155). "

"C. . . . Notes to provide other types of information vary in importance and are not generally indispensable. These include notes: 1) To reveal the contents or partial contents (particularly bibliographies) of a work in one volume. 4) To provide bibliographical history of the work; relationship to other works, etc. (see 144E2). "

"D. Style. Rule 149 provides fixed forms for certain notes. Informal notes are used for any other data that need to be supplied. They may take any of the following forms: 1) Statements composed by the cataloger, . . . 2) Quotations from the work being cataloged. . . .

"Notes are factual and unbiased. . . . "

". . . The form of the citation is as follows: the source
of a quoted note is preceded by a dash; the source of a statement not quoted, by 'cf.' The source, not included within quotation marks, consists of the author's name, in direct form,
and the title, both in sufficient fullness for identification. . . .
Commonly used and easily recognizable words are abbreviated. . . .

"E. Order. Various considerations affect the order of
notes, making an invariable order undesirable. In certain
cases, various notes are combined or grouped together to produce a clear, logical entry. . . .

"In general, the following order will prevail: 1) Notes
that refer to the elements in the formalized description, in
the same order as they appear there: title, subtitle, authorship, edition, imprint, collation and additional physical description. 2) Notes that provide bibliographical history; relationship to other works (. . . sequels. . . supplements, indexes . . . abridgments, adaptations, dramatizations, parodies,
etc.) and to other editions of the same work. "

"f) The author or editor of earlier or subsequent editions if there has been a change of author heading.

"Based on the 3d ed. of Guide to the study and use
of reference books by Alice Bertha Kroeger as revised by I. G. Mudge.

"g) The title of a sequel to the work being cataloged or
of an earlier work which the work being cataloged continues.

Sequel: Men against the sea
Sequel to Mutiny on the Bounty

"h) Information in regard to the original publication of
works issued as reprint editions if the information can be ascertained from the works and is significant. Information in regard to the original publication of works which first appeared
as part of another publication, if this can be given in a specific form leading to the earlier work. "

Reprinted from the Physical review, vol. 70, nos.
5-6 . . . September 1-15, 1946.

Contents note (A. -A. 1967. 149)

It is not often necessary to give contents for collections of short stories, poetry, or plays on cards made locally if the library has copies of the printed indexes of collections. The H. W. Wilson Company's <u>Cumulative Book Index</u> includes contents from many of the collections, which it lists. More information on these indexes is given in the section on analytical entries in Chapter VII.

"A. Scope. 1. Either all of the contents or a part of them are specified in the catalog entry if it is necessary to bring out important parts of the work not mentioned in the title, or to give a fuller and more detailed description of the contents than the title supplies. If an added entry is to be made for an item in the work, the presence of this item is specified in the contents or partial contents note. The complete contents are listed in the entry for collections of works by the same author (especially if they are on different subjects) or for collections of works by different authors, unless the articles are numerous and slight. If the collection contains the complete works of an author in one volume, however, the contents are not listed.

"2. Contents are especially necessary for works in several volumes, whether they are single works (with a formal division of matter that can be described) or collections of works by one or more authors.

"4. Partial contents are noted if one or more selected items in the work need to be specified. . . . Bibliographies are noted unless they are obviously of little value. . . . Appendices are noted only if they contain matter that is important enough to be specified. Supplements or other appended matter not printed with the work are always noted (see 155).

"B. Position. The contents note (because of its length and the fact that in an open entry[8] it will have additions) is the last note in the catalog entry. If specific items are noted in addition to the 'Contents' or 'Partial contents' paragraph, they precede the latter, generally in the order of the items in the work.

"C. Form. 1. The specification of one or more items in a work consists of the precise heading of the item as it is found in the work (generally as a caption or heading of the piece or in a table of contents), a quoted statement from the work, or a statement phrased by the cataloger.[9] If one to three selected items are noted, the inclusive pagination of the

items is generally specified, unless a single item described
is scattered throughout the work. In other cases, the contents
are arranged in one paragraph, beginning with the word 'Contents' or the phrase 'Partial contents.' The items are given
in the order in which they appear in the work. In works of
more than one volume, the parts of the work are designated,
the terms being those used in the work itself, except that
Arabic numerals are substituted for Roman numerals unless
both are required for clarity. If the parts are unnumbered,
volume or part numbers are supplied. If the number of bibliographical volumes does not correspond with the number of
physical volumes and the collation statement needs amplifica-
tion the number of physical volumes follows the titles in the
contents.

"2. For works of one volume, the items in a contents
paragraph are separated by a dash; for multi-volume works
the dash precedes the volume number and items within the
volumes are punctuated as separate sentences.

"3. Introductions described in the title are not mentioned again in the contents paragraph. Prefatory and similar un-
signed matter is also omitted.

"4. In listing works by different authors, the title precedes the name of the author, as indicated in the examples
below, . . . Initials are used for one or more forenames.
Brackets are not used to show that the words 'by,' or 'and,'
or their equivalents have been supplied.

"5. Paging is given in the contents paragraph only for
bibliographies, and for a particular item that occupies a dis-
proportionately large portion of the work. If given, it is cited
within parentheses.

"6. If the volumes of a set are of different editions, the
editions and . . . dates are given in the contents paragraph.

"7. Contents of a set in many volumes may be paragraphed, one paragraph to a volume, with 'Contents' centered
as heading. . . ."

> Bibliography: v. 1, p. 351-358; v. 2, p. 234-235.
> Bibliography: p. 18-25 (3d group)
> Chronological list of the author's works: p. 469-475.
> Includes bibliographies.

> Appendices (p. 157-200): A. The Anglo-Japanese

alliance. -B. The Russo-Japanese peace treaty. -C.
The Japan Korean agreement.

Contains biographies of: G. F. Dick; G. H. Dick;
Ehrlich; Jenner; Koch; Pasteur; Salk; Schick.

Contents. -How these records were discovered. -A
short sketch of the Talmuds.-Constantine's letter . . .

Contents. -A memory of two Mondays, by A. Miller. - The Browning version, by T. Ratligan. -27 wagons
full of cotton, by T. Williams. -Sorry, wrong number,
by L. Fletcher. -Glory in the flower, by W. Inge . . .

Contents. -v. 1 From Aeschylus to Turgenev. Rev.
ed. for colleges. 1951-v. 2 From Henrik Ibsen to Eugene Ionesco. 3d college ed. 1960.

Contents
[1] American Peace Society. Should the United
States of America join the Permanent Court of International Justice? [1931]
[2] Bustamente y Sirvén, A. S. de. The World
Court and the United States. [1929]

19. Author entry for work of more than one volume with different copyright dates for different volumes and with contents

```
973
C45    Channing, Edward, 1856-1931.
           A history of the United States.
       Macmillan [c1905-25]
           6 v. illus.

           Contents. -v. 1 The planting of a
       nation in the new world, 1000-1660. -
       v. 2 A century of colonial history,
       1660-1760. -v. 3 The American Revolution,
       1761-1789. -v. 4 Federalists and Repub-
       licans, 1789-1815. -v. 5 The period of
                            (Continued on next
                                          card)
```

Supplements, indexes, etc. (A. -A. 1967. 155)

"Scope. The rules below provide for the description of continuations, supplements, and indexes that are so dependent upon the works to which they are related that they are best described by means of an addition to the catalog entry for the main work. A continuation or supplement which has an author and title differing from those of the original work is generally described according to the rules for cataloging other monographs, [10] with a note, if necessary, to show its relation to the original work. It may, however, be described according to the most appropriate of the following forms.

"A. Supplements described in detail. 1. A dash, . . . to represent the repetition of the author heading . . . is added to the catalog entry following all of the paragraphed notes relating to the main work. . . . It is followed by the title of the supplement or index, the author statement (if necessary to show the compiler or other person responsible for the work), the adition statement, imprint, collation, etc., as for an independent work. "

20. Extension card also shows general index added to card for main work

---

```
973                          2
C45    Channing.

       transition, 1815-1848. -v.  6 The war for
       Southern independence.

973    --- --- Supplementary volume, general
C45    index, comp. by Eva G. Moore.    Mac-
       millan [c1932]
            155 p.
```

"2. If the title of the supplement or index includes the title of the main work and can be separated from it, the title of the main work is represented by a second dash (see Card 20) . . . following the dash that represents the author. "

Extension cards. When there is not space on the card for all of the information, added cards known as extension or second cards are made. Whenever an extension card follows,

"Continued on next card" is typed (or stamped with a rubber
stamp) aligned with the hole in the card, and immediately to
the right of it. The call number and the first or filing word
of the first card are repeated on all extension cards and the
number of the card is written in the center of the card, on
the line above the heading. On an author or main card, the
filing word at the top of the extension cards would be the author's surname; if the name of an organization, however, the
full heading would be repeated as so many organizations begin
with the same word, the name of the country, and so forth.
On extension cards for added entries repeat the entire added
heading, then proceed as usual.

Extension cards may be tied to the first card with heavy
white thread. A pencil may be slipped in while the thread is
being tied, so that the cards may be turned easily without
being cut. Tying makes it easier to handle the cards before
they are filed, and if for any reason they have to be removed
from the catalog for additional information or a correction
they can be kept together.

Names of organizations as authors. Chapter V gives the
rules covering the forms of names of organizations to be
used as headings in the catalog. The author card for a government document would be just like that for a book with a personal author, except that the heading would frequently be the
official name of the government body, adapted to agree with
the rules in Chapter V.

Note that the name is given on the same line as if it
were a personal author. There are periods at the end of the
main heading and each subheading, and each subheading is preceded by two spaces, e.g., Canada. Court rules. Supreme
Court.

Capitalization (A.-A. 1967. Appendix II. English. 2.)

"The abbreviation indicating incorporation, or limited
liability, appearing after the name of a firm or other body
is not capitalized."

inc., ltd.

"If a word in the name of a corporate body consists of
a prefix joined by a hyphen to a common noun, the latter is
not capitalized."

Mid-century Book Society

21. Author entry for a government document

---

385. 2
U58   U. S. Congress. House. Committee on
           Foreign Affairs.
      Special mission to Panama to study
    the Panama Railroad Company; report by
    Thomas S. Gordon.   U. S. Govt.
    Print. Off. 1951.
      22 p. maps.

As in the case of government documents, publications of societies, associations, institutions and miscellaneous bodies are cataloged as are works of personal authors except that the name of the society, association, etc. , is used as heading.

The same book with two different titles. Mireille Cooper's The Happy Season, published by Pellegrini & Cudahy in New York in 1952, was published in London in 1951. The content of the English and the American editions is the same, but the English edition has the title Swiss Family Burnand. If the library has a copy of one title, an entry is made under the author for that title and a reference is made from the author and the other title so that the reader will be sure to find the book. A note on each entry informs the reader of the changed title.

If on the other hand the library has a copy of the book under each of its titles, each title will be cataloged separately, with the appropriate note on each entry giving the information as to the other title.

Notes. Order   (A. -A. 1967. 144 E 2)

"a) The original or earliest known title of a work reissued in the same language with a changed title [is given as a note]. "

22. Main entry for book with changed title--book in library

```
        Cooper, Mireille (Burnand) 1893-
             The happy season.    New York,
        Pellegrini & Cudahy [1952]
             214 p.    illus.

             First published in London in 1951
        under title:  Swiss family Burnand.
```

23. Main entry for book with changed title--book in library

```
        Cooper, Mireille (Burnand) 1893-
             Swiss family Burnand.    London,
        Eyre & Spottiswoode, 1951.
             220 p.    illus.

             Published in New York in 1952
        under title:  The happy season.
```

Information in catalog entries for fiction. Since the reader who wants fiction uses the catalog only to find whether or not a certain book is in the library or what books the library has by a certain author, cards for fiction may be simpler than for nonfiction. For this reason most public libraries do not classify fiction nor assign a book number, and catalog it more simply than nonfiction when they type the cards. Some school and college libraries, however, prefer to classify their fiction as literature and to catalog it exactly as they do their nonfiction. Others do not classify fiction, but catalog all books the same way whether fiction or nonfiction.

24. Reference for book with changed title--book not in library

```
        Cooper, Mireille (Burnand) 1893-
            Swiss family Burnand.
            see her
            The happy season.
```

The simplest form of entry may contain only the author's full name, without dates, and the title. Many librarians prefer, however, to follow the same policy regarding author's dates for fiction as for nonfiction. Some librarians find the copyright date or the date of publication useful as the date answers the reader's query as to which of the titles is the most recent.

If more information regarding the book, e.g., the publisher, is desired on the catalog entries, it is better to catalog fiction and nonfiction alike. But if this information is available in trade catalogs and bibliographical tools which are at hand, time may be saved by making simple catalog entries such as Card 25 and by referring to these printed aids for the occasional calls for such information.

If the printed catalog cards described in Chapter X are used for fiction there are very few books for which the author's name and dates have to be established. If only author and title, or author, title, and dates are given for fiction, however, it may be less expensive, takes less time, and is as satisfactory to type the cards for fiction in the library as it is to order Wilson or Library of Congress printed catalog cards.

On the title card the information given on the author card

is simply reversed, the title given on the top line, the author on the line below. As the reader frequently remembers the title rather than the author, title entries for fiction are important.

Another type of fiction is the anonymous book the author of which is unknown. This is the easiest of all to catalog. Obviously there can be no author card, and the only items that could go on the title card are the title and the copyright date. The latter item may be omitted. When the author is known but his name is not given on the title page, the book is cataloged as any other work of fiction, and a note states that the book is published anonymously.

25. Main entry for fiction

```
Edmonds, Walter Dumaux, 1903-
    The Boyds of Black River.      [c1953]
```

References

1. See p.133-35 for information regarding dates of books.

2. The term, tracing, is discussed in Chapter VII.

3. U. S. Government Printing Office, Style Manual. Rev. ed. Jan. 1959; Washington, D. C., 1959, 3.19.

4. Loc. cit., 3.17.

5. Loc. cit., 3.2-3.5, adapted.

6. A. L. A. Glossary of Library Terms (Chicago, A. L. A., 1943), p. 124.

7. "A series issued in two or more sequences and called

'second series, ' 'new series, ' or by a similar designation has this designation included, with the customary abbreviations, as the series numbering, not as a separate series or sub-series. '' Footnote 9, p. 213, A. -A. 1967.

8. "A catalog entry which provides for the addition of information concerning a work of which the library does not have a complete set, or about which complete information is lacking. '' A. L. A. Glossary of Library Terms (Chicago, American Library Association, 1943), p. 94.

9. "The word 'Bibliography' (without quotes) is to be preferred to the precise heading found in the work unless the latter is necessary to show the scope of the bibliography or unless the author of the bibliography is to be named in one note. '' Footnote 12, p. 223, A. -A. 1967.

10. "The term 'monograph' is used in these rules to embrace all non-serial publications, regardless of content or format, including collections, . . . '' Footnote 1, p. 191, A. -A. 1967.

Chapter VII
Added Catalog Entries

Introduction. An added entry is a "secondary entry, i. e., any other than the main entry. There may be added entries for editor, translator, title, subjects, series, etc. . . . an added entry card is a duplicate of the main entry, with the addition of a special heading. "[1]

Added entries (A. -A. 1967. 33)

"Added entries supplement the main entry by providing additional direct access to bibliographical items that are represented in the catalog. The preceding rules have indicated the added entries that are required in the typical circumstances with which each rule deals.

"A. . . . Make an added entry under any person or corporate body associated with the publication if it is believed that some catalog users might reasonably consider the person or body to be primarily responsible for it. Added entries are particularly important whenever the main entry is under a corporate body, under a special heading denoting the form of the material, or under title. "

"H. . . . Make an added entry under a person or body that has any other relationship to the publication that is important for retrieval purposes and that would not otherwise be brought out. . . ."

"J. 1. . . . If the only clue to a person's name is the appearance in the publication of initials or abbreviations of the name, make two added entries: one in direct order, and one transposed to bring the supposed initial or abbreviation of his surname into first position. . . .

On title page: von M. B.
Added entries: M. B.
B. , M.

"2. . . . Make an added entry under a concise phrase that characterizes the person and provides the only clue to his identity.

150

On title page: by a physician
Added entry: A physician

On title page: by an American
Added entry: An American

"3. When the author is indicated only as author of another work, transpose the statement to bring the title into first position. "

On title page: by the author of Early impressions
Added entry: Early impressions, Author of

Title entries. Title entries are made for all books of fiction and may or may not be made for all books of nonfiction. Consider Henry Bamford Parkes' The United States of America: a history and Foster Rhea Dulles' Yankees and Samurai. The former title is neither striking nor distinctive and may be used for many different histories of the United States. Undoubtedly many readers, however, will remember the latter and look for it in the catalog.

"P. . . . Make a title added entry for every work of known authorship that is published anonymously, and for all other works [except]:

"1) works with common titles that are incomplete or meaningless without the author's name, such as 'Collected works, ' 'Autobiography, ' 'Letters, ' 'Memoirs, ' 'Bulletin, ' 'Proceedings, ' 'Report, ' etc. , . . . "

Publications with introductory words commonly used in titles e. g. , "Introduction to, " "The principles of, " "A story of, " do not require title added entries;

"3) works with titles that are essentially the same as the main entry heading or a reference to the heading (e. g. , Royal Dublin Society. The Royal Dublin Society, 1731 to 1941);

"4) works with titles consisting solely of the name of a real person, except when they are works of the imagination;

"6) works with titles that are identical with a subject heading under which they are entered, if the subject heading as used has no subdivision, or with a see reference that leads directly to such a subject heading.

"Make a title added entry also for any title other than the main title (cover title, partial title, etc.) by which the work is likely to be known. "

There are two possible forms for title entries, namely, the short form and the unit card form. The short form title card has classification number, book number, title, and author. Title cards may be just like the main entry, however, with the brief title added above the heading of the unit card. This form is in accordance with the statement made above that "an added entry is a duplicate of the main entry, with the addition of a special heading. " If the unit card is used, the reader need not refer to the author card.

26. Title entry - short form

```
327. 73
D88           Yankees and samurai.
        Dulles, Foster Rhea, 1900-
```

27. Title entry - unit card

```
327. 73      Yankees and samurai.
D88      Dulles, Foster Rhea, 1900-
              Yankees and samurai; America's role
        in the emergence of modern Japan: 1791-
        1900.     Harper [c1965]
            275 p.    illus. , map, ports.

        Bibliography, p. 255-268.
```

28. Title entry for book with changed title - book in library

```
                The happy season.
          Cooper, Mireille (Burnand) 1893-
                The happy season.    New York,
          Pellegrini & Cudahy, 1952.
                214 p.  illus.

                First published in London in 1951 under
          title: Swiss family Burnand.
```

29. Reference card for book with changed title - book not in library

```
                Swiss family Burnand,    see
          Cooper, Mireille (Burnand) 1893-
                The happy season.
```

In the preceding chapter the author card for Cooper's
The Happy Season is given as an illustration of what is done
with books published under different titles. Corresponding
cards would be made for the titles.

The latter part of the title of some books is better known
than the full title, e. g., The Tragedy of Macbeth. In such
cases a catch or partial title card is made. This card begins
with the first striking word of the title, for example, Macbeth.

If the card is a unit card, the full title is given after the
author entry.

> Macbeth.
> Shakespeare, William, 1564-1616.
> The tragedy of Macbeth.

> Robinson Crusoe.
> Defoe, Daniel, 1661?-1731.
> The life and strange surprising adventures of
> Robinson Crusoe.

There are other books for which full and partial titles
should be brought out in the catalog, e. g., J. George Frederick's A Primer of "New Deal" Economics. This work
should have title cards as follows:

> A primer of "new deal" economics.
> Frederick, Justus George, 1882-
> A primer of "new deal" economics

> "New deal" economics.
> Frederick, Justus George, 1882-

Subject entries. There are usually more inquiries for
material on a specific subject than there are for books by a
particular author or with a special title. The most used cards
in the catalog are the subject cards, that is, the cards which
indicate on the top line the subject of which the book treats.
For this reason a subject entry should be made for every
book which deals with a definite subject. Sometimes a book
includes several different subjects and requires two, three,
or even more subject entries. Subject entries are not necessary for books containing a single poem or a single play, or
for a collection of all or part of the works of an individual
author. Chapter II, "Choice of Subject Headings," deals with
the question of ascertaining what a book is about and what subject headings best express its contents. There is also the possibility of making general subject references for entire groups
of books, e. g., books on birds, airplanes, etc., or for all
books of a certain form, e. g., books of American poetry. See
Sample Cards 1 and 2.

If one turns back to Card 1, one will note that the classification number for this general subject reference is given
in the same position as on the main card, described in Chapter VI; the subject heading in the same position as the added
title on Card 27. A line is skipped and a paragraph, beginning on the second line below the heading and at the same in-

dention as the heading, tells where books on the given subject may be found. The second and succeeding lines of this paragraph begin at the first indention. Another line is skipped; then the second paragraph about the use of the shelf list is given with the same indentions as the first paragraph.

On the subject card the subject heading is given on the third line from the top of the card, the line above the author or main heading (two lines above if the length of the heading requires it), beginning at the second indention, so that the author heading may be more prominent. If the subject heading occupies more than one line, succeeding lines begin at the third indention. Subdivisions of a main heading may be separated from it by a space, dash, space or other punctuation marks agreed upon locally, as a long dash (e. g., U. S. --History). This heading is usually given in red ink or in full capitals in black ink to make it stand out conspicuously. In all other respects the subject card is a copy of the author card.

30. Subject entry

```
327. 73     JAPAN - RELATIONS (GENERAL) WITH
D88            THE U. S.
          Dulles, Foster Rhea, 1900-
               Yankees and samurai; America's
          role in the emergence of modern Japan:
          1791-1900.     Harper [c1965]
               275 p.   illus., map, ports.

          Bibliography, notes: p. 255-268.

               1.  Japan - Relations (general) with
          the U. S. 2.  U. S. - Relations (general)
          with Japan.   I. Title.
```

Added entry for joint author, compiler, editor, etc. Added entry cards may be made for the second of two joint authors, for a compiler, editor, illustrator, translator, or for the person who writes the introduction to the book of another, provided these added entries are likely to be useful. If there are more than two joint authors or joint editors, added entries are made only for the first one. An added entry under Kaufman would be useful for Hart and Kaufman's You Can't Take It With You. This play is frequently referred to as Hart and Kaufman's play, and some readers will look un-

der Hart, some under Kaufman. The abridgment given on
page 68 will need an added entry under Lanier, since it is
spoken of as Lanier's Boy's King Arthur. Also, though the
main entry for The Book of King Arthur and His Noble
Knights is under Macleod, Card 118, an entry is needed under Malory for the reader who is interested in everything
Malory has written.

(A.-A. 1967. 33) "D. . . . If the work is entered under the name of a person, make an added entry for an editor
if he has added significant material or if the work has been
issued in many editions with different editors, " e.g., Shakespeare's plays.

"E. . . . If the main entry is under the name of a person, make an added entry under a translator if the translation is in verse or if the work has been translated into the
same language by many different translators."

"F. . . . Make an added entry under an illustrator if
his contribution is considered to be an important feature of
the publication."

If a writer, Pope or Longfellow for instance, translates
another's work, an added entry would enable the student to
consider not only Pope's or Longfellow's original writings but
his translations as well. The student of The Iliad may be
interested in the Pope translation and think of it as Pope's
Iliad, though knowing it is Homer's Iliad. Occasionally an
added entry is necessary for a compiler or an editor, for the
same reason. If the library is likely to have a call for illustrations by a well-known artist, e.g., Sir John Tenniel, an
added entry under his name would make it possible to find examples of his illustrations. If the library has a copy, and it
should have, of the H.W. Wilson Company's Children's Catalog, it may be used to locate books with illustrations by a
particular artist and no added entry need be made under illustrator.

To make added entries of the kind mentioned, the full
name in its best-known form (see Chapter III, "Choice of Personal Names") with dates, if the library uses them, is written on the line above the author. Begin at the second indention,
so that the heading of the main entry may remain in a prominent position. If this added heading occupies more than one
line, succeeding lines begin at the third indention. The abbreviation, comp., ed., illus., or tr. (or the full word if preferred), is given one space after the comma at the end of the

heading (Card 32). In the case of an added entry for a joint author or for the individual who writes the preface or introduction for another's work, no designation follows the name (Card 31).

31. Added entry for a joint author

```
812          Kaufman, George S            1889-
H32      Hart, Moss, 1904-
             You can't take it with you, a play by
         Moss Hart and George S. Kaufman.
         New York, Farrar & Rinehart [c1937]
             207 p.   illus.
```

32. Added entry for a translator

```
220          Moffatt, James, 1870-1944, tr.
B58      Bible.
             A new translation of the Bible,
         containing the Old and New Testaments
         [by] James Moffatt.   (Concordance ed. )
         Harper [c1950]
             2 v. in 1.   illus.
```

Another type of added entry is one for the author and title of a work which has been dramatized by another writer (Card 33). The name of the author and the title of the original work are added above the unit card at the second and third indentions respectively.

33. Added entry for the author and title of a work dramatized by another writer

```
                     Purdy, James Malcolm
                        Malcolm.
   812      Albee, Edward, 1928-
   A32          Malcolm; [play] adapted by Edward
            Albee from the novel by James Purdy.
            New York, Atheneum [c1966]
                138 p.   illus.



            I.  Purdy, James Malcolm
```

Added entries, except title and subject cards, are made
sparingly in the small library where the collection is accessible.

References [instead] of added entries (A. -A. 1967. 126)

"A. Added entries common to many editions

1. When the same added entry is required for
many editions of a work, it may be replaced by
appropriate references when it appears that the
advantage of greater simplicity and savings in
time and catalog space offset whatever incon-
venience may result for the user of the catalog.

Hamlet
Shakespeare, William, 1564-1616.

Editions of this work will be found under the
author's name.

Analytical entries (A. -A. 1967. 156)

"An analytical entry is an entry for a part of a work or
series of works for which another, comprehensive, entry is
made. The part analyzed may be a complete volume, biblio-
graphically independent from the set of which it forms a part,
or it may be a mere page or two which is inadequately described (either from the author or the subject approach) by the

catalog entry for the work as a whole. If the part analyzed is an independent work, it is cataloged according to the rules for separately published monographs, with a series note indicating its relationship to the more comprehensive work. . . ."

Some books are made up of two or more separate works of an author, or of different authors; or they may treat of several distinct subjects or phases of a subject. For example, the two-volume edition of De la Mare's Collected Poems contains his well-known poems for children, published under the title Peacock Pie. In this collection the library has the work, Peacock Pie, whether or not it has the separately bound edition. How can this be shown in the catalog? By making author and title analytical entries for it. Law's Science in Literature contains an essay by Madame Curie on her discovery of radium. This material on radium is as important as any that will be found in many libraries. It can be brought out by means of a subject analytical entry, i. e., a subject entry for a part of a book. Small collections and special libraries need to have their material analyzed freely, since the analytical entry may represent the only work by the author, the only copy of the essay, play, etc., or the only material on the subject. Frequently the analytical entry is used to call attention to an extra copy of popular material already available in another form.

It should be emphasized again that advantage should be taken of work already done. The H. W. Wilson Company's Children's Catalog, eleventh edition, includes 11, 496 analytical entries; their Standard Catalog for High School Libraries, eighth edition, includes 12, 850 analytical entries. Printed indexes such as Firkins' Index to Short Stories, Logasa and Ver Nooy's Index to One-Act Plays and other similar indexes, although they may seem expensive would be more economical in the long-run than preparing analytical cards for collections of short stories and plays.

For an author analytical entry the name of the author of the play, essay, or other separate work is given on the unit card on the second line above the author of the book, the title on the line below the author of the part, followed by: "p. 00-00:". For a title analytical entry this is reversed and the title is given on the top line, the author of the analytical entry on the next line followed by the same phrase and punctuation, namely: "p. 00-00:".

Note on Card 34 that the regular unit card is used as it is for all added entries, with the appropriate heading added.

The author of the analytical entry is given on the second line of the card, the title on the third line, followed by: a comma, the paging, and a colon (in case of a work of two or more volumes, the volume number precedes the paging, e. g. , v. 2, p. 56-112:). The indentions deserve special attention. In order that the author of the main book may stand out as well as the author and title of the particular part, the author in the added heading (i. e. , the analytical author) is given at the second or title indention and the title of the part analyzed at the third indention. If the name of the author of the analytical entry takes two lines, it begins on the first line and continues on the second line, third indention; and if the title of the analytical entry runs over, it comes back to the second indention.

34. Author analytical entry

```
                    Sheridan,  Richard Brinsley Butler,
                       1751-1816.
                       The school for scandal, p. 182-
  808. 82             265:
  C67     Cohen                    2

          The school for scandal. -Ibsen, Henrik.
          A doll's house. -Rostand, Edmond. Cyrano
          de Bergerac. -O'Neill, Eugene. The Em-
          peror Jones. -Further explorations.
```

If the author of the analytical entry and the author of the book are the same, an author analytical entry is unnecessary, as the person searching for the play or short story will look under the author's name, then in the contents listed on the card, for collections of plays, short stories, etc.

The two title analytical cards (numbers 35 and 36), like the author analytical card (number 34), are unit cards with the title and author of the respective analytics added as headings, followed by the paging. On Card 35, the author of the analytical entry and the author of the book are the same. It would be absurd to give the same author twice in succession, hence the title of the analytical entry is simply added in the regular place for an added title heading, and is followed by the paging as for all other analytical entries. In the second example, Card 36, since the authors are different, the same items are given as for the author analytical entry, but in reverse order. If the title runs over, the second line begins at the same indention, i. e., the third indention; and if the author's name runs over, it continues on the next line beginning at the third indention.

35. Title analytical entry-book and analytical entry by the same author

821	Peacock pie, v. 2, p. 95-218:
D33	De la Mare, Walter John, 1873-
	Collected poems, 1901-1918.
	Holt [c1920]
	2 v.
	Contents. -v. 1 Poems, 1906. The listeners, 1914. Motley, 1919. -v. 2 Songs of childhood, 1901. Peacock pie.

36. Title analytical entry - book and analytical entry by different authors

	The school for scandal, p. 182-265:
	Sheridan, Richard Brinsley Butler,
808. 82	1751-1816.
C67	Cohen 2
	The school for scandal. -Ibsen, Henrik. A doll's house. -Rostand, Edmond. Cyrano de Bergerac. -O'Neill, Eugene. The Emperor Jones. - Further explorations.

For a subject analytical entry the subject heading is
given as on any subject card. The heading is followed by the
phrase regarding the paging. If the author of the chapter or
section whose subject is being brought out in the catalog in
this way is different from the author of the book, his name
comes on the line below the subject, and the phrase regarding the paging follows that. If the work is in more than one
volume and the analytical entry is for an entire volume, the
volume number is substituted for the paging (e. g., v. 2:). If,
however, the analytical entry is for only a part of a volume,
both volume and paging are given (e. g., v. 2, p. 101-137).

37. Subject analytical entry including title of the part ana-
    lyzed

                       BOONE, DANIEL, 1735-1820.
973   Roosevelt, Theodore, 1858-1919,
L82   p. 18-28:
          Lodge, Henry Cabot, 1850-1924.
                 Hero tales from American history,
          by Henry Cabot Lodge and Theodore
          Roosevelt.   New York, Century Co.
          [c1922]
                 335 p.   illus.

                 Daniel Boone and the founding of
          Kentucky.

On subject analytical entry cards it is observed that the
title of the part analyzed is omitted because the name of the
author and the subject heading are more important than the
title and there is not space for all three at the top of the
unit card. Dropping the author, title, etc., of a typed unit
card another line would make all other items too low on the
card. If the title is very important, an exception may be
made by omitting the notes and contents of the unit card from
this copy of the card and substituting a note giving the title
of the analyzed part.

Series entries. A series entry is defined as "1. A number of separate works issued in succession and related to one
another by the fact that each bears a collective title generally
appearing at the head of the title page, on the half title, or
on the cover; normally issued by the same publisher in a uni-

form style, frequently in a numerical sequence. . . . 2. Each of two or more volumes of essays, lectures, articles, or other writings, similar in character and issued in sequence, e. g. , Lowell's Among my books, second series. 3. A separately numbered sequence of volumes within a series or serial, e. g. , Notes and queries, 1st series, 2d series, etc. " (A. -A. 1967. App. I Glossary)

Added entries. Series (A. -A. 1967. 33N)

"Make an added entry under the series for each separately cataloged work (adding after the title the numerical designation of the work as part of the series if it is numbered) if it can be reasonably assumed that the work might be cited as part of the series or if the series might be reasonably cataloged as a collected set. The decision should be influenced by the importance of the series, the nature of the issuing body, and the scope and numbering of the series. Added entries are rarely made, however, if all the volumes in the series are by the same person.

"Thus, added entries are not generally made for 1) series with titles that include the name of a trade publisher . . . or that do not have a subject limitation and which may have only format in common. . . . "

The title of the series is given (see Cards 38-39) on the fourth line from the top at the first indention; if it runs over, the succeeding lines begin at the second indention. Following a comma, the words ed. by and the name of the editor of the series as found in the book are given. There is a period at the end. If there is no editor, or it seems unnecessary to give the editor's name, the phrase is omitted. The classification number is given on the next line, and below that, on the same line with the book number, are given: the author's name inverted, beginning at the second indention, with his dates omitted to conserve space; after four typewriter spaces, the title of the work, omitting explanatory and alternative titles; then after four typewriter spaces, the date. The second line of the entry for each individual work begins at the second indention. Other volumes in the series are added to the card in the same form. A line skipped, as shown on Card 38, makes it easier to read the entry for any one volume. For a numbered series in which the volumes are preferably read in a certain order (see Card 39), the volume numbers are given at the first indention, and the surname of the author of the individual book at the third indention.

38. Added entry under series — short form


```
          Rivers of America.
975. 1
C21            Canby, Henry Seidel.    The Brandy-
               wine.    [c1941]
978. 9
C77            Corle, Edwin.    The Gila.
               [c1951]
975. 62
R82            Ross, Malcolm.    The Cape Fear.
               [c1965]
```

39. Added entry under series, giving volume number and
    editor of series — short form


```
          The Chronicles of America series, ed.
               by Allen Johnson and Allan Nevins.
970
H94      v. 1  Huntington, Ellsworth.    The red
               man's continent.    [c1919]
973. 16
R53      v. 2  Richman, Irving Berdine.    The
               Spanish conquerors.    [c1919]
```

Another way to make a series entry is to write the name
of the series above the heading of the unit card. Thus a series entry is made for each book in the set, and these cards
file together in the catalog alphabetically by author.

Special entry under series is necessary for important
subject series, i. e. , for series in which all the books deal
with the same subject, e. g. , "Rural Science Series, " "The
Chronicles of America Series. " School libraries especially
will find these entries useful. Even the smallest public library

which owns "The Chronicles of America Series" would probably find a series entry useful.

40. Added entry under series —unit card

```
973. 917     The Chronicles of America series,
B86             v. 52.
             Brogan, Denis William, 1900-
                The era of Franklin D. Roosevelt; a
             chronicle of the New Deal and global
             war.    New Haven, Yale University
             Press [1950]
                382 p.  illus.    (The Chronicles of
             America series, v. 52)

             "Bibliographical note": p. 365-372.
```

Another kind of series for which an added entry under
the series title is useful is an author's series, e. g., "The
Leatherstocking Tales, " by James Fenimore Cooper (see
Card 42). Added entries under series titles are also useful
for standard works in an attractive format, for example,
"Scribner Illustrated Classics. "

41. Added entry under series —biography

```
             Golden hind series.
92
F92             Frobisher, by William McFee.
             [1934]

92
H39             Hawkins, by Philip Gosse.    [c1930]

92
R16             Raleigh, by Milton Waldman.
             [c1928]
```

42. Added entry under series—author the same

> The Leatherstocking tales, by James
>   Fenimore Cooper.
>
> The deerslayer.
>
> Last of the Mohicans.
>
> The pathfinder.
>
> Pioneers.

---

43. Reference from the name of the editor of the series

>   Nevins, Allan, 1890-   ed.
>   See
>   The Chronicles of America series.

Card 43 shows the form to be used for a reference card from the editor of a series to the entry under the title of the series.

Some book indexes, e. g., the Cumulative Book Index, include entries under series and the libraries which have these indexes might use them for series rather than making added entries. This would mean checking the Index to see if it includes an entry for the series before deciding not to make one.

Extension cards for added entries. Extension cards for added entries follow the same rule for the added heading, if it is a person's name, as for main entries; otherwise, the entire added heading and the heading on the unit card are given as usual. Extension cards are omitted for added title entries and for analytical entries, unless the part given in the added heading is mentioned on an extension card, in which case the extension card is made. The phrase "Continued on next card" is omitted in these cases.

Name reference cards. On page 70 it is stated that the librarian should choose one form of an author's name and always enter his works under that form, and that a reference should be made from any other forms with which the public may be familiar. This applies to all name entries in the catalog: author, subject, editor, compiler, etc. These reference cards (number 44-46) are very brief. They should be made for all names which might be searched for in the catalog under any other form than the one chosen for entry. The form of name not used for entry is given on the fourth line from the top, at the second indention, the word See, at the third indention on the succeeding line. The form of name that has been adopted for entry is given on the next line at the first indention. If the name referred from runs over, the next line begins at the third indention; and if the name referred to runs over, the next line begins at the second indention.

44. Name reference card — pseudonym

```
┌─────────────────────────────────────────────────────────┐
│                                                         │
│                                                         │
│            Gorham, Michael, pseud.                      │
│            See                                          │
│      Folsom, Mary Elting, 1914-                         │
│                                                         │
│                                                         │
│                                                         │
│                                                         │
│                                                         │
│                                                         │
│                                                         │
└─────────────────────────────────────────────────────────┘
```

45. Name reference card—heading for anonymous classic

```
                    Roland
                    See
            Chanson de Roland




```

46. Name reference card—name of an organization

```
                    Congress
                    See
            U.S.    Congress




```

Subject reference cards. Cards 3 and 4 in Chapter II are illustrations of see and see also reference cards. Note that both the term not used and the term used as a subject heading are given in full capitals, as are the subject headings on Card 30. If red ink is used for the headings on the subject cards, it should also be used for the subject references. The indentions and spacing are the same as for name references.

Tracing of secondary entries (A.-A. 1967. 151) ". . . Each catalog entry includes a record, or 'tracing,' of all of the

secondary entries that are to be made for the work. . . ."
It is necessary in order that all the cards may be found and
taken out of the catalog if it is decided to make a correction
on or addition to them, or if the book is withdrawn from the
library. The headings for the other cards decided upon as
necessary for the book are traced on the main entry card as
soon as it is made. These added entries are typed by a typist
who has been taught how to make them.

Rules for tracing. The record of the added entries, in a
single paragraph, is typed on the front of the main entry card,
just above the hole. The first line begins at the second indention. On printed cards the tracing is put on each card, as all
cards are made from the same copy, but in typed cards it
should be omitted on the added entry cards. If necessary,
part of the tracing can be put on the back of the card, in
which case type the word "Over" on the front of the card,
just below the hole.

"A. . . . The subject headings are listed first, numbered consecutively with Arabic numerals, followed by the other
secondary entries, numbered with Roman numerals except for
the series entry which is unnumbered and enclosed in parentheses. . . . added entries for persons or corporate bodies
. . . are listed in the order in which they appear in the catalog entry, . . . Added entries for title entry, the partial title
if such entry is to be made, [titles of analytical entries] and
for the series follow in this order. Each is traced to show
the form in which it is to be found in the catalog. Unless the
title is to be found as it appears in the catalog entry, the
word 'Title' in the tracing is followed by the selected form of
the title. "

"C. If the series is entered as it appears in the series note, only the word 'series' is given in the tracing. Any
variation between the series note and the series entry is
shown. "

Note: (S. P. E. tract no. 36)
Tracing: (Series: Society for Pure English. Tract no. 36)

If author and title analytical entries are made for all
the plays, essays, or stories listed in contents on the main
entry card, instead of tracing each one, a statement to that
effect may appear below the other tracing, e. g., "Author and
title analytical entries made for each play, " or "See contents
for tracing. "

The reference card for the author or the editor of a series is traced on the back of the series card by giving his name in full. For example, the tracing for a reference card for "Cooper, James Fenimore, 1789-1851" (see Card 43 for form of this card) is written on the back of the card.

Name and subject reference cards do not need to be traced on any catalog card, as they are applicable to all books by or about an individual or on a subject and do not pertain to one particular book. The subject reference cards are traced by checking the printed list of subject headings, or on the subject authority card in the card subject authority list described in Chapter II. Name reference cards are traced on the name authority card, if such cards are made for all names with cross references; if not, they may be traced on the author card for the first book cataloged with which that person is associated, just as they would be on the name authority card. Later if that book is withdrawn from the library and consequently its cards from the catalog, that tracing is transferred to another author card.

Examples of tracing.

Gunther's Inside Asia.
1. Asia - Biography. 2. Asia - Politics. 3. Chiang, Kai-shek, 1886-   4. China. 5. Gandhi, Mohandas Karamchand, 1869-1948. 6. Statesmen.
I. Title.

Numbers 1, 2, 4 and 6, in the above example of tracing, are subject entries for the entire book; numbers 3 and 5 are subject analytical entries. Note that the word "Title" is used to trace the title, which may readily be determined by looking at the card.

Burt's Powder River.
1. Cattle. 2. Dakota Indians. 3. Powder River.
4. Wyoming - History. (Series).

No title card would be made for Burt's Powder River, as it would be the same as the subject entry.

Hart and Kaufman's You Can't Take It with You.
I. Kaufman, George S., 1889-   II. Title.

Albee's Malcolm.
I. Purdy, James Malcolm. II. Title.

An added entry is made under James Malcolm Purdy as he

is the author of the novel on which the play is based, but only one title entry is necessary as it is the same for both the novel and the play.

Cohen's <u>Milestones of the Drama.</u>

1. Drama - Collections. I. Sheridan, Richard Brinsley Butler, 1751-1816. School. II. Title. III. Title: The school for scandal.

The added entry for Sheridan is an author analytical entry; number III is the record of a title analytical entry. Author analytical entries are traced by the heading for the author, followed, if not apparent from the card, by the first word, not an article, of the title of the analytical entry.

The shelf list. The shelf list is "A record of the books in a library arranged in the order in which they stand on the shelves. "[2]

Uses of a shelf list. The shelf list is used—

To take the inventory to see if any books are missing.

To show how many copies of a given book the library owns.

To show what kind of books are in a given class as an aid in classifying.

To show the librarian who is making out book orders how many books the library already has in any given class.

To serve in a limited way as a classed catalog. [3]

To give source, date, and cost if no accession record is kept.

To serve as a basis for a bibliography or reading list on a specific subject.

To serve as a record for insurance.

Rules for shelf listing. The shelf-list card is a unit card; i. e., it is a duplicate of the main card, except that the notes, contents, and tracing may be omitted. This saves space for the <u>shelf list information.</u> If an accession book is used, the accession number, described in Chapter XII, is added to this card. If an accession book is not used the price of the book is added to the shelf-list card. The price is needed in public libraries in order to know what to charge a borrower who loses a book. It may be the actual cost or the list price and is also of value in estimating the collection for insurance purposes. Many libraries also give the source and date of acquisition on the shelf-list entry, but Miss Esther Piercy states that these items serve no apparent purpose; if the library is reordering it places the order with its current dealer. [4] Although the date may be wanted if it is not included as part of the accession number (e. g., 1966-1) and if the library uses accession numbers.

If no accession book is kept, but an accession number is used, this number is added to the shelf-list card, as shown on Cards 47-48, followed by the name of the source, the date received, and cost. Some libraries consider the accession book unnecessary duplication of other records, but like the convenience of having one number which stands for the book.

If an accession number is used, it begins on the second space from the left edge of the card on the second line below the last line of the description-imprint, collation, or series note, as the case may be. If there are two or more copies or volumes of a work, the accession numbers are listed on the shelf-list cards in numerical order. The volume numbers or the copy numbers are written at the first indention opposite their respective accession numbers. Thus all copies and volumes of one work go on the same shelf-list card, and there are as many shelf-list cards as there are titles in the library, i. e., different works in the library. Copy numbers may be omitted if the librarian wishes, as long as accession numbers are used.

If accession numbers are not used, the source, date, and cost of the book are given instead. Abbreviations which will be clear to the librarian, e. g., B. & T. for Baker and Taylor, may be given for the source; if the book is a gift, the name of the donor is given, e. g., Mrs. J. H. Jones. The number of the month, day, and last two figures of the year are given, separated by hyphens, e. g., 2-16-52. The date follows the source, with one space between; then the cost, or, if it is a gift, the word gift.

Note that one ditto mark is sufficient for both source and date, but that the cost, or word gift, is repeated for each volume or copy.

Shelf-list cards for nonfiction are arranged exactly as the books are arranged on the shelves, first numerically by classification number and second alphabetically by author, except individual biography, which is arranged alphabetically by the subject of the biography. Since the figures in all book

47. Shelf-list entry showing accession numbers for a two-
volume work of which the library has two copies

```
821
D33    De la Mare, Walter John, 1873-
              Collected poems, 1901-1918.
          Holt [c1920)
              2 v.

3016    v. 1
3017    v. 2
3511    v. 1
3512    v. 2
```

48. Shelf-list entry showing source, date, and cost of a two-
volume work of which the library has two copies

```
821
D33    De la Mare, Walter John, 1873-
              Collected poems, 1901-1918.
          Holt [c1920]
              2 v.

1201    B. & T. 2-16-52 $2.00 v. 1
1202       "              $2.00 v. 2
1622    Jones, Mrs. J. H. 6-7-53 gift v. 1
1623       "                     gift v. 2
```

numbers are regarded as decimals, B219 would precede B31,
e. g.: 973   973   973 for Bancroft's History of the United
         B21 B219 B31
States of America and Bassett's A Short History of the United
States, respectively. If book numbers are not used, the name
of the subject of a biography may be added on the top line of
the card just as it is on the subject card, as an aid in filing
the cards by the subject of the biography.

In a public library the adult and the juvenile shelf-list cards are filed separately. The juvenile shelf-list cards as well as the juvenile catalog cards are marked with a location symbol in connection with the classification number, e. g.,
+   J   Also the shelf-list cards for the reference col-
973 or 973.
lection are marked with a location symbol   R   *
                                              (e. g., 394 or 394)
to distinguish them and are filed separately. The books, of course, have these location symbols added to the classification number.

Some libraries have one shelf-list card for all editions of works of fiction and so-called "Easy Books" for children, in which case the various editions are shown on the shelf-list card after each line of entry—accession number or source, date, and cost, e. g., the name of the publisher and information about the illustrations. Miss Piercy emphasizes this point.

When to shelf list. If the library is not yet cataloged, the fiction shelf list may serve also as an author list and the nonfiction shelf list may serve as a subject catalog (since it brings together all of the botanies, all of the United States histories, etc.) until such time as the library can be cataloged. Before beginning the cataloging of an old library, be sure that there is a correct shelf list to use as a basis for the work. In a new library, if it is not possible to catalog the new books as rapidly as they are being bought, it is well to accession (if an accession record is to be made), classify, and shelf list them at once. Later, using the shelf list as a check, catalog the different classes. In a well-organized and well-established library it is best to make the shelf list and catalog cards for each book when it is added to the library.

If printed catalog cards are used whenever they can be secured, they are used for the shelf list also. The H. W. Wilson Company prints a special shelf-list card.

References

1. American Library Association, Division of Cataloging and Classification, A. L. A. Cataloging Rules for Author and Title Entries (2d ed., ed. by Clara Beetle; Chicago, American Library Association, 1949), p. 229.

2. A. L. A. Glossary of Library Terms (Chicago, American Library Association, 1943), p. 126.

3. A classed catalog has its entries arranged by classification numbers rather than alphabetically as in a dictionary catalog, and there is an alphabetical subject index. This classed arrangement brings together all the entries on a given subject.

4. E. J. Piercy Commonsense Cataloging (New York, The H. W. Wilson Company, 1965), p. 78.

Chapter VIII

Cataloging Sets, Serials, and Independent Publications
Bound Together

Sets. The cataloging of sets differs as do the sets themselves. If there is a common title for the entire set, if one volume gives the contents for two or more volumes and the last volume contains the index to the set, then, needless to say, the set must be given one classification number and be cataloged as one work. If the common title is distinctive the set will be known by that title, and this fact is another argument for keeping the volumes together. If the volumes are bound alike and have a common title, but each volume is complete in itself, has a distinctive title, an index, etc., there is no reason for keeping them together. Besides, the average reader will not select a volume from a set as readily as he will pick up an individual book. For example, a set of the Waverley Novels, the different volumes all bound alike--on the back of each volume: "The Waverley Novels, Vol. XXI" (or XII, etc.)--does not attract readers as does a binding reading "Rob Roy," even though "Vol. XI," or even "Waverley Novels, Vol. XI," appears below "Rob Roy." If this volume XI is shelved with other editions of Rob Roy, it is likely to be chosen for reading more often than if it is one of twenty-five books in the same binding shelved together.

To consider examples of different kinds of sets:

The Works of
John Milton
Volume I
Part I
New York
Columbia University Press
1931

All of the volumes of this set of Milton's works have identical title pages, except for the volume number and date. Volume I has two parts, bound separately but with the table of contents for both in Part I. The two parts are paged consecutively. The same is true of Volumes II and III. But Volumes IV to XVIII are each bound separately. Each one has the copyright statement on the back of the title page, running from 1931 to 1938 in the different volumes.

This set of Milton has a two-volume index with the same binding and style of title page as the set, but it is not included in the volume numbering of the set. The title page is given below:

An Index
To the
Columbia Edition of the
Works of John Milton

By Frank Allen Patterson
Assisted By
French Rowe Fogle

Volume I. A-K

New York
Columbia University Press
1940

The title page of the second volume of the index is the same as that for Volume I, except that it has: "Volume II. L-Z." These index volumes will be cataloged in the same way as the index for Channing's History of the United States, described on pages 142-143. Obviously this set of Milton's works will have to be cataloged as a set because of the way in which the works are divided among the different volumes and because of the index. If a set is incomplete, the dates, the number of volumes, and the number of parts would be written in pencil, so that they may be easily changed when another volume is added.

Note that as there are twenty-one physical volumes in this set of Milton's works (Card 49) but only eighteen from the point of view of the division of the works, it is stated as "18 v. in 21."

Works with dependent titles (A.-A. 1967. 19)

"A. Enter a work that has a title that is indistinctive and dependent on the title of another work under the same author and/or title as the work to which it is related if it falls in . . . the [category] given below . . ."

1) Auxiliary works the use of which is dependent on one particular edition of the main work (e.g., certain indexes, manuals, etc.).

49. Main entry for a set *means only 18 vols. are from point of view of division of the works*

828
M66   Milton, John, 1608-1674.
                Works.   New York, Columbia Uni-
           versity Press [c1931-38]
                18 v. in 21.   illus.

                ---- An index to the Columbia edition
           of the Works of John Milton, by Frank
           Allen Patterson, assisted by French
           Rowe Fogle.   New York, Columbia Uni-
           versity Press [c1940]
                2 v.

A type of title page which is found rather frequently in
such works of fiction as the Waverley Novels, is the following:

The
Waverley Novels
By
Sir Walter Scott, Bart.

Vol. XXXV
Redgauntlet. — I.

Edinburgh
Adam and Charles Black
1879

Other volumes of this work have the same information on
their title pages; the individual volume title and the volume
numbers are different. On this particular title page the title
of the series is more prominent than that of the work. Yet
Redgauntlet is one of Scott's well-known novels and will be
asked for by title. If fiction is cataloged in the library as
nonfiction is, "The Waverley Novels" would be given as a
series note. But if fiction is cataloged very simply with only
author, title, and date, as recommended in Chapter VI, the
card for the above book would not show that it is one of the
Waverley Novels. Regardless of how little detail is given on
the catalog cards an added entry under the name of the series, "The Waverley Novels," will be found useful.

The Standard Catalog for High School Libraries, eighth edition, in its notes for Cooper's "Leatherstocking tales" states that The Deerslayer is the first of the tales; The Last of the Mohicans, the second; The Pathfinder, the third; and The Pioneers, the fourth. The notes also state that The Pathfinder is the sequel to The Last of the Mohicans; and that it is followed by The Pioneers but does not list the fifth, The Prairie. The editor's note of Everyman's Library edition of The Last of the Mohicans states ". . . one of the five 'Leatherstocking tales.' . . ."

As has been pointed out, the average reader is not attracted by books which belong to sets, consisting of many volumes bound alike. Yet the reader is apt to be much interested in reading all the volumes in a series in which the same characters appear. The Leatherstocking Tales is a series of this type and should have a series entry. Having read and enjoyed the first work the reader is likely to continue until he has read them all.

Sequels. Closely akin to the series, "The Leatherstocking Tales," are sequels such as Nordhoff and Hall's Men Against the Sea, the second volume of a trilogy, the first volume of which is Mutiny on the Bounty. Such books are cataloged as are any other works with notes stating the sequence (Card 50). Such notes are very desirable, since readers are usually anxious to read sequels. Men Against the Sea would have as a note: "A sequel to Mutiny on the Bounty. Followed by Pitcairn's Island." Pitcairn's Island would have as a note: "A sequel to Mutiny on the Bounty, Men against the Sea."

50. Main entry for book with a sequel

```
          Nordhoff, Charles Bernard, 1887-1947.
            Mutiny on the Bounty, by Charles
          Nordhoff and James Norman Hall.     Lit-
          tle [c1932]
            396 p.

            The first volume of a trilogy.
          Followed by Men against the sea, Pit-
          cairn's Island.
```

Related works [with dependent titles and different authors] (A.-A. 1967. 19)

"B. . . . Enter [such a] work under its own author and/ or title according to the general rules. Make an added entry under the author and title or under the title of the work to which it is related, as appropriate. . . ." "No added entry is necessary for the work to which it is related in the case of a sequel by the same author, or in the case of the Bible."- Footnote 19, page 41.

Title page:

John Jasper's gatehouse, by Edwin Harris. A sequel to the unfinished novel, 'The mystery of Edwin Drood, ' by Charles Dickens

Enter under Harris with an added entry (author-title) under Dickens

"The title of a sequel to the work being cataloged or of an earlier work which the work being cataloged continues" is given as a note. - (A.-A. 1967. 144E 2g)

Serials (A.-A. 1967. Glossary)

"A publication issued in successive parts bearing numerical or chronological designations and intended to be continued indefinitely. Serials include periodicals, newspapers, annuals (reports, yearbooks, etc.), the journals, memoirs, proceedings, transactions, etc., of societies, and numbered monographic series. "

The World Almanac is such a serial. The title page of the 1967 edition reads:

THE WORLD
ALMANAC
1967

AND BOOK OF FACTS

FOUNDED 99 YEARS AGO

EDITED BY

Luman H. Long

Published Annually by

NEWSPAPER ENTERPRISE ASSOCIATION, INC.

The World Almanac Division

230 Park Ave., New York, N. Y. 10017

© Newspaper Enterprise Association, Inc., 1966

Printed in the U. S. A.

The title pages for the 1966 edition and on back to 1961 are very similar, having the same first four lines as the above, with the exception of the year; and having for instance, "Seventy-sixth year of issue, " "Seventy-seventh, " etc.; Edited by Harry Hansen"; the imprints: "New York World-Telegram and The Sun, A Scripps-Howard Newspaper"; "N. Y. 15. "; and the respective copyright dates.

The reader consults the catalog to see if The World Almanac is in the library, and if it is, what volumes the library has. All numbers of the Almanac are cataloged on one set of cards and only items of importance common to all numbers are given. A library which had been cataloged and had the issues from 1961 on, all of which have the same imprint, would add the 1967 issue to the cards and add a note regarding the change in publisher. A library which was being cataloged for the first time would catalog The World Almanac from the title page of its most recent issue, probably ignoring past changes in imprint even though it had some of the older volumes.

51. Main entry for an almanac

```
R
310
W92   The World almanac.      New York, World-
          Telegram.

          Annual
          Library has

      1950-58

      1964-67
```

52. Main entry for an almanac—extension card

```
R
310                    2
W92   The World

        1967-          issue published by
Newspaper Enterprise Assoc. Inc.
The World Almanac Division.
```

To take another example of a serial:

WHO'S WHO

IN AMERICA

A BIOGRAPHICAL DICTIONARY OF

NOTABLE LIVING MEN AND WOMEN

A COMPONENT VOLUME OF

WHO'S WHO IN AMERICAN HISTORY

REVISED AND RE-ISSUED BIENNIALLY

(Compilation begun 1898 - Published continuously since 1899)

Volume 34

(1966 - 1967)

MARQUIS - WHO'S WHO
INCORPORATED
(The A. N. Marquis Company - Founded 1897)

Marquis Publications Building

210 EAST OHIO STREET

CHICAGO, ILLINOIS, 60611

USA

The back of this title page lists the copyright dates of all issues of this work, ending "Copyright, 1966."

The title page of volume 33 differs only in the volume number and the dates and in the addition of the phrase: "A nonprofit foundation," just below "Marquis - Who's Who," following the word, "Incorporated."

53. Main entry for a biennial publication

```
R
920
W62   Who's who in America.      Chicago, A. N.
          Marquis Co.

          Biennial
          Library has

      v. 33-34    1964/65-1966/67
```

The volume numbers are especially helpful in cases where each volume covers more than one calendar year. Note that the location symbol R, meaning the books are shelved in the reference collection, is placed on the line above the classification number on Cards 51-54.

Besides serials which are entered under their titles, there are those which are published yearly, biennially, etc., by a government department or an association, for example:

STATISTICAL
Abstract of the
United States
1966
87th Annual Edition
Prepared under the direction of
EDWIN D. GOLDFIELD
Chief, Statistical Reports Division
U. S. DEPARTMENT OF COMMERCE
John T. Connor, Secretary
BUREAU OF THE CENSUS
A. Ross Eckler, Director

At the foot of the title page or on its verso is the statement:

For sale by the Superintendent of Documents, U. S. Government Printing Office, Washington, D. C., 20402; Price and binding. The years, number of the edition, name of the secretary of the department, and price are practically the only variations from title page to title page. Such a publication would have the same sort of author heading as any other government document. Aside from the fact that it has an author, it is cataloged as is The World Almanac or Who's Who in America.

54. Main entry for a serial with an author

```
R
317. 3
U58    U. S.  Bureau of the Census.
              Statistical abstract of the United
       States.      U. S.    Govt.  Print.  Off.


              Annual.
              Library has

       1959

       1964-66
```

Periodicals. Sets of bound periodicals may be cataloged just as almanacs and other serials are cataloged. The title pages have most features in common with the serials discussed on the preceding pages.

The librarian of a small public, school, or even special library with sets of bound periodicals may catalog them in this way, or may not catalog them at all. As they are conspicuous by their make-up, they are easily located on the shelves in a one-room library; and they are used through the general or special periodical indexes rather than through the catalog.

Note that the library has statement for Current History and Forum (Card 55) gives the months as well as the years covered by the volumes. This form is used when the volumes do not coincide with the calendar years. Since Current History and Forum ceased publication with volume 53, number 1, June,

1941, this volume number and final date are typed, rather than written in pencil as the last dates on cards 53 and 54, thus closing the entry. When Current History and Forum united with Events in September, 1941, to form Current History, a new volume numbering began. The library having this periodical would add the latest volume, "v. 47, June-Dec. 1964" in pencil to facilitate changing the statement when the next volume is received. The notes on Cards 56 and 58 explain the formation of the periodicals. Because the periodical Current History (Card 57) has a different name and a new volume numbering begins, it is cataloged as a separate periodical.

General encyclopedias are examples of sets that may or may not be cataloged. Unless the library has a number of encyclopedias the reader does not go to the catalog to locate them, but goes directly to the shelves. Like bound periodicals they may be easily located in a small library. Shelf-list cards, however, should be made for all bound periodicals, encyclopedias, and other works, whether cataloged or not, in order that the library may have a record of such works and of what volumes of each it has.

55. Main entry for a periodical

```
909. 82
C97     Current history and Forum.       New York,
            C-H Pub. Corp.

         Monthly.  illus.
         Library has

     v.  51-53, no. 1  Sept. 1939-June 1941


                                (Continued on next
                                              card)
```

56. Main entry for a periodical--extension card

```
909. 82                        2
C97    Current.
            Current history combined with The
       Forum and The Century magazine, May 23,
       1940, under the title:  Current history
       and Forum; Current history and Forum
       was superseded by Current history,
       September, 1941.
```

57. Main entry for a periodical

```
909. 82
C976   Current history.       Philadelphia,
            Events Pub. Co.

            Monthly.
            Library has
       v. 1-         Sept.  1941-

       v. 20-        Jan.  1951-

       v. 46-47      Jan.  1964-Dec.  1964
```

Rules for Cataloging Serials and Periodicals

"The general principles for cataloging serials are the
same as those for cataloging monographic publications. . . .
It is essential to record such information as. . . changes of
name of issuing bodies, connection with preceding or succeeding publications, and statement of indexes . . . to mention
only the more important. . . . If the serial is still being published or the library has only a part of the set, an 'open' en-

58. Main entry for a periodical--extension card

---

909. 82   2
C976   Current.

      Formed by the union of Current
history and Forum with Events.

---

try is prepared according to the rules below; the aim is to
prepare an entry that will stand the longest time and will permit the making of necessary changes with the minimum of
modification. . . . "

"Certain types of publications that are not true serials
but that are issued frequently in new editions may be cataloged according to the rules of description for serials. These
include certain directories, guidebooks, handbooks, etc., even
though they may be of personal authorship. "-A. -A.   1967. Ch.
7. Introductory notes.

Variations from the cataloging of monographic publications (A. -A.   1967.   160)

"A. A serial that changes its title or that is entered
under a corporate body that changes its name during the course
of publication is normally cataloged with a separate entry for
each new title or new name of the corporate body. [1] A note
relates the new title to the serial it continues, " e. g., "Preceded by; Continued as. "

"B. A serial publication in several volumes with varying
bibliographical details is described from the latest volume,
with the variations from the volume noted, whereas a monographic work in several volumes is cataloged from the first
volume, with variations noted.

"C. The subtitle is frequently omitted. . . . "

"F. The catalog entry for a serial publication should show which parts of it are in the library's collection. . . .

"G. An important feature for the characterization of a serial, and occasionally for its identification, is the frequency of its publication.

"H. If the statement of holdings does not show the duration of publication, supplementary notes are essential to show it. This includes the facts of suspension and resumption of publication. "

Classification number. Classification number is given as usual. If book numbers are used in the library they are assigned for serials as for any other book. If the serial is entered under its title, the book number is derived from the first word of the title not an article. The book number for The World Almanac would be W92, for Who's Who in America, W62.

Author. Reports of institutions, governments, bureaus, associations, and the like, are entered under the institution, bureau, or association as author (see Chapter V), with the title in its usual place. If there is a change in the author, the work may be recataloged under the new author with a reference from the former author and title; or if many volumes have been cataloged previously, the work may be left under the former author with a reference from the new author and title.

Body of the entry: organization and source of data
(A. -A. 1967. 161)

"A. The body of the entry consists of the following elements, in the order given here: title, subtitle (if required), volume designation and dates of the . . . [volumes in the library], and imprint. . . . If the publication has no title page, the title is taken from the cover, caption, masthead, editorial pages, or other place. . . . The source of the data is specified if it is not the title page, cover, caption or masthead. . . .

"B. . . . in the case of a serial which has ceased publication, if an earlier title has continued for a much longer period of time than the later title [the earlier title is chosen rather than the later one.]''

Recording of the title (A. -A. 1967. 162)

"A. A short title is generally used in cataloging serial publications if this makes it possible to disregard minor variations in the wording on various issues. . . . Subtitles are omitted unless necessary for identification or for clarification of the scope of the publication. . . .

"B. When the title of a serial publication entered under a corporate body includes the name of the body . . . the name . . . is omitted unless . . . [it] is given in a significantly different form from that in the heading and cannot be omitted without distorting the title (e. g., Report of the Librarian of Congress entered under U. S. Library of Congress).

"C. If a number appearing as part of the title is considered to be the volume designation it is omitted from the title . . . e. g., Report of the first annual meeting becomes Report of the annual meeting.

"D. If any other word or phrase preceding the title might be construed and cited as part of the title, an author-title and/or title reference with this form of the title is made to the catalog entry for the serial. " On all cards the title begins on the fourth line at the first indention, succeeding lines at the second indention.

Imprint (A. -A. 1967. 164)

"A. . . . 1. The imprint in the catalog entry for a serial publication is limited to the place of publication and the name of the publisher. . . .

"B. Place of publication. Changes in the place of publication that do not warrant specific description are indicated by the abbreviation 'etc. ' following the place of publication. . . .

"C. Publisher. 1. If the name of the publisher is essentially the same as the title of the publication, as is often the case with periodicals, it is omitted. . . .

"2. Minor changes in the name of the publisher as it appears on the various volumes, and changes of publisher not warranting specific description, are indicated in the imprint by the use of 'etc.' after the name of the publisher. . . ."

Collation (A.-A. 1967. 165)

"A. . . . The collation statement describes the completed set for serials that have ceased publication. . . . Illustrative matter is described for the set as a whole. If the serial is still in process of publication, the collation describes the set as it is at the time it is cataloged."

"E. Illustrations. Only those types of illustrations that are, or probably are, important to the set as a whole are included in the description of a serial publication. . . ."

Holdings (A.-A. 1967. 163)

"A. 1. The statement of the volumes 'held' by the library is given immediately after the title. . . ."

v. 27-35   1952-60

If the library is receiving the volumes regularly the last volume number and the latest date are written in pencil that they may be easily changed when the next volume is received. If there is a gap or gaps in the set these are indicated, e.g.,

v. 27-29, 30-33, 36-   1952-54, 1956-58, 1961-

Many libraries give the statement of the numbers or volumes or years of a serial that a library owns beginning with the phrase library has on the second line below the imprint or, if frequency is given in a note, on the line below the frequency note beginning at the second indention. On the line below, beginning at the first indention, are given the volumes or the years, or both, of the issues in the library in straight columns. They are put on the same line with a dash between the numbers if the volumes are consecutive, giving the latest one in pencil so that it may be changed when the next number comes. A line is skipped to indicate each gap, not each volume lacking, and statements that need to be changed are written in pencil. Such statements as "Forty-third issue," "Third edition," and "Second annual report," may be written "v. 43, v. 3, v. 2." Sample cards 51, 53-55 and 57 illustrate the form of the holdings.

Yet another method is to purchase the printed record cards from Demco, Gaylord, or some other library supply house and tie the card or cards to the main entry card. These

record cards are ruled in columns or squares and have printed on them e. g. , "Year, " "Volume, " or are just blank
cards ruled. The library checks or writes in each square the
years or volume numbers as they are received.

Notes (A. -A. 1967. 167)

"A. 1. . . . Many of the supplementary notes necessary
to the cataloging of serial publications are presented in a conventional style. . . . At times unnecessary repetition can be
avoided, without sacrifice of clarity, by combining two or
more conventional or other notes.

"2. In describing bibliographical changes in a serial
publication, reference is generally made to the date of the
volume or issue showing the change rather than to its volume
designation. . . . Dates may be described by the month, day
and year, by the month or season and year, or by year
alone, . . .

"B. Frequency.

"1. If the frequency of publication can be described by
a single adjective or brief phrase, it is given immediately after the collation, unless it is obvious from the title of the
publication; e. g. , Library quarterly.

v. illus.   annual
v. illus.   monthly (except July and August)

"2. If there are numerous changes in frequency of publication, the information is represented by the general note,
'Frequency varies. ' "

Notes other than that of frequency are given on a separate extension card, since library has statements may take
up more space if there are many gaps in the set. Later, if
the first card should be filled up, a second and, if need be,
a third card could be inserted between the first card and the
card giving the notes.

"C. Report year. If the period covered by an annual
publication is other than that of the calendar year, the fact
is noted. "

Report year ends June 30.

"E. Suspension of publication. If a serial suspends publication with the intention of resuming at a later date, the entry is left open and a note is used to show date, or the volume designation, of the last issue published. If publication is
resumed, the note shows the inclusive dates of the period of
suspension. "

> Suspended with v. 11.
> Suspended with Dec. 1942.

"F. Numbering. Irregularities and peculiarities in the
numbering of a serial publication are described, unless they
are limited to the numbering of the parts of a given volume."

> Issues for Feb. -Mar. 1939 have no vol. number-
> ing but constitute v. 1, no. 1-2.

"G. Connection with preceding publications. The relationship between a serial and its immediate predecessor or
predecessors is indicated. A serial that appears under a different title or different name of corporate author but continues
the numbering of its predecessor is considered to 'continue'
that publication; if the numbering has not been continued, however, it 'supersedes' it. "

"Q. Connection with later publications. If a serial is
continued, superseded, or absorbed by, or merged with,
another publication, this fact is noted. "

Special numbers (A. -A. 1967. 169)

"Special numbers of serial publications present, as such,
no particular problem of description. They are cataloged as
separate works, with the relationship to the regular numbers
shown, cataloged with analytical entries, or simply noted informally. If they are to be shelved with the regular numbers
and are of minor importance, they may be disregarded, " e. g.:

> Bertram, Anthony, 1897-
>   Contemporary painting in Europe; introd. by
> Anthony Bertram.   New York, The Studio [1939]
>   114 p.   illus.

"Special autumn number of the Studio, 1939. "

Shelf listing serials. To make the shelf-list card for a
serial the same rules are followed as for other shelf-list cards

The library has statement is omitted. If accession numbers are used they are given in parallel columns opposite their respective volume numbers or years (see Cards 59 and 60).

59. Shelf-list entry for a serial

```
R
310
W92    The World Almanac.     New York,  World-
          Telegram.

1102   1950
3106   1956
3612   1958
4523   1959
5502   1960
6512   1964
7000   1966
```

60. Shelf-list entry for a serial (alternative method)

```
R
310      The World almanac.     New York,  World-
W92           Telegram.

Pub.   2-9-50    $1. 00    1950
  ,,   2-15-56   $1. 25    1956
  ,,   2-8-58    $1. 25    1958
  ,,   3-1-59    $1. 25    1959
  ,,   2-16-60   $1. 25    1960
  ,,   2-13-64   $1. 50    1964
  ,,   2-8-66    $1. 65    1966
```

The unit card may be used for the shelf list, adding an extension card or cards as needed.

Bound withs. Two or more works of the same author or works of different authors are sometimes bound or published together in one volume. If the book has a title page for each

work as well as table of contents, a preface, and separate
paging, each work may be called informally a bound with.
The book is cataloged as a separate book, but on the cards
for each work there is a note of the other work or works
with which it is bound. The true test of such a volume is
that it could be cut into two or more works, each of which
if bound separately would be a complete volume, not showing
in any way that it had ever been bound with another.

A similar sort of work may have one title page which
gives all or at least some of the different titles; or it may
have a common title for the volume and the individual titles
may be given only on half title pages preceding the different
sections of the book. The half title is a brief title on a page
preceding a title page, or a separate work where there are
several in one volume. It does not include the imprint. The
title pages for two such volumes follow:

How to Live

By
Arnold Bennett

A Special Edition for the Bookman Subscribers Only, Contain-
ing "How to Live on Twenty-Four Hours a Day,"
"The Human Machine," "Mental Efficiency,"
"Self and Self Management."

A BOOK OF
GREAT AUTOBIOGRAPHY

Christopher Morley
Joseph Conrad
Selma Lagerlöf
Helen Keller
William McFee
W. N. P. Barbellion
Walt Whitman
Etsu Inagaki Sugimoto

The first of these examples, the volume of Bennett's
works, includes four of his essays, published separately,
brought together in one volume under a common title. The
one title page lists all the essays and each of them has a
half title, a table of contents, and is paged separately. But
all of the copyright dates, in this case a different copyright
date for each work, are given on the back of the title page.
The second example, A Book of Great Autobiography, also

has only one title page on which is given the common title for the volume and the list of authors whose works are included in the volume. Each work is separately paged and preceded by a "Publisher's Note." Some works of these types have continuous paging throughout the volume.

While examining these title pages and half titles, the librarian must keep in mind such questions as these: What is there in these volumes that readers would want? Under what would they look in the catalog? A reader may be looking for The Human Machine, A Daughter of the Samurai, Helen Keller's The Story of My Life, something by Walt Whitman. Title analytics would be needed for each of the essays in the volume by Bennett; and both author and title analytics for each of the works in A Book of Great Autobiography. The main entry for the latter work would be under the title (see Card 61).

61. Main entry for several works with common title--not a bound with

```
920
B72    A Book of great autobiography: Christo-
          pher Morley, Joseph Conrad, Selma
          Lagerlöf, Helen Keller, William
          McFee, W. N. P. Barbellion, Walt
          Whitman, Etsu Inaguki Sugimoto.
          Garden City, N. Y., Doubleday, Doran
          [c1934]
          1 v.   (various pagings)
```

Similar, yet different, is this bound with:

WHEN WORLDS

COLLIDE

By

EDWIN BALMER

and

PHILIP WYLIE

J. B. LIPPINCOTT COMPANY
PHILADELPHIA   NEW YORK

On the back of this title page is given:

Copyright 1932, 1933, by
Edwin Balmer and Philip Wylie

The title page is followed by the Table of Contents, then the
text. Next in this volume is a half title page: After Worlds
Collide, then the title page:

AFTER WORLDS

COLLIDE

By

EDWIN BALMER

and

PHILIP WYLIE

Authors of "When Worlds Collide"

J. B. LIPPINCOTT COMPANY
PHILADELPHIA   NEW YORK

And on the back of this title page: Copyright, 1933, 1934, by
                                        EDWIN BALMER and
                                        PHILIP WYLIE

The paging for this book is: When Worlds Collide, viii, 344
p.; After Worlds Collide, xiii, 341 p.

These works would be cataloged as any other work except for the notes, each of which refers to the other title.
The classification number and the book number, if they are
used, would be the same for both since there is only one
physical volume on the shelf.

Notes of works bound together (A.-A.   1967.   146)

"A. If several works issued independently are subse-
quently bound together, the entry for each work in the volume
bears a note to show the presence of the other work or works.
For the first work in the volume, the note is simply a matter
of physical description and need not have prominence, . . .

When wks. are bound together

62. Main entry for the first work in a bound with

```
813
B19    Balmer, Edwin, 1883-
           When worlds collide, by Edwin
       Balmer and Philip Wylie.      Lippincott
       [c1933]
           344 p.

           Bound with: the authors' After
       worlds collide.
```

63. Main entry for a work other than the first in a bound with

```
813
B19    Balmer, Edwin, 1883-
           After worlds collide, by Edwin
       Balmer and Philip Wylie.      Lippincott
       [c1934]
           341 p.

           Bound with: the authors' When
       worlds collide.
           Sequel to When worlds collide.
```

For the second or any succeeding work in the volume, for which the note may be necessary to identify the work on the shelves or to explain a call number that appears to be incorrect, a prominent position is desirable.

"Bound with the author's (or authors')"

"B. If two or more distinct works, each with its own title page and paging, are issued together in one cover, the description is the same. . . .

"C. The citation of the other work or works in the volume, to be added to the above, takes the following form: the author's name in catalog entry form, with forenames (if more than one) represented by initials, brief title. . . . " If the author is the same then use "the author's (or authors'). " "If there are more than two titles bound together all are cited only in the entry for the first item in the work. "

The added cards are traced on each main entry card as usual. In addition the main card or cards for the other work or works in the volume are traced simply by giving the author headings in full, if the authors differ; where the authors are the same as in the case of Balmer and Wylie, by the first author's surname and the first word of the title bound with it, e. g., Balmer After. There is only one card for the shelf list as there is only one book on the shelf and one call number. The shelf-list card is made for the first work in the volume, in this case When Worlds Collide.

References

1. "The Library of Congress generally catalogs as a single serial the various publications that result from changes of title, or changes in the name of the corporate body under which a serial is entered, so long as the volume numbering is continuous. The entry is normally under the latest title or name of corporate author. "

Chapter IX
Audio-Visual Materials

Introduction. Audio-visual materials, i.e., motion pictures, filmstrips, records, slides, maps, and pictures, are found in most libraries today. Pictures are generally put in a vertical file, either by themselves or with pamphlets and clippings, and do not need to be classified or cataloged. As films are rented or borrowed rather than bought by the smaller libraries, they are not included in this chapter. Filmstrips, maps, musical and nonmusical records, and slides are found in the smaller as well as in the larger libraries and for the fullest use they need some kind of classification and cataloging.

Rufsvold's Audio-Visual School Library Service[1] is still a useful, general book on the selection, care, processing, and use of this type of material. The National Information Center for Educational Media's Index to 35 mm educational filmstrips,[2] is a guide to the source and content of filmstrips. This Index is in three parts: Subject Matter Section, Alphabetical Title Descriptive Section, and Producer-Distributor Production Credit Section. The Alphabetical Title Descriptive Section, which gives the most information about the filmstrips, includes in its entries: title, number of frames, whether in black and white or color, the producer, the distributor and the date of the filmstrip. The third section gives the name and address of the producer, elsewhere given in abbreviation. If the library, or a library in the vicinity, has this Index it would be helpful to look up the entries for the filmstrips to be cataloged and get the essential information, as the filmstrip itself may not give all of it. NICEM indexes

James I. Wyer stated an important principle in organizing materials in a library, "have all materials on the same subject in the fewest places."[3]

Classification. Books are classified so that those dealing with the same or related subjects may be found close together. They can be examined at the shelves. On the other hand, records must be put on a record player, filmstrips and slides on a projector, and maps spread out on a table. Furthermore, the librarian usually gets the audio-visual material for the

patron, as filmstrips are in a special cabinet and are easily
mixed up, and records are on special shelves. For these
reasons it does not seem worthwhile to arrange nonbook materials by a subject classification system.

A few librarians prefer to classify their record albums
and let the patron choose his records as he does his books.
As he knows that printed material on United States history is
together on the shelves under 973, he can also learn to go
to that number on the shelves where the album records are
kept and find together those on United States history.

But for the majority of libraries an accession or an
identification number is the most satisfactory way of arranging nonbook materials. The records, filmstrips, etc., can be
arranged in order as they are received by the library; no
space is wasted, and no shifting is necessary later to fit a
new acquisition in its proper place in a classified collection.

The identification number consists of a letter or letters
indicating the type of material, e.g., FS for filmstrip, and
a number given to the item when it is received by the library.
The identification or call number for the first record added
to the library would be R1; and for the first record album,
RA1; for the first filmstrip, FS1; and for the first map, M1.
This number is put on the record, album, filmstrip, map,
or set of slides, and it is also placed on the shelf list and
catalog cards in the same position as the classification number on the cards for a book.

Cataloging. If the material requires equipment, e.g., a
record player or a projector for its use, or if it is difficult
to handle, as a map, cataloging is important as a catalog
is more easily consulted than the materials themselves. In
cataloging the four types of materials discussed in this chapter, consider their similarity to books rather than their differences. Books are entered under author or title; so are
these materials. Book entries include publisher and date;
records have the trade name of the firm and the serial identification. "The rules for entry, heading, and description for
books and book-like materials . . . apply also in the cataloging of non-book materials . . . to the extent that they are
pertinent . . . " (A.-A. 1967. p. 258).

What is it the user needs to know about the filmstrip,
map, record, or slide that differs from what he needs to know
about a book? Is the filmstrip in black and white or in color,

how many frames[4] has it? On what scale was the map drawn; what are its measurements? How many records and how many sides of the record are used for a piece of music; what is the speed, i. e., the number of revolutions per minute? The person who wishes to use slides wants to know their size, whether or not a study guide is included, etc.

The items in the description of a book, filmstrip, map, record, or slide are given in groups in a predetermined order, with the same indentions and spacing. It is more convenient, especially in a small library, to have the catalog entries for all types of materials in one file. But, that the user of the catalog may know whether he is getting a book, record, or filmstrip, the cards show clearly the type of material described. The library may have a stamp, MAP, FILMSTRIP, etc., and use it above the call number, or an appropriate symbol, such as those suggested in the section on classification, may be used to identify the material. The Library of Congress printed catalog cards for records and filmstrips have the word Filmstrip or Phonorecord in italics immediately after the title and the library using these cards would do well to do the same, even though its call number has descriptive letters, such as FS and R. It is also desirable to show the approximate age level. This information may be given in the upper right-hand corner of each card, e. g., p for primary, a for adult. A list of abbreviations commonly used in cataloging audio-visual materials is given at the end of this chapter.

The next chapter tells how to order and use Library of Congress printed catalog cards, which are suggested for records, filmstrips, and maps whenever they are available. Unit cards should be typed following the specific directions given under each type of material in this chapter; and the general rules about items to include, spacing, indentions, and general style of the cards, given in the preceding chapters, should be used for the few maps, records, and filmstrips for which printed cards are not available. The rules given here are based on the Anglo-American Cataloging Rules.

Records, musical and nonmusical. The "Glossary" of the Anglo-American rules defines a "phonorecord" as "Any object on which sound has been recorded"; a phono-disc, -tape, [etc.] as "A recording of sound on the object named at the end of each of these terms." Chapter 13 of the Anglo-American rules gives details for cataloging music scores and Chapter 14, "Phonorecords," provides "the additions and exceptions that must be made to the rules" in the chapters on

entry and descriptive cataloging of separately published monographs and on music. This chapter also includes the technical
specifications necessary to enable a reader to know whether
or not the record can be reproduced on an instrument available to him.

Mary D. Pearson's Recordings in the Public Library[5]
gives material on how to arrange recordings, how to catalog
them; lists of sources of equipment and supplies, selected
bibliography of cataloging aids, glossary of technical terms,
a suggested modification of the Dewey Decimal Classification
for recordings if the library classifies them; and suggests
what information on the Library of Congress printed catalog
cards may be omitted.

Miss Pearson states that an alphabetical arrangement,
first by author, second by title, is satisfactory for a collection under 5,000 and not likely to exceed that number. Esther
J. Piercy in Commonsense Cataloging[6] says that the small
college or public library may well use the accession method
of arrangement, i.e., assign a number to each record as it
is acquired, but for school library collections she would use
a subject arrangement.

For the smaller libraries in which this manual would be
used the so-called accession method seems best regardless of
the type of the library. A number is assigned to each record
as it is added to the library; this number preceded by the letter R, if it is a single record, is the call number for that
record, e.g., R29 would be the call number for the twenty-
ninth record added to the collection. RA would indicate a record album, RA16, the sixteenth album added.

The items to be included in the catalog entry for a phonorecord are: name of the author, usually the composer for musical records, author or narrator for nonmusical records; conventional title; title; trade name of the publisher, serial number (i.e., album and record numbers) for identification, performers, medium, number of albums, sides, size, speed, title
of record on reverse side. Miss Piercy states that a contents
note may be given if there are more than two works. Record
sleeves and disc labels supply the information for records as
the title page does for books.

Headings for the main entry and the one appearing on all
the unit cards is similar to what would be used for visual materials. The rules and examples in Chapters III-V apply to rec-

ords as they do to printed materials; the form on the card would be the same. Nonmusical records are treated much as their corresponding literary counterparts. Separate works on opposite sides of a record are cataloged individually with appropriate notes on each as for books bound together (see Chapter VIII, pages 196-198 and Cards 62-63). (Children's records are usually best known by title, hence may be entered under title.) If the record is a famous classic, e. g., Grimm's Snow White, told by Thorne Thomsen, author entry would be used.

Title. The title of the work is taken from the label of the record, or the cover of the album, and is given as the title of a book is given.

Conventional titles are formulated for musical works on phonorecords, unless the work is entered under its title or the arranger. The conventional title is given on the line below the composer and is in brackets. It is given in order that all the editions and arrangements of a composition may be brought together in the catalog. It includes: the title of the first edition of the work, or is based on that title; the instrument or instruments on which it is played, the number of the composition if that is necessary to identify it; the opus number; and the key.

Examples of conventional titles for phonorecords are:

Conventional title: [Sonata, piano, no. 21, op. 23, C major]
Title on record label: Sonata No. 21 in C major, op. 23 ("Waldstein")
Conventional title: [La traviata. Selections]
Title on record label: Duets from La traviata
Conventional title: [Operas. Selections]
Title on record label: Great Baritone Arias

Note that the items in the conventional title are given in a definite order, regardless of how they are given in the title of a particular record.

Imprint (A. -A. 1967. 252C)

"1. If the publisher is known to be primarily a record publisher, the imprint consists of the trade name of the publisher and the serial identification (e. g., album and record numbers) followed by a period. . . ."

Decca DL 8146.

"2. If the publisher is not known to be primarily a record publisher, the imprint consists of the place, the name of the publisher. . . . The serial identification [follows]. "

>Louisville, Ky., Louisville Philharmonic Society . . .
>   LOU 545-8.

"3. Notation for serial numbers is given as it appears on the work being cataloged. For consecutive serial numbers only the first and last are transcribed, separated by a dash. When nonconsecutive, all of the numbers are transcribed, separated by commas. "

>USC 233-236.
>London LL 1585, 1682.

Miss Pearson does not consider it necessary to give the imprint.

>Collation (A.-A. 1967. 252D)

"1. Phonodisc. The number of volumes (albums) if more than one, and/or sides, or fractions of the latter are indicated. . . . This is followed by the diameter to the nearest inch . . . and speed (revolutions per minute). The term 'microgroove' or 'stereophonic' is added when applicable. "

>6 s. 12 in. 33 1/3 rpm.
>2 albums (12 s.) 10-12 in. 78 rpm.

"3. Phonotape. The extent (number of reels) is followed within parentheses by the diameter of the reel; speed (inches per second) is given if available. If the width of the tape is other than 1/4 in., it is given after the diameter of the reel; e.g., (14 in., 1-1/4 in. tape). The term 'stereophonic' is added when applicable. "

>1 reel (5 in.) 3-3/4 in. per sec. stereophonic.

"7. Visual materials accompanying phonorecords. Frequently manuals, pamphlets, analytical booklets, etc., are issued to be used in conjunction with aural materials. . . . If the visual matter is secondary in importance to the phonorecord, the description of the former is given in a note. . . ."

>Series statement (A.-A. 1967. 252E)

"Series statement. The form of the series statement follows that for visual materials. . . ."

Notes (A.-A. 1967. 252F)

"3. Participant, performer, and medium

"a. Names of participants, performers, and of perform-ing groups are always given, followed, after a comma, by the medium of performance. . . . Performer-medium units are separated by semicolons. "

> Budapest String Quartet.
> James Melton, tenor; Robert Hill, piano.

"b. In the case of collections with several performers, this note may be combined with the contents note. . . ."

"4. Text: languages, authors, etc. If the language of the performance is not apparent from the uniform and trans-cribed titles, it is given, if known. . . ."

> Lily Pons, soprano, with orchestra; sung in French.

"8. Abridgments. If the existence of omissions is known without special search, it is noted. "

> Without the recitatives.

"9e. Phonotape. A note is made to state the number of tracks it contains, and any other details which may determine the playback equipment. The cataloger will be dependent on information from the container. "

> Single track.

"g. Supplementary visual materials

> Program notes on slipcase.
> Program notes by William Mann and libretto, with
>   English translation by Edward J. Dent ([8] p.) laid
>   in container.

"10. Contents. The scope and form of the contents note established in rule 149 obtains also for phonorecords. The con-tents note and the performer note may be combined when it is nec-essary, as in the case of certain collections, to relate a per-former to a particular work. "

> Contents. Louise: Depuis le jour, by G. Charpen-
> tier; (Mary Garden, soprano, with orchestra)-Tosca:
> Vissi d'arte, by G. Puccini (Maria Jeritza, soprano,
> with piano).

"11. 'With' note, when a separate entry has been made
for each of two or more works issued together, a 'With'
statement is used as the final note, the works being listed
in the order given in the publication. The titles, in the case
of a musical performance, are given in their uniform style. "

> Debussy, Claude, 1862-1918.
>> [Prélude à l'après-midi d'un faune] Phonodisc.
>> Prelude: The afternoon of a faun. Music Trea-
> sures of the World MT-20.
>> 1/2 s. 12 in. 33-1/3 rpm. microgroove.
>
> Music Treasures Philharmonic Symphony: Max
> Schönherr, conductor.
>> With: Grieg, E. H. Peer Gynt (Suite) no. 1-2. -
> Strauss, Richard. Til Eulenspiegels lustige Streiche.

Serials (A. -A. 1967. 252G)

"Serials. Phonorecords that are issued serially are described according to the preceding rules. . . . "

> Sonorama. Phonodisc no. 1- Oct. 1959-   [Paris,
>> Sonopresse]
>>> no. 7 in. 33-1/3 rpm. microgroove. month-
>>> ly.

Nonprocessed phonorecords (A. -A. 1967. 253)[7]

". . . The entries are as brief as possible, giving all of
the essential data without citation of source and without the
use of brackets, except for uniform titles.

"A. Title and physical medium. The title may be given
as found in the recording, in accompanying documents, or in
other sources; if no title can be found, as succinct and descriptive a title as possible is formulated by the cataloger.
When a uniform title is required for music, it is the only title
used. The title is followed by a statement of physical medium.
. . . "

> Frost, Robert, 1874-1963.
>> Address to high school students, discussing good
> writing. Phonotape.
>
>> (Title formulated from accompanying typewritten
> statement.)

"B. Imprint. Data normally given in imprint position
for processed phonorecords is omitted. Date of recording is

given in a note. "

"C. Collation. The rules for collation of processed phonorecords are followed. "

"D. Notes.

1. Data needed to amplify the catalog entry are given in notes as for processed phonorecords. . . . Of particular importance are notes which name the participants, give the available details concerning the event, give duration when known, and supplement collation where necessary. "

Added entries (A. -A. 1967. 251)

"A. Added entries are made under performers (vocal and instrumental soloists, narrators, etc.) and under performing groups, but not under the individual members of performing groups.

"B. Added entries under series are made only for subject or other special series. "

The form is the same as for books, simply add the appropriate headings to the unit card. Subject headings are taken from Sears List of Subject Headings. For children's records Rue and LaPlante's list would be used for subject headings if it were used for children's books. The heading "Symphony" in Sears would be used for books or other printed material about symphonies or for recordings, as the differences in the call number would show whether a given entry were for a book or a record. Subject entries and subject analytical entries would be made on the same basis as for printed matter. Nonmusical records of famous personalities, e. g., General of the Army, Douglas MacArthur: the Life and Legend of 'The Old Soldier' would have an entry under MacArthur, either as main entry for it is chiefly his words, or as subject; it is his personality which has value.

"D. Other added entries are made according to the provisions of rule 33, p. 150. In the case of analytical added entries, the physical medium . . . is added at the end. " Miss Pearson states that series entries are rarely needed.

The same location, form and style of numbering are used for tracing added entries for records as are used for books.

64. L. C. printed catalog card for recording

Marian Anderson sings great spirituals.
[Phonodisc] RCA Victor   ERA 62.

   2 s.   7 in.   45 rpm.

   Title from slipcase.
   Marian Anderson, contralto; Franz Rupp,
     piano.
   "Extended play. "
   Program note on back of slipcase.

   Contents. --Nobody knows the trouble I see,
                (Continued on next
                       card)

---

65. L. C. printed catalog card for recording

Marian Anderson sings great spirituals.
   (Card 2)

   arr. by Lawrence Brown. --Hear de lam's a-
   cryin', arr. by Lawrence Brown. --Soon-a
   will be done, arr. by Edward Boatner. --
   Were you there? Arr. by H. T. Burleigh.

   1. Sons (Low voice) with piano. 2. Negro
   spirituals.   I. Anderson, Marian, 1902-
   II. Rupp, Franz, musician.

                               R 53-116

      Library of Congress   [8]

    The shelf-list cards for phonodiscs would be the same
as the unit card through the collation and series note, if any;
with the source, date, and cost of each copy of a record
added on the second line below the collation or series note
as on the shelf-list card for a book. These shelf-list cards
would be filed separately as the records are shelved apart
from the books.

    Filmstrips. As each filmstrip is added to the library
assign a number. This number preceded by the letters FS
forms the call number, e. g., FS6 would be the call number

for the sixth filmstrip added to the library. This number would be written on the container for the filmstrip and on the catalog and shelf-list cards.

If two or more distinct filmstrips are presented on one strip, a separate entry is made for each title, with an appropriate note, as is done when two or more books are bound together, a method described in Chapter VIII, pages 196-198. On the other hand two or more filmstrips presented on a single strip should be cataloged as a single work if they can be considered as forming a whole.

The information needed to describe a filmstrip for the catalog is found on the filmstrip itself, in the accompanying booklet, or in such aids as the Educational Media Index.

The main entry of a filmstrip is "under the title . . . followed, after any alternative title or subtitle, by the designation . . . (Filmstrip). " (A.-A. 1967. 220A). Write the title, given on the filmstrip or in the descriptive material, with hanging indention.

The items to be included in the catalog entry are: the title; name of the producer and date; physical description of the filmstrip; series to which it belongs; credits, i. e., persons or organizations not mentioned in the description to whom credit should be given; a summary of its contents; and the tracing of the added entries (see Card 66).

66. L. C. printed catalog card for filmstrip

> The Extension of set and number ideas (Filmstrip) Jam Handy Organization, 1966.
>
> 24 fr. color. 35 mm. (Using sets and numbers, no. 10)
>
> Produced in cooperation with Ginn and Co.
> Summary: A review and extension of all concepts presented in the primary mathematics series entitled Using sets and numbers.
>
> 1. Arithmetic-Juvenile films. I. Jam Handy Organization, inc. Series: Using sets and numbers (Filmstrip) no. 10)
>
> Jam Handy Organization   Fi A 66-2884
> for Library of Congress   [1 1/2]

Production. "The name of the individual, company, institution, or organization responsible for the [filmstrip's] coming into existence--either directly or as sponsor--[corresponds to the publisher of a book and] follows the title [in 'imprint place']. . . . "--(A. -A. 1967. 223 B. 1) "If a filmstrip was made by an individual, company, . . . [etc.] other than the one responsible for its coming into existence, the name of such individual, company, . . . [etc.] is given following the phrase 'Made by.' "--(A. -A. 1967. 223 B. 2) "The year in which a [filmstrip] was released is given following the name of the company which released the [filmstrip]. The releasing company may be the producing company, or it may be a releasing agent. . . . "--(A. -A. 1967. 223 D. 1)

Following the imprint information in the usual place for the collation give the physical description of the filmstrip which includes the "number of frames, . . . color, . . . or black and white, and width of the film in millimeters. "--(A. - A. 1967. 224A) "For synchronized recordings accompanying filmstrips, information regarding physical description is given after the phrase 'and phonodisc': or 'and phonotape' ": . . . "a. For phonodiscs: number of sides, diameter in inches, playing speed in revolutions per minute. . . . The term 'microgroove' is added when applicable. b. For phonotape recordings: number of reels, diameter of the reels in inches (within parentheses), speed (inches per second) if available. If the width of the tape is other than 1/4 inch, it is given after the diameter of the reel; e. g., (14 in., 1-1/2 in. phonotape). "-- (A. -A. 1967. 224 C. 2)

> 81 fr. color. 35 mm. and phonodisc: 2 s. 16 in. 33-1/3 rpm. 19 min. microgroove.
> 48 double fr. color. 35 mm. and phonotape: 1 reel (10 in.), 7-1/2 in. per sec., 10 min.

This information about the filmstrip would be followed by the name of the series, if any, in parentheses.

Notes, given in their usual place, include information about accompanying material such as teachers' manuals.

Credits. (A. -A. 1967. 227)

"A. Credits are recorded for certain individuals or organizations who have participated in the artistic or technical production of the . . . [filmstrip]. Frequently, no credits are available for filmstrips . . . or if available are limited to the commentator or collaborating authority. "

"B. The following credits, when prominently named, are given in this order:

> producer[8] (associate producer if no producer is given).
> director.
> writers of the story, . . . or narration.
> narrator or commentator.
> collaborating authority.
> [filmstrip] editor.

67. L. C. printed catalog card for filmstrip

Alaska: America's frontier State (Filmstrip)
     McGraw-Hill Book Co. , 1965. Made by Centron
     Corp.

   44 fr. color. 35 mm. (United States geog-
raphy--social studies series. Set 2)

     With guide.
     Credits: Adviser, Clyde F. Kohn.
     Summary: Describes the geographic fea-
tures of Alaska, the distribution of its population, the importance of fishing in the area,
the military bases located in the State, and
the potential resources which are awaiting
                              (Continued on next
                                          card)

---

68. L. C. printed catalog card for filmstrip

Alaska: America's frontier State (Filmstrip)
     1965. (Card 2)

   development.

      1. Alaska--Descr. & trav. --1959-
I. McGraw-Hill Book Company.   Series:
United States geography--social studies series
(Filmstrip)   Set 2.
                                Fi A 66-2801

McGraw-Hill Book Co.
for Library of Congress [1 1/2]

Summary (A. -A. 1967. 228)

"As a contribution to the general objective of reducing
to a minimum the occasions for consulting and handling films,
the summary should describe accurately and objectively the
content of the film, and should be specific enough to serve
as a basis for the assignment of subject headings. . . . For
some films, the title and/or series title may make a summary unnecessary."

Continuations (A. -A. 1967. 229)

"A. Collected series and newsreels"

"1. Filmstrips issued in a series or as a continuation.
. . . and cataloged as a collection are described according to
rules 223-224, 227-228, with adaptations as required, such
as giving the inclusive dates of release if the entry is closed.

"2. The physical description that follows the release
dates consists of the number of . . . filmstrips . . . and the
other elements that are common to all separately issued parts
with specification of any variations that can be succinctly
noted. Other variations are given in the first note or following
the special titles in a contents note."

4 filmstrips (28 fr. each) b&w. (pt. 1 in color)
35 mm. and 4 phonodiscs (1s. each), 12 in., 78 rpm.,
5 min. each.

"3. Changes in title or producing company are noted.

"4. The contents note may be given separately following a summary, or it may substitute for a summary."

Added entries, similar to those for books, are made
for joint producers, sponsors, the releasing agent in the
United States if it is a foreign filmstrip, alternative or partial titles when distinctive, titles of separate parts if important and not used as a separate entry, series if important, and subjects. There is no entry for the person who
writes the script or illustrates the work, though he may be
mentioned under credits. The form of these added entries is
the same as that of added entries for books: the heading is
added above the title on the unit card and the entries are
traced on the front of the main entry.

Maps. Use the letter M and the number of the map to

form the call number, as is done for filmstrips and records, e. g. , M14 would be the fourteenth map added to the map collection. The librarian may prefer to classify maps by area, in which case M940, for example, would be used for maps of Europe.

Another method of caring for maps in the small library is to arrange them alphabetically by area, thus making it unnecessary to assign any type of call number or to catalog them. The area heading would be written on the folded map, or on a label on the map, in the upper right hand corner and the maps would be arranged alphabetically. To illustrate, maps may be arranged by: (1) continent, (2) country, (3) state, province, etc. , (4) county, (5) city or town. For instance:

> North America. United States. North Carolina. Wake. Raleigh

A library might omit from its arrangement for the maps of the area in which it is located: the name of the continent, even the country; for instance: N. C. Durham. Durham.

If there is no catalog entry for the maps a shelf list might be useful, in order to have a list of the maps in the library. These cards would be filed alphabetically by the name of the area. Each entry would include the area on the top line as the filing medium, then the author, title, perhaps the place and publisher, and the date and number of maps.

"A map, a series or set of maps, an atlas . . . is entered under the person or corporate body that is primarily responsible for its informational content. If the content has both geographic and subject aspects, the aspect that constitutes the principal feature of the work determines the rules of entry to be applied. If the subject aspect is the principal feature, the rules of entry for books . . . are applied . . . , if the geographic aspect is the principal feature, rule 211 [given below] is applied. "--(A. -A. 1967. 210)

The items to include in an entry for a map are very similar to those in a book entry. They are: author; title; place of publication, publisher, and date; collation, which includes the number of maps and their size; series; notes; and the tracing of the added entries. Information for cataloging a map is usually found on the map itself, sometimes within a fancy border or in the margins.

". . . A map, series or set of maps, or an atlas, etc. ,

the content of which is mainly confined to geographic information, is entered under the person or corporate body that is
explicitly indicated as primarily responsible for its geographic
content. . . . "--(A. -A. 1967. 211A) "When the primary responsibility . . . is not explicit, the main entry is chosen according to the [following] order of preference": surveyor,
cartographer, engraver, the corporate body including a map
publisher that prepared the maps, the title. "--(A. -A. 1967.
211B) If there is no individual or organization which can be
considered responsible for the map, enter under the title, using hanging indention as is customary when the main entry
is under the title. Following the author, in its usual place,
give the title. The title is taken from any part of the front
of the map.

The place of publication, name of the publisher, and
date of the map are given in imprint place; if not found on
the front of the map, they are put in brackets, if they can
be ascertained. The copyright date is the date of first choice.
If the map is entered under the publisher as author the publisher statement is omitted in the imprint.

The collation is given in the usual place. If there is
only one map, put "map" or "col. map, " if more than one
give the number, e. g., "4 maps. " If one map is printed on
several sheets, it is described as a single map, e. g., "map
on 6 sheets. " The height and width of the map are given in
inches, to the nearest half inch. The height is always given
first. The Anglo-American rules, 1967 and the printed Library
of Congress catalog cards give the measurement in centimeters, not inches. The library which plans to use the printed
cards whenever they are available would do well to give the
measurements in centimeters for the cards made locally. The
measurements are taken from the outer border lines of the
map. If a map is folded, especially if folded within a cover,
or has a panel that should come on the outside, give the
measurements for it folded as well as spread out.

map 28 x 27 in. fold. to 10 x 5 in.

"If the size of the map is less than half the size of the sheet
on which it is printed, both sizes are indicated. "--(A. -A.
1967. 212C)

If a map belongs to a series give a series note as for
any other material.

The first and most important note gives the scale of the

map. This shows the relation that exists between a unit of
distance on the map and that same distance on the earth's
surface. It is usually given on the map expressed as a fraction or a ratio and is called the natural scale, e. g., $\frac{1}{125,000}$
or 1:125, 000; or it may be a linear scale, e. g., 1 mile to
the inch. This latter is determined by measuring with a foot
ruler the distance marked as one mile on the linear scale
drawn on the map. If the scale is not given, a note would
read: Scale not given.

Another item which may be important for a map is the
projection from which the map was drawn. This is taken
directly from the map, e. g., "polyconic projection." "The
name of the map projection is given if stated and if sufficiently unusual to affect the use of the map. The prime mer-
idian is named if other than that of Greenwich."--(A. -A.
1967. 212E. 5) Notes also give information as to what types
of data the map shows, e. g., air routes, population distribution, railroads, etc. Information of a type not usually found
on that kind of map is especially important for notes; for
instance if a highway map shows points of historic interest,
bring it out in a note, as all highway maps do not have such
information; but, since all highway maps do show the type of
surface of the highways, this fact would not be noted on the
card.

Notes also cover such items as: name of surveyor, engraver, cartographer, dates; for instance: "With international
boundaries as of September 1, 1939, the day Germany invad-
ed Poland."

"A separately issued text, accompanying a map, is noted. [e. g.] With this is issued: Street-index and guide."--(A. -
A. 1967. 212 E. 9)

Inset maps, if important, are given in a partial contents note.

Insets: Alaska--Hawaiian Islands.

If very important the inset map is cataloged separately as an
analytic.

Atlases (A. -A. 1967. 215)

"The cataloging of atlases varies from general book

69. Main entry for map showing measurements when folded,
    scale, insets

Canada. Dept. of Mines and Technical Sur-
        veys. Surveys and Mapping Branch.
    Canada and northern United States high-
way map.   Ottawa, 1966.
    col. map   27 x 38 in. fold. to 9 x 4-3/4 in.

Scale 1 inch to 45 miles.
The Western sheet is on the face of the
map, the Eastern sheet on the verso.

                              (Continued on next
                                         card)

---

70. Extension card shows note listing insets

                          2
Canada. Dept. of Mines and Technical
        Surveys. Surveys and Mapping
        Branch.
    Insets: Highways of Yukon and Northwest
Territories-Highways of Western United
States-Island of Newfoundland-Highways of
Eastern United States.
    Insets on reduced scales.

1. Canada - Maps.

---

cataloging practice in only two respects, as follows:

"A. Collation

"1. To distinguish an atlas from a set of loose maps
and to aid in identifying copies and distinguishing between editions, the collation given represents the pages or leaves of
text and the number of maps, or the pages or leaves of

71. L. C. printed catalog card for map

> United Nations. Economic Commission for Asia
> and the Far East.
>   Oil and natural gas map of Asia and the
> Far East. Compiled under the sponsorship
> of the United Nations Economic Commission
> for Asia and the Far East (E. C. A. F. E.)
> from data supplied by countries in the E. C.
> A. F. E. region, member governments, and
> by oil companies. [New York] United Na-
> tions, c1962.
>
>   col. map on 4 sheets 83 x 110 cm.
>   (Continued on next
>   card)

72. L. C. printed catalog card for map

> United Nations. Economic Commission for Asia
> and the Far East.   Oil and natural gas
> map of Asia and the Far East. c1962.
> (Card 2)
>
>   Scale 1:5, 000, 000.
>   "Lambert conical orthomorphic projection
> with two standard parallels at 40° N. and 10°
> S."
>   Shows oil and gas fields, and geologic
> formations, exclusive of U. S. S. R.
>
>   Map 63-311

maps . . . according to the makeup of the atlas. "

      (1) 1., 148 col. maps. 26 x 40 cm.
      xiii p., 30 1. of col. maps 40 cm.

"2. Maps not forming a separate section are described
in the same manner as maps in works that are not atlases. "

      48 p. maps. 31 x 42 cm.

"B. Scale. If all the maps, except index maps, are of

one or two scales, a supplementary note states the scale.
This note is placed with notes on physical description. ''

> Scale of maps 1:2, 500, 000 or 1:5, 000, 000
> Scale of maps 1:4, 800 or 1 inch to 400 feet, and 1:
> 3, 600 or 1 inch to 300 feet.

73. L. C. printed catalog card for map

United Nations. Economic Commission for Asia
and the Far East.   Oil and natural gas
map of Asia and the Far East. c1962.
(Card 3)

    "United Nations publication. Sales no.: 62-
1-16. "

    1. Oil fields--Asia--Maps. 2. Gas, Nat-
ural--Asia--Maps. 3. Petroleum--Geology--
Asia--Maps.

G7401. H8 1962. U5   Map 63-311

Library of Congress   [1]

---

74. L. C. printed catalog card for atlas

Hagstrom Company, inc. , New York.
    Hagstrom's Atlas and official postal zone
guide of the city of New York; five boroughs:
Manhattan, Bronx, Brooklyn, Queens [and]
Richmond, Staten Island. 10th ed. New York,
1966.

    71 p. illus. , maps (part col.) 34 cm. (Its
Atlas no. 2088A)

    Scale of sectional maps ca. 1:33, 000.
First ed. published in 1941 under title:
Atlas of the City of New York.
        (Continued on next card)

      [2]   Map 67-289

Card 74 is for an atlas. Notice that it is entered under the
company responsible for it; that the title, imprint, and collation are given in their usual positions.

75. L. C. printed catalog card for atlas

Hagstrom Company, inc., New York.
    Hagstrom's Atlas and official postal zone
guide of the city of New York. (Card 2)

    1. New York (City)--Maps. 2. Postal ser-
vice--New York (City)--Maps. I. Title. II.
Title: Atlas and official postal zone guide of
the city of New York.

G1254. N4H2   1966   Map 67-289

Library of Congress   [2]

Added entries are made "under any person or corporate
body that has a significant share in the responsibility for the
work";--(A. -A. 1967. 211A); for a distinctive title; the series and the subject or subjects. Analytical entries are made
for important inset maps.

Slides. Assign a number to each unit or series of slides
as they are added to the library, adding this number to the
abbreviation SL to form the call number, as is done for records, filmstrips, and maps. Miss Rufsvold points out that the
individual slides, like the individual records in an album, may
have their number in the series added, e. g., SL92(8) for the
eighth slide in the series numbered 92. The title is used for
the main entry of a slide as it is for filmstrips. The unit
card would include: title, using hanging indention; place, name
of producer, and date; number of slides, if a set; size of the
slides; and whether black and white or in color; in the usual
place for title, imprint, and collation. For sets list the number and subject of each individual slide in a contents note.

Added entries are made for subjects only and they are
traced just as they are for books. The shelf-list card is the
same as the unit card, with the omission of notes and contents
and the addition of the source, date received, and cost of the
slides.

Sample cards 76 and 77 show the items described as
the ones needed for slides. Note that the style of card is the
same as that for books.

7 6. Main entry for a set of slides

SL52 Farm animals.   Chicago, Society for
           Visual Education, n. d.
           10 2x2 in. slides. col.

           Contents. -Bf193 Cattle, Guernseys in
farmyard. -Ah360 Beef cattle in pasture. -
Da29 Pig. -Aa115 Sheep in pasture. -Bf160
White billy goat.-Bf67 Horses, team of. -
Ar190 Colorado turkey farm. -Bf138 Farm
unit, chickens scratching for their food. -
Bf198 Duck, white Muscovy. -Bf146 Three
                                         (Continued on next
                                                       card)

---

77.   Extension card for a set of slides

                              2
SL52 Farm animals.

           geese at edge of pond in typical poses.

              1. Domestic animals.

           Simplified care of audio-visual materials.

       The small library may not have the time to do even the
simple cataloging of audio-visual materials described in this
chapter. Records can be kept in albums or in envelopes, in
cabinets, or on shelves with upright partitions close together
to hold the records erect or in one of the metal racks found
in some of the record stores. As in the case of filmstrips
and slides some kind of index or catalog is essential. If a

good plan is worked out, the necessary rules adopted and the work kept up-to-date, it does not take long to catalog such audio-visual materials and it does save time in locating the right one and also saves wear and tear on the materials. A method of arranging maps by area is suggested in the section on maps in this chapter and may be preferred to classifying, assigning an accession or an identification number and making catalog cards for them.

Records, filmstrips, and slides, however, must have some kind of card index or catalog. If a good plan is worked out, the necessary rules obtained, printed catalog cards used whenever obtainable, and the work kept up-to-date, it does not take long to catalog such audio-visual materials and it does save time in locating the right one and also saves wear and tear on the materials.

Abbreviations. The abbreviations used in cataloging records, filmstrips, maps, and slides are given below, rather than in Appendix II, since they are needed only for this chapter. They are taken from the work by Rufsvold, the Anglo-American rules, 1967, Appendix III, and the H. W. Wilson Company's Filmstrip Guide.

Type of material:		Age level:	
FS	Filmstrip	a	adult
M	Map	c	college
R	Record, single	e	elementary
RA	Record, album	jh	junior high school
SL	Slide	p	primary
		ps	preschool[9]
		sh	senior high school
		t	teacher

Abbreviations used in the description of the material:

b&w	black and white	min.	minute, minutes
fr	frame, frames	mm.	millimeter, millime-ters
ft	foot, feet		
guide	teacher's manual	rpm.	revolutions per minute
in.	inch, inches	s.	side, sides
		sec.	second, seconds

References

1. M. I. Rufsvold, Audio-Visual School Library Service (Chicago, American Library Association, 1949).

2. National Information Center for Educational Media, Index to 35mm Educational Filmstrips (New York, McGraw-Hill, 1968).

3. American Library Association, Pamphlets and Minor Library Materials (Chicago, American Library Association, 1917), p. 6.

4. A frame is "the area of film that constitutes one exposure" (A. L. A. Glossary).

5. M. D. Pearson, Recordings in the Public Library (Chicago, American Library Association, 1963).

6. E. J. Piercy, Commonsense Cataloging (New York, Wilson, 1965), p. 108-109.

7. Nonprocessed phonorecords are chiefly those made in the library, not by a commercial company, most frequently tape recordings.

8. "If this individual has been named in the production statement . . . as solely responsible for the film's coming into existence, his name is not repeated here. " Footnote 6, p. 289, A. -A. 1967.

9. This abbreviation is not found in any of the sources listed above, but as no abbreviation was found for this term, ps was adopted, as it is similar to those used for related terms.

Chapter X
Printed Catalog Cards and the Use
of Centralized Services

No library, however small, should do all of the cataloging and classification processes locally. It is necessary for
the librarian to know where and how he can secure printed
catalog cards with their suggested classification numbers and
added entries. He should also know what is available in the
way of centralized processing and cataloging, including that
offered by commercial firms. But whether he does his own
processing and cataloging or utilizes the work of others he
should know how to classify, catalog, and process materials.

Since 1901 printed catalog cards have been available at
a reasonable cost. Today there are cataloging centers in state,
regional, and county libraries and commercial cataloging companies where libraries can have the bulk of their processing,
cataloging, and classifying done for them. The individual library must continue to compare every classification number
with its shelf list that the classified collection may present
a consistent whole over the years, material on like subjects
together, policies uniform. Likewise catalog entries must be
checked to assure uniform headings for the same person, organization, or subject.

This chapter discusses in some detail the use of Library
of Congress and the H. W. Wilson Company printed catalog
cards and those available from the centralized services. The
Library of Congress prints and sells catalog cards for adult
books, documents, recordings, filmstrips, maps, slides, etc.
In 1966 the Library of Congress began printing annotated catalog cards for children's literature. The H. W. Wilson Company
prints and sells catalog cards for titles which the editors of
the Standard Catalog Series select from reports of representative libraries and which include outstanding fiction, nonfiction,
and juvenile books. The time that it takes to get these printed
cards depends upon the location of the library and whether the
cards are available when the order is received. A recent
sampling showed an average of twenty days for the Wilson
cards and thirty days for the Library of Congress cards; it
may take longer. Consider how long it would take the local

library to prepare the copy and have these cards made and
remember the times suggested were averages. Since the
cards are somewhat different and the procedure in ordering
them differs, they will be treated separately.

Library of Congress printed cards. Differences will be
found, not only in Library of Congress cards, Wilson cards,
and the sample typewritten cards in previous chapters, but
between Library of Congress cards printed at different times,
as shown by the first two figures of the card number (e. g.,
66-13912 means that the card was issued in 1966). These latter differences are the results of changes in the cataloging
practices of the Library of Congress and should be ignored.
Since the older cards and the most recently printed ones both
describe the material accurately, variations in the details of
certain items do not matter.

Card 78 for Maurois' Prometheus gives the author heading in the form adopted by the Library of Congress. The subtitle is included as it is short and shows the subject treated.
These printed cards always give the place of publication, the
publisher's name, and the date of the work, in this case the
imprint date and the copyright date as they differ. The sample Library of Congress cards in this chapter and in Appendix
I show some of the variety of ways in which the date may be
given: imprint date; copyright date; date found elsewhere in the
book than on the title page or in a reliable bibliography; the
nearest approximate date; e. g., 1962, [c1962], [1963], [1963,
c1961], [1961?], [195-?]. The brackets, as usual, indicate
that the enclosed material is not on the title page.

Note that different sizes and styles of type are used to
emphasize or make less conspicuous the different items. The
collation gives the last numbered page of each section of the
work, information about the illustrations, and includes the
size, i. e., the height of the book in centimeters, e. g., 25cm.

Card 79 includes the authors in the title, as the book
was written jointly by two authors; the word "by," the edition, and the date are in brackets as they are not on the title
page; the series including the number of this book in the series; and a note about the bibliography. This manual and the
Wilson printed cards ignore the edition if it is the first. Compare Card 79 with Card 89, a Wilson printed card for this
same book.

78. L. C. printed catalog card

```
        Maurois, André, 1885-
            Prometheus; the life of Balzac. Translated
        by Norman Denny. [1st ed. ] New York,
        Harper & Row [1966, c1965]

            573 p. illus. , ports.   25cm.

            Bibliography: p. 563-564.



            1. Balzac, Honoré de, 1799-1850.   I. Title.
        PQ2178. M333   1966        843. 7    66—13912

        Library of Congress        [66f7]
```

79. L. C. printed catalog card--joint author, series note

```
        Berry, Frederic Aroyce, 1906-
            Your future in meteorology [by] Frederick
        A. Berry and Sidney R. Frank. [1st ed. ]
        New York, Richards Rosen Press [1962]

            155 p.   20cm.   (Careers in depth, 18)

            Includes bibliography.

            1. Meteorology as a profession.    I. Frank,
        Sidney Raymond, 1919-    joint author.   II.
        Title.

        QC869. 5. B4              551. 5069  62—11570‡
        Library of Congress        [67f7]
```

Cards 80-81 show the punctuation and capitalization of the
name of an organization as heading. Note that the words,
"Red Cross, " the name by which the organization is best
known are given first, then a period, then the official name:
U. S. American National Red Cross. Compare Cards 80-81
with Cards 91-92, Wilson cards.

Card 82 gives the edition note as given on the title page,
using standard abbreviations.

80. L. C. printed catalog card--name of an organization as
heading--bibliography mentioned in note

Red Cross. U. S. American National Red Cross.
Home nursing textbook, prepared under
the supervision of Nursing Services, American Red Cross. [6th revision] Philadelphia,
Blakiston, 1950.

ix, 235 p. illus. 23 cm.

First published in 1913 under title:
American Red Cross textbook on elementary
hygiene and home care of the sick.
Bibliography: p. 225-227.
(Continued on next
card)

81.

Red Cross. U. S. American National Red
Cross. Home nursing textbook. 1950. (Card 2)

1. Hygiene.   2. Nurses and nursing.
I. Title.

RT61. R38 1950   649   50--4804
Library of Congress [67u^{3}3]

Card 83 shows the title on the top line with hanging
indention extending through the imprint. Most libraries and
certainly the smaller libraries would not give the series note
and Wilson cards do not do so as this is a publisher's, not
a subject series. Note that this card does not give contents.
Presumably as there are only six plays, all found in other
collections, the Library of Congress did not consider contents
necessary. On Card 84, however, the Library of Congress
does give the contents. Compare Cards 83 and 84.

82. L. C. printed catalog card--edition note

> Allen, Durward Leon, 1910-
>   Our wildlife legacy. Rev. ed. New York,
> Funk & Wagnalls [1962]
>
>   422 p. illus. 22 cm.
>
>
>
>   1. Wild life, Conservation of--U. S.   I.
> Title.
>
> SK361. A66 1962   799   62--7980‡
>
> Library of Congress [67p3]

83. L. C. printed catalog card--main entry under title

> Six modern American plays; introd. by Allan G.
>   Halline. New York, Modern Library [1951]
>
>   419 p. 19 cm. (The Modern library of the
> world's best books, 276)
>
>
>
>   1. American drama--20th cent.   I.
> Halline, Allan Gates.
>
> PS634. S57   812. 5082   51--8900‡
>
> Library of Congress [67c^{2}10]

At the bottom of the cards is the tracing (see Cards 78-
79, 81-83) for the added entries made for the Library of Congress
catalog. Below the tracing and to the left of the hole are
given the Library of Congress classification and book numbers, e. g. , PR6031. R6A19; on the same line to the right of
the hole is given the suggested Dewey Decimal Classification
number, e. g. , 822. 91.

The Library of Congress card number, e. g. , 51-118 rev,

84. L. C. printed catalog card--note giving different title for
    volume 1--contents included

Priestley, John Boynton, 1894-
    Plays. New York, Harper, 1950-52.

    3 v. 23 cm.

    Vol. 1 published under title: Seven plays.

    Contents. --[v. 1] Dangerous corner. Eden
    end. Time and the Conways. I have been here
    before. Johnson over Jordan. Music at night.
    The linden tree. --v. 2. Laburnum Grove.
    Bees on the boat deck. When we are married.
    Good night, children. The Golden Fleece.
    How are they at home? Ever since para-
    dise. --v. 3. Cornelius. People at sea. They
                        (Continued on next card)

Priestley, John Boynton (Card 2)

    came to a city. Desert highway. An in-
    spector calls. Home is tomorrow. Sum-
    mer day's dream.

    PR6031. R6A19 1950   822. 91   51--118 rev

    Library of Congress   [r52k5]

---

which is to be used in ordering Library of Congress cards,
is given in the right hand corner of the card. Such symbols
as [r52k5] to the right of the hole and below the Dewey
Decimal Classification number indicate facts as to the edition
of the card and have no significance for the catalog.

        Some cards, as numbers 85-86, Hooper's The Discovery of
Wrangel Island, indicate that the Library of Congress has a
second copy by giving two long dashes followed by "copy 2"

85. L. C. printed catalog card--series note including author
   and title of series--note the tracing of the series

```
        Hooper, Samuel L
              The discovery of Wrangel Island.  San
        Francisco, California Academy of Sciences,
        1956.

              27 p.  illus. , port. ,  map, facsim.  26 cm.
        (Occasional papers of the California Academy
        of Sciences, no. 24)


              1.  Hooper, Calvin Leighton, 1842-1900.
        2.  Wrangel Island, Siberia.  3. Corwin
        (Revenue cutter)     I. Title.     (Series:
                              (Continued on next card)
```

86.

```
        Hooper, Samuel L   The discovery of Wrangel
        Island.  1956. (Card  2)

        California Academy of Sciences, San Fran-
        cisco.  Occasional papers, no.  24)



        Q11. C18  no. 24                      A 56--4043
        ——  ——  Copy 2.         G830. H6

        Indiana.  Univ.  Libr.
        for Library of Congress  [61f 1/2]†
```

(_____ copy 2) below the Library of Congress classification number.

   Ordering Library of Congress cards. The Card Division
of the Library of Congress[1] issues lists of publishers and
dealers who are participating in the Cards-with-Books Programs, i. e. , including a set of Library of Congress cards in
each book sold to a library. Despite this service from many
publishers, the librarian should write to the Card Division

and ask for a copy of the Library's instructions for ordering
printed cards and a supply of the forms to be used for each
order. Request a supply of order slips for an estimated three-
month period. The directions for making out orders are detailed and clear and should be followed exactly.

The price of Library of Congress cards varies slightly
from time to time, as each year the price is compared with
the cost of production and any necessary adjustments made.
The price also varies with the method of ordering. Current
prices vary from 10¢ to 15¢ for the first card for a work and
6¢ for each additional copy of the same card provided three
or more copies of the same card are ordered at the same
time.

Wilson printed cards. The printed cards of the H. W.
Wilson Company reproduce the entries for books in their
printed book catalogs, including the very helpful annotations.
Unlike the Library of Congress cards, all the cards of a set
are not exactly alike, but have title, etc., added at the top.
The sets for each book are available in two forms. One form
has the subject headings and the classification number added
in the proper place at the top of the card; both forms have
the subject headings in the tracing and the classification number in the lower right hand corner of the card, thus they are
available as suggestions but are not in the way if the particular library has used or prefers to use another form of subject heading or a different classification number. The illustrations in this manual show the two forms. Punctuation is omitted from the printed book catalogs published by Wilson to save
expense and space; the cards are printed from the same copy,
hence have little or no punctuation. Entries for individual
books give a short form of name for the publisher which is
given in full in the "Directory of Publishers" at the end of
each issue of the book catalog.

Card 87 gives the author heading as it is found on the
title page; the ampersand (&) is used in the title as it is used
on the title page. The publisher's name is given in short form
as found in the list of abbreviations in the "Directory of Publishers, " followed by the date of the work, the total number
of pages, and the fact that the book is illustrated. Below in
note place is the annotation and its source, followed by the
tracing. The Dewey Decimal Classification number is given
at the lower right. Bold face type is used for the author's
name. Smaller print makes it possible to get the annotation
on the first card. The rules for cataloging as given in this

book do not include annotations.

87. Wilson printed catalog card

> Thurber, James
>   Lanterns & lances. Harper 1961
>   215p illus
>
>   Contains 24 pieces in which the well-known
> humorist is largly concerned with the survival
> of our English language, currently being sub-
> jected to much erroneous use. (Publisher)
>
>
>   1 English language--Errors   I Title   817
>
>   61W11, 317   (W) The H. W. Wilson
>   Company

88. Shelf-list card

> Thurber, James
>   Lanterns & lances. Harper 1961
>   215p illus
>
>
>
>   1 English language--Errors   I Title   817
>
>   61W11, 317   (W) The H. W. Wilson
>   Company

Card 88, the shelf-list card, omits the annotation, leaving space for the special shelf-list information.

Comparing Cards 78 and 87 one sees that the Library
of Congress has searched the author's name and added the author's date of birth, gives the place of publication and the
publisher's full name, "Harper & Row, " and brackets the
dates to show that they were not on the title page. Paging is
given as on the Wilson card and information about the illustra-

tions, followed by the height of the book in centimeters. The
tracing is in the same form on both cards: the heading for
the subject entry and a title card.

    89. Wilson printed catalog cards--joint authors and series
          note

          Berry, Frederick A
            Your future in meteorology [by] Frederick
         A. Berry and Sidney R. Frank. Rosen, R. 1962
         155p (Careers in depth)

            Partial contents: The United States Weather
        Bureau; A career in the Navy Weather Service;
        Air Force weather careers; Private meteorol-
        ogy practice; Meteorologists--who and what are
        they; Meteorological schools; Job-hunting; Me-
        teorology as a way of life; Women in meteor-
        ology; Scholarships; Self-evaluation test
        A selective bibliography: p147-55
                           (Continued on next card)

   90.

      Berry, Frederick A Your future in meteorology.
        1962. (Card 2)

      1 Meteorology as a   profession I Jt.
                            auth. II Title 551. 5

      62W17, 524   (W) The H. W. Wilson
                            Company

      Cards 79 and 89 are for the same book, even the same
edition, but as it is the first edition it is not given on the
Wilson card. The Library of Congress has searched the author's name and so gives Frederic not Frederick, fills in the
middle name, and adds the author's date of birth; gives the

place of publication and the publisher's full name, "Richards Rosen Press, " and brackets the date to show it is not on the title page. Both cards give the series, but only the Library of Congress card adds the number of this book in the series. The Wilson card gives the paging for the bibliography, the Library of Congress card has the general statement: Includes bibliography. The Wilson card gives "partial contents, " the Library of Congress card does not. Both cards have the same tracing, except that the Wilson card does not give the joint author's name, just "I Jt. auth. " The Wilson card has a shorter Dewey Decimal Classification number, suitable for the smaller library.

Cards 80 and 91 are likewise for the same book. The author headings are the same, but the cards have the main title and subtitle in a different order. The Library of Congress card gives the edition note in its usual place, following the title; the Wilson card includes this information in the annotation. The Wilson card gives the number of the last page only; the Library of Congress card gives the number of the last page of each section. The tracing differs in that the Library of Congress having changed the order of its title information, bringing the phrase, "Home nursing textbook, " first gives only "I. Title. "; The Wilson card gives I Title which stands for the title as it appears on the title page; and II Title: Home nursing textbook, the catch title, which may be remembered and looked for by many readers.

91. Wilson printed catalog card--name of an organization as heading--title card

```
   American Red Cross Home nursing textbook

 Red Cross.  U.S.  American National Red Cross

   American Red Cross Home nursing textbook;
 prepared under the supervision of Nursing Ser-
 vices, American Red Cross.  Blakiston 1950
   235p illus

   "This is the sixth revision of the official
 Red Cross textbook on home nursing that has
 been issued under various titles since the pub-
 lication of 'Elementary Hygiene and Care of
                            (Continued on next
                                       card)
```

92. Wilson printed catalog card--name of an organization as
    heading--title card

American Red Cross Home nursing textbook.
Red Cross. U. S. American National Red Cross.
1950. (Card 2)

the Sick, ' prepared by Jane A. Delano and Isabel
McIsaac, in 1913. " Foreword
"Provides information to guide the home-
maker in keeping the family in good health, as-
sisting in case of illness and supporting community action in the promotion of health. " Huntting
Supplementary reading: p225-27

1 Hygiene 2 Nurses   and nursing I Title
II Title: Home nursing   textbook [610. 7] 649. 8

---

93. Wilson printed catalog card--edition note

Allen, Durward L
    Our wildlife legacy. Rev. ed. Funk 1962
422p illus

    First published 1954. The 1962 edition has been
"brought up to date with the most recent develop-
ments in science and technology, wildlife population, and legislation. " Bk Buyer's Guide
    The author explains what is happening to our
American birds, mammals and fish and presents
the basic principles of wildlife conservation.
(Publisher)
    Bibliography: p379-408

Usually the call number is at the left of the author
heading but the cards for Critics' Prize Plays have the classification number at the left of the first word of the title,
since the title is used as the main entry for this work. Note
in the tracing: "(12 author and title anals). " The printed
cards for the author and title analytical entries (Cards 94 and
95) have both author and title added at the top of the card.
The paging follows the title on the author analytical entry and
the author's name on the title analytical entry, so as to immediately precede the main entry for the book, "Critics. . . "
The punctuation of the contents on these cards differs from

94. Wilson printed catalog card--author analytical entry

Anderson, Maxwell, 1888-
High Tor p83-161

812. 08 Critics' prize plays; introduction by G. J.
Nathan. World pub. 1945
377p

"This collection contains text and original casts for the six plays chosen for
recognition by the New York Drama critics' circle from 1935 through 1943. An introduction briefs the standards for the
award and the personnel of the committee."
Bkl

---

that used on the typewritten and on the Library of Congress
cards (see Cards 19, 84 and 89). That is only a minor difference of form and of no importance.

Library of Congress cards used as author analytical entries would have the author of the analytical, title, and paging typed on the card above the top printed line.

If the library's policy differs--and this would not happen

95. Wilson printed catalog card--title analytical entry

High Tor
Anderson, Maxwell, 1888-   p83-161

812. 08 Critics' prize plays; introduction by G. J. Nathan.   World pub. 1945
377p

"This collection contains text and original casts for the six plays chosen for recognition by the New York Drama critics'
circle from 1935 through 1943. An introduction briefs the standards for the award
and the personnel of the committee. " Bkl

---

often in a school or small public library--regarding the need
for an added entry for a joint author or perhaps an illustra-
tor--the Wilson card or cards for these entries would not be
used and the tracing would be changed accordingly.

It is also possible to use Wilson cards whenever available, filling in with an occasional set of Library of Congress
cards or typing one's own cards, following the form of the
cards given in Chapters VI - VIII. If Library of Congress
cards are used there may be variations in the name headings,
suggested subject headings and Dewey Decimal Classification
numbers and it will be necessary to check these items carefully with the library's catalog, shelf list, and policy and
make the necessary changes.

Ordering Wilson cards. Some publishers and book dealers furnish Wilson cards with the titles they sell. If, however,
one wishes to use the Wilson printed cards regularly, he
should write to: The Catalog Card Department, The H. W. Wilson Company, 950 University Avenue, Bronx, New York, 10452
for a copy of its latest Checklist of Sets of Catalog Cards and
its supplements. The pamphlet and the monthly supplements
give simple, clear directions for ordering the cards and include a printed order form. The company sells sheets of twenty-five coupons at $3.00 per sheet to be used in purchasing
the cards which are sold in sets only. The current price is
12¢ for each set with one additional 12¢ coupon to be sent with
each order. If the book requires more than the average number of analytical entries, the additional cards are sold separately in sets at the price indicated in the Checklist.

Advantages of using printed catalog cards. When one con-
siders the cost of blank cards and the time required to do the
cataloging printed cards are not expensive. A professional committee of the Northern Section of the School Library Association of California[2] surveyed preparation and cataloging time
and concluded that it takes three and three-fourths times as
long to catalog, classify and assign subject headings for books
if no printed cards are used. Besides there is no waste of
cards or expenditure of time in making and revising typed
cards.

Miss Veda Fatka[3] estimated on the basis of her work in
her library that she saved $29.60 and thirty-seven hours on
every 103 books cataloged by using printed catalog cards.

The copy for printed catalog cards is prepared by expert catalogers, with all that this implies in regard to author

headings, items included on the cards, suggestions as to subject headings, classification numbers, and added entries to be made. The Library of Congress cards give considerable bibliographical information about the book which may be of great value. The Wilson cards give annotations which are very useful. Printed cards are uniform as to blackness and are very legible. Their use saves time in preparing the entry, in typing and otherwise reproducing the cards, and in revising typewritten cards. One printed card may be compared with the book to see if it matches the particular edition which the library has; then only the call number and the typewritten headings added to the other cards need to be checked for accuracy. Printed cards are especially useful for books which require several subject cards or numerous analytical entries. The Library of Congress cards do not specify cards for analytical entries; but the necessary extra cards may be ordered and by adding call number, headings, and paging the cards are quickly made into analytical entries. The Wilson cards for analytical entries have the headings and the paging printed on them.

Typewritten reference cards and short form series cards have to be made by each library for its own catalog. If the unit card is used for series entries, printed cards may be used. The simple form of cataloging for fiction recommended in this manual makes the process of cataloging by the library as quick or quicker than ordering Library of Congress printed cards and adapting them for the catalog. It is recommended, therefore, that typewritten cards be used for fiction even though Library of Congress cards are ordered for all nonfiction. On the other hand, if the Wilson cards are to be used for nonfiction, it is recommended that they be ordered for fiction as well, since they include annotations and are very easy to order.

The question of whether to use Library of Congress cards depends largely upon the kind of library. The library for adults and the more scholarly library would do well to use Library of Congress cards with their added bibliographical information. The school or children's library having chiefly books which are listed in the Wilson Standard Catalog Series and for which printed Wilson cards are available would do well to use Wilson cards, ordering Library of Congress cards only for books for which Wilson cards are not available. The mixture of Library of Congress cards, Wilson printed cards, and typewritten cards in the same catalog does not reduce the usefulness of the catalog.

Adapting printed cards for use in the catalog. The librarian compares the cards with the book which they are to represent in the catalog to see that they agree, and with the catalog or authority file to see whether or not the form of heading agrees with what has already been used. If, for example, the printed card has the author's real name on the first line and it seems better to use the pseudonym, write it on the line above the real name--beginning at the first indention--followed by a comma, one space and pseud. of.

If the library has entered a few books under another form of the name, e. g., Mulock, Dinah Maria, instead of Craik, Dinah Maria (Mulock), it would be better to change those and adopt the form used on the printed cards. If on the other hand there are many cards in the catalog by the author, the headings on the printed cards may be changed. A line can be drawn through the author heading and the preferred form written above, beginning at the first indention, as usual.

Changes may be made by crossing out or erasing items and typing or writing in the corrections. As few corrections as possible should be made, however, so as not to spoil the appearance of the cards. It is unnecessary to cross out any item given on the printed card if it applies to the book in question.

If the publisher given in the imprint is not the publisher of the edition to be cataloged, the statement on the card should be changed. If the date given on the edition to be cataloged is not the copyright date, c should be added and the date changed if necessary. In the case of incomplete sets, date and volume should be changed with pencil so that the card may show what the library has and yet be easily changed when the other volumes are added.

After the librarian makes the corrections or additions which may be necessary in order that the printed card may represent the book correctly, the next step is to add the call number. For most books published since 1930 the Decimal Classification number appears to the right of the hole in the card and may be used if it is not too long and is in agreement with the policy of the library and the edition of the Dewey Decimal Classification in use. For instance, if the number suggested for a biography is 923 it would not be used if the plan recommended for the small school or public library in Chapter I is followed; i. e., to use 920 for all collective biography and 92 or B for all individual biography.

The next step is to examine the tracing. Does the library need all of the added entries listed? Are the subject headings those listed in the printed list of subject headings adopted by the library? Does the amount of material on the subject make necessary the subdivisions of the subject given? If the library has only a few books on a country and is unlikely to ever have many, the name of the country alone may be sufficient for all of the books about it, e. g. , FORMOSA; or the general subdivisions HISTORY and DESCRIPTION AND TRAVEL may be sufficient rather than the more specific subdivisions such as, CZECHOSLOVAK REPUBLIC. HISTORY, 1938-1945. or IRELAND. DESCRIPTION AND TRAVEL. 19th CENTURY.

If all of the added entries given in the tracing on the printed card are not used, underscore the number of each item of tracing which is used. If the subject heading given on the card is not the same as that listed in the printed subject headings list used by the library, use the heading from the printed list and type it with the tracing on the front of the card. If there is insufficient space at the end of the tracing, type it on the back, and type the word "over" below the hole on the front of the card.

On the Library of Congress cards which are to be used as added entries the call number is added, any necessary alterations are made and in addition the appropriate headings are added. No change is made in the tracing on the added entry cards, as only the main entry is consulted for tracing. To make a Library of Congress card into an author analytical entry, estimate in advance the number of lines the added heading will require. If contents or any other extra information has made extension cards necessary, use a full set of cards, i. e. , first, second, third, etc. , for the main and all other entries except for title cards and for analytical entries. For title cards use the first card only, drawing a line through the words, "Continued on next card. " For analytical entries, use the card which contains the part of the contents for which the entry is made, crossing out "Continued on next card. " See also Card 34 in Chapter VII.

The Wilson printed cards will rarely need any alteration, as they are more often made for the edition of the book which the library has. The Dewey Decimal Classification number is suggested for the same type of library as that

for which the cards were ordered; however, two or, occasionally, three numbers may be given and a choice has to be
made. The cards for Keith's White Man Returns have [919. 11]
991. 1 and Profile of Youth by members of the staff of the
Ladies' Home Journal has [136. 7] 136. 73 or 301. 15. Choose
the number which will put the book with similar books in the
library.

Likewise the added entries for joint authors, editors,
and subject headings on the Wilson cards are selected for
greatest usefulness to the type of library which customarily
orders their cards. The suggested subject headings on these
cards are chosen from the Sears List. Hence it will not often
happen that the indicated entries need not be made or that
the subject headings will need to be shortened. It is best in
many libraries, however, to order the cards that do not have
subject headings printed at the top of the subject cards nor
the classification number in its place in the upper left-hand
portion of the card, as the subject headings and classification
number may not agree with those used by the library and may
have to be modified.

Whether it is the first set of printed cards to be added
to the catalog or the thousandth, any cards added have to be
first checked with the catalog to assure uniformity of name
headings.

Centralized services. The service which the Library of
Congress and the H. W. Wilson Company provide for libraries
through their sale of printed catalog cards is centralized cataloging. The A. L. A. Glossary of Library Terms[4] defines centralized cataloging as "(1) The preparation in one library or
central agency of catalogs for all the libraries of a system."
This has long been the practice of the majority of public library systems and many of the larger public school systems
in which the Catalog Department or a central office does the
cataloging for the central library and the branches or individual school libraries. The Glossary also defines centralized
cataloging as "(2) The preparation of catalog cards by one library or other agency which distributes them to libraries."
Libraries have been able to take advantage of these centralized services for over half a century. Beside The Library of
Congress and the H. W. Wilson Company today, some publishers and book dealers send printed catalog cards with their
publications, if the library so desires. A library which belongs to a regional, county, city school or public library system frequently can order its books through the headquarters

office and receive the catalog cards with the books.

The present trend is towards centralized processing as well as cataloging and this field is developing very rapidly. The terms: "cataloging, " "preparation, " and "processing" as applied in different libraries vary in their inclusiveness. This variation is reflected in the articles on centralized processing and cataloging. "Cataloging" as used in this chapter and in the articles cited includes "classification. " It is more often used in connection with books, but to cite one example, the Library Department of the Fulton County [Georgia] School System includes nonbook materials in its central processing and cataloging service. J. W. Henderson[5] states that "processing includes ordering, cataloging and preparation of library materials, " adding that the "preparation" which is done by a clerk includes: Stamping the title page with the library's mark of ownership; putting the accession number in the book; making the book card, book pocket, holdings record and shelf-list record for the headquarters library and the shelf-list record for the regional library.

The American Association of School Librarians in its Standards for School Library Progress[6] states that "Centralized processing should be introduced if three or more schools, in the system, as it saves time and effort and provides uniformity within the school system. If not a librarian in each school centralized processing makes possible a well-organized and functioning library collection. "

Centralized processing and cataloging agencies are found at the state, regional, county and city level. To mention some of these agencies there are: The State Catalog Card Service in the State Department of Education at Atlanta, Ga.; the West Virginia Library Commission; the Southwest Missouri Library Service; the Weld County Library, Greeley, Colorado; the Library Section of the Los Angeles City Schools. The participating libraries send their book orders to the central agency and receive the books ready for the shelves with the catalog and shelf-list cards ready to file. The Georgia agency uses Wilson printed cards of they are available, if not, the agency prepares and duplicates the cards.

The State Library Catalog Center in Ohio catalogs the books for the State Library and for other libraries according to the individual library's needs, so-called "custom-built" cataloging. Other agencies state frankly that the subscribing library must accept their classification, subject headings,

cataloging form, processing procedure, and the choice and
quality of materials used as determined by the Center.

The extent of the processing varies; for instance, the
North Carolina State Library Processing Center states that
stamping the book with the property stamp of the library, assigning an accession or copy number to the book and adding
such information to the shelf list is the responsibility of the
individual library.

One commercial agency supplies Library of Congress
or Wilson cards, whichever the library prefers. If neither
Library of Congress nor Wilson cards are available, the company, having secured the library's prior approval, sends
cards which its professional library staff has prepared. Another firm states that each book will be completely processed,
ready to go on the shelf; the catalog cards ready to file; adding that a Dewey Decimal Classification number will be on
the spine of the book, book pocket in the back of the book,
and a complete set of the agency's printed catalog cards,
which represent a merger of the best information on Library
of Congress and Wilson cards, will accompany each book. Yet
another commercial center issues a list of 800 titles covering
books suitable for the kindergarten through grade six; and a
1200 title list for junior and senior high school libraries. The
North Carolina State Library Processing Center requests that
the libraries subscribing to its services select their books
from a given list of sources as this helps the Center to identify the title and to pre-catalog it. This list is quite inclusive
and has been expanded several times. Beginning with the selection of materials the participating library modifies its procedures. The individual library, however, after selecting the
materials and sending in its orders has no more work to do
until the books, ready for use, are received.

Cost of centralized processing and cataloging. The cost
of centralized processing and cataloging varies with the work
to be done. One state agency describing its centralized cataloging in 1962 stated that it could provide catalog cards at
21¢ a set; its custom cataloging and processing at 92¢ for
each title of fiction, $1.17 for each title of nonfiction. A
library which will accept the classification and cataloging of
the state library and the same processing procedure for accessioning and book pockets and cards can have its books processed and cataloged for 75¢ a volume. Yet another state agency offers its cataloging service on a "cost, self-sustaining
basis." The cost includes card stock, postage and the labor

in printing cards. One regional library service center processes and catalogs books for public libraries for 75¢ a volume
and for school libraries for $1.00 a volume. A commercial
firm which delivers the books, fully processed and cataloged,
states that "All prices will be net and will include complete
processing charges, and will be in many instances a few cents
less than list and in some cases a few cents above the list
price." A survey of central processing and cataloging in 1963
showed estimates ranged from 25¢ to $2.00 per volume.[7]

In comparing the cost of centralized processing and cataloging with the cost of doing the work in the individual library
one should include consideration of the space available, any
special furniture or equipment required for the work as well
as reference books needed for ordering and cataloging; supplies, e.g., book cards and pockets, date due slips, blank
catalog and shelf-list cards; materials for marking books on
the spine; and necessary professional and clerical staff. Mr.
Everett L. Moore[8] points out that certain routines must be
performed before and after sending out the order to a cataloging center or commercial firm and the cost of this should
be added to the costs of the service in making one's decision
to use an outside agency. To give a few illustrations of work
which must be done in the individual library: filing the catalog and shelf-list cards; checking name and subject headings
against the usage of the library; assigning copy numbers.

Mrs. Catherine MacQuarrie[9] found that among the factors affecting the cost are: size of the library's collection;
type of material, e.g., serials, documents, material in foreign languages, and audio-visual materials take more time
for the professional side of the work hence are more expensive to catalog; use of printed cards; having subject entries
for fiction; analyzing short story collections; and the use of
Cutter numbers.

Mrs. MacQuarrie states that "In four [public] libraries,
all with collections of approximately 100,000 volumes, the
range was from 76¢ to $1.00 per title. In college libraries
ordering less than 3,000 titles per year, the average cost
per volume for ordering, cataloging, and preparing, as indicated by the survey, was $3.76." The survey forms were
also sent to the school libraries but the librarians though interested in the results of the survey were unable to supply
the necessary information.

"The exact number of minutes of professional time it

takes to catalog a title" seemed important as it is a basic
figure not affected by variations in salaries. It was found that
in public libraries the "overall average for cataloging a title
is 45 minutes, or 10 titles per day." This average included
four groups of libraries divided according to their size. In
the group including one medium-large and four small public
libraries "it takes from 14 to 19 minutes to catalog a title."
It was found to be impossible to compute ordering in public
libraries on a cost basis as there were too many variations
in the libraries studied. The use of plastic jackets seems to
be the time-consuming part of the process. These average
figures must be used cautiously. They serve as a target to
aim towards in setting work standards but cannot be used as
a criterion for any particular library since too many vari-
ables enter into individual library costs and work-time.

Mrs. MacQuarrie concludes "As determined by this
cost analysis it is questionable whether, from a strictly dol-
lar and cents viewpoint, it would profit a public library in
this area to contract for outside technical processing. The
problems of space, staff, and promptness in cataloging and
delivery of books to the service outlet might justify having
the work performed on a commercial basis although the re-
sultant costs might be greater than if the library continued
to perform its own technical work in its entirety. Whether
the freeing of a professional worker for other duties would
be sufficiently worthwhile to outweigh the additional costs is
another question. . . . Libraries that are unable to hire a
professional cataloger probably would be better off using an
outside agency than to make do with non-professional catalogers; new libraries that are just organizing their collections
and libraries adding new branches with new collections could
benefit from hiring the work done and freeing the staff for
other duties. "

This study of libraries in Southern California shows
clearly that libraries everywhere, small as well as large,
should study closely the services of commercial companies
and of non-profit organizations of libraries in their areas before deciding to do or to continue doing all of their own processing and cataloging with or without printed catalog cards
from other libraries or agencies.

Harry C. Bauer[10] in his "Three by Five" says: "one
writer wrote the book, one publisher published the book, but
12, 000 catalogers cataloged the book. " To quote from Mac-
Quarrie's[11] cost survey again ". . . all these libraries in

Southern California hire catalogers, order clerks, and preparation clerks; each catalogs almost identical collections of
new books. ''

Advantages and disadvantages of centralized processing
and cataloging. The chief gain is in the time saved by the
local library's professional staff which can be used for more
services to the readers. Many books are purchased by all the
public libraries or all the school libraries in a state and instead of each school librarian's having to send her order to
one or more jobbers, classify and catalog the same book, the
central agency sends in one order for all of the copies wanted,
decides on the classification, adapts printed catalog cards or
prepares card copy and reproduces it by mechanical means.
There are better discounts when more titles and more copies
are included in one order. Thus there is a saving of expense
as well as of time. A central agency can afford a better reference collection for use in ordering and cataloging books
than an individual library. Better classification and better cataloging are possible when the work is done by experienced, able
catalogers, not just fitted in with other duties by a general librarian. The needed machines, mechanical devices--too expensive for the individual library--are feasible for the central
agency and on large jobs save time and expense. Centralization helps to make catalogs uniform, hence lessens the problems of cataloging when regional libraries are created. The
catalogs are kept more up-to-date when the work is done by a
central agency.

The major disadvantage, perhaps, is in adapting centralized processing and cataloging to the needs of the participating libraries. There is, of course, some loss of local control
of subject headings; there are the necessary changes to be
made in the library's classification numbers, in subject and
name headings in order to conform to the central agency's
forms in the case of libraries which have previously done
their own classification and cataloging. Some writers cite the
delay in getting the books to the libraries as a disadvantage
of centralized processing and cataloging, others cite this as
one of the advantages of centralization, the books are ready
for the shelves sooner.

The time of delivery by the commercial firms, listed
in Miss Barbara Westby's ''Directory''[12] varied, e. g., ''Not
specified; Depends upon type of book and type of processing;
New titles arrive ready to shelve on or before publication
date; Ten days; Two weeks; Two months. ''

Two very important considerations, especially in the case of a commerical centralized processing and cataloging agency, are: (1) is the agency qualified from the professional librarian's point of view to perform the services which are offered; and (2) is the agency likely to continue to offer such services indefinitely? Undoubtedly failure of an agency which would make it necessary for the libraries subscribing for the service to seek another agency or do their own processing and cataloging, would be very hard on the libraries dependent on this service.

The uncataloged and unclassified small public or school library, the one which is only partially classified and cataloged, or the one with a completely classified and cataloged collection whether it be well or poorly done, should most certainly consider having the processing and cataloging done elsewhere. Your state library agency and larger libraries in your vicinity can tell you what agencies are available and help you to evaluate their services for your library.

The governing board of your library or your principal would want to know the cost of such services, what work is included, the extent to which your library would have to conform to all the procedures of the libraries served by the agency, and the effect of such centralized service on the length of time before a book would be delivered to your library. Established libraries will want to check their present processing costs with those of the center. Other questions which would need consideration are: What is the minimum number of books which must be ordered at one time? Will such service be a substitute for a clerical assistant, either part or full time? Will it release more of the librarian's time for reader services? When could the necessary funds for initiating this service be made available?

Suppose a small library has a good, accurate catalog; its books are well classified but it is becoming increasingly difficult for the librarian to find time to do this part of the work. The state central library agency offers good centralized processing and cataloging service, but it is not custom cataloging. The library taking advantage of it must accept the agency's classification numbers, subject headings, catalog method and processing. What would be involved in adopting this service? All new shelf-list cards when filed would have to be examined for classification and in some cases the numbers for the books already in the library would have to be changed to conform with the new numbers which means change the numbers on the back of the book, book pocket and card, the shelf-list and catalog cards. But it would be better to adopt the new number for books in that class at once as in time the majority of the books will have that number. Likewise subject headings and the tracing for them will have to be changed; also some name headings. At first these changes will take additional time, mean additional expense, but very soon there will be little of this work to be done.

Although much of the assistance in processing and cataloging libraries is directed at the school and smaller public libraries, such service is also available for college libraries. One commercial firm states that "you can order all books from all publishers . . . and we ship them to you ready for immediate circulation." This would seem to fit any type of library. An advertisement in the ALA Bulletin by one of the largest book wholesalers in the country gives a long list of well-known publishers whose books they can supply with processing kits which contain catalog cards, book pocket, book card, spine label. Are not many of the titles found in college libraries also in public and high school libraries?

References

1. Card Division, Library of Congress, Building 159, Navy Yard Annex, Washington, D. C. 20541.

2. W. B. Hicks & A. M. Lowrey, "Preparation and Cataloging Time in School Libraries." School Library Association of California. Bulletin 30:7-10 (May, 1959).

3. Veda Fatha, "Cost of Cataloging vs Printed Cards in the School Library, " Wilson Library Bulletin 33:239 (November, 1958).

4. A. L. A. Glossary of Library Terms (Chicago, American Library Association, 1943).

5. J. W. Henderson, "Centralized Processing of Library Materials in West Virginia and Other Matters, " Survey. [1959?].

6. Chicago, American Library Association, 1960, p. 112.

7. Mary Lee Bundy, "Behind Central Processing." Library Journal 88:3539-3543 (Oct. 1, 1963).

8. Everett L. Moore, "California Junior College Libraries." Library Resources & Technical Services 9:312 (Summer, 1965).

9. Mrs. Catherine MacQuarrie, "Cost Survey: Cost of Ordering, Cataloging and Preparations in Southern California Libraries," Library Resources & Technical Services 6:337-350 (Fall, 1962).

10. Wilson Library Bulletin 35:393 (Jan., 1961).

11. MacQuarrie, op. cit., p. 343.

12. Barbara Westby, "Commercial Cataloging Service: a Directory," Library Journal 89:1509-1513 (April 1, 1964).

Chapter XI
Arrangement of Cards in a Catalog

Introduction. Next in importance to making the cards for the catalog is their arrangement in the trays of the catalog case. Unless all cards with the same heading are found together and all cards are arranged according to some definite plan, a card catalog is of very little use. One of the most important mechanical points is to watch that the trays do not become overcrowded. A good rule is never to fill a catalog tray more than two-thirds full; space is needed to shift cards so that the one being examined may be handled easily.

Another important matter is to label the trays so that the reader can easily locate the tray which contains the author, title, or subject for which he is searching. Adequate guide cards, preferably cut in thirds, should indicate the approximate location of the desired card.

A very good method of arranging guide cards in the catalog is to have the authors' surnames on the left, main subject headings in the center, and subdivisions of the subject on the right. This plan enables the caption on the guide card to be short and near enough to the top of the card so that it may be read. So far as possible there should be a guide card for every inch of tightly held cards. A very minor point is to have a blank card in the front of each tray so that the first card will not become soiled.

One of the signs telling how to use the catalog, which may be purchased from a library supply house, may be placed in a poster holder on top of the catalog if it is a low cabinet, or hung beside it. Be sure that the printed directions fit the catalog.

Some large libraries file cards in the catalog once a week; small libraries may file oftener or less often than this. It is not worthwhile to file a few cards if there will be more tomorrow; if it might be a week or more before there are others, those ready may be filed so that the readers may have the use of these new cards.

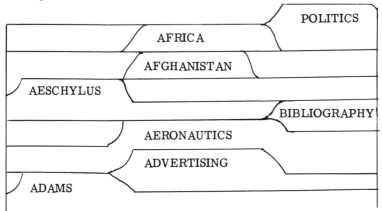

POLITICS

AFRICA

AFGHANISTAN

AESCHYLUS

BIBLIOGRAPHY

AERONAUTICS

ADVERTISING

ADAMS

Before filing cards, they should be sorted into catalog and shelf-list cards, and counted for the library reports.

After this preliminary sorting the cards are arranged for the catalog alphabetically, according to the rules used in this catalog. The next step is to interfile the cards with those already in the catalog trays, leaving the new cards above the rod. Later go over these new cards, making sure that they are in their right alphabetical place. Next pull out the rod and allow the cards to drop into place, locking them in with the rod.

Filing should not be continued for a long period. Since filing cards requires close attention, the eye becomes tired and mistakes are likely to occur. If the same person both files and revises, several hours should elapse between the filing and the revising.

There is no dictionary catalog with all cards filed absolutely alphabetically, word by word or letter by letter. In all catalogs there will be at least a few logical exceptions and in certain areas a chronological or numerical arrangement. Before beginning to file in an unfamiliar catalog, observe what alphabeting code was used. Whatever code has been used, continue to follow it unless it is unsatisfactory, and be sure that the change will be an improvement before deciding to refile an entire catalog.

Rules for Arranging Cards in a Catalog

The rules given below should prove adequate for filing cards in the dictionary catalog of a small library. These

rules are listed by number in the A L A filing rules. [1] Many
of the illustrations in this chapter are from the same source.
If more information on filing catalog cards is desired, it will
be found in this filing code.

There are two fundamental methods of filing alphabetically; namely, word by word and letter by letter.

Word by word filing:	Letter by letter filing:
Book	Book
Book collecting	Bookbinding
Book of English essays	Book collecting
Book of famous ships	Bookish
Book scorpion	Book of English essays
Bookbinding	Book of famous ships
Bookish	Books
Books	Books and reading
Books and reading	Book scorpion
Books that count	Booksellers and booksell-
Booksellers and bookselling	ing
	Books that count

In word by word filing, each word is a unit, and thus
Books that count precedes Booksellers and bookselling, since
Books precedes Booksellers; while in letter by letter filing
no attention is paid to words but each letter is considered.
Thus Books that count follows Booksellers because bookst
follows bookse. To take another example: Book scorpion pre-
cedes Bookbinding in word by word filing as Book precedes
Bookb, but in letter by letter filing Bookbinding precedes
Book scorpion because bookb precedes books.

Basic rule (ALA 2d ed. abr. 1)

"A. Arrange all entries . . . alphabetically according to
the order of the English alphabet. . . .

"B. Arrange word by word, alphabeting letter by letter
within the word. . . . Apply the principle of 'nothing before
something,' considering the space between words as 'nothing.'
. . . When two or more headings begin with the same word,
arrange next by the first different word."

"Every word in the entry is regarded, including articles,
prepositions and conjunctions, but initial articles are disregarded."

I met a man

Image books
Imaginary conversations
In an unknown land
In the days of giants

"C. In a dictionary catalog, interfile all types of entries (author, title, subject, series, etc.) and their related references, in one general alphabet."

Abbreviations (ALA 2d ed. abr. 6)

"A. Arrange abbreviations as if spelled in full in the language of the entry, except Mrs., which is filed as written."

Dr. Jekyll and Mr. Hyde
Doctor Luke
Dr. Norton's wife
Doctors on horseback
Documents of American history

Miss Lulu Bett
Missis Flinders
Mister Abbott
Mr. Emmanuel
Mistress Margaret
Mitchell, Margaret
Mrs. Miniver
Much

St. Denis, Ruth
Saint-Exupéry, Antoine de
Saint Joan
St. Lawrence River
Ste Anne des Monts
Sainte-Beuve, Charles Augustin
Saintsbury, George Edward Bateman

Ampersand (ALA 2d ed. abr. 8)

"B. Arrange the ampersand (&) as 'and,' 'et,' 'und,' etc., according to the language in which it is used."

Aucassin and Nicolete, . . .
Aucassin & Nicolette: an old French love story. . . .
Aucassin et Nicolette, . . .
Aucassin und Nicolette; . . .

Analytical entries

<u>Author</u> (ALA 2d ed. abr. 26)

"B10. Arrange an author analytic by the <u>title of the ana-</u>
<u>lytic.</u> If there are no main entries for the work in the cata-
log, file an author analytic in its alphabetical place, . . . Arrange analytics made in the form of author-title added entries
after main entries for the work, the analytics subarranged by
their main entries. "

   Huxley, Thomas Henry, 1825-1895.
    <u>On a piece of chalk,</u> p. 157-187:
  Law, Frederic Houk, 1871-
   Science in literature . . . .

   Huxley, Thomas Henry, 1825-1895.
    Science and education . . . .

<u>Title</u> (ALA 2d ed. abr. 33)

"B1. . . . Arrange title analytics by the entry for the
analytic if different from the main entry for the whole book. "

   Peabody, Josephine Preston, 1874-1922.
    The piper . . . .

    Peacock pie, v. 2, p. 95-218:
  De la Mare, Walter John, 1873-
    Collected poems . . . .

    Peacock pie.
  De la Mare, Walter John, 1873-
    Peacock pie . . . .

    Peacocks and pagodas.
  Edmonds, Paul.

<u>Subject</u> (ALA 2d ed. abr. 32)

"B. Arrange subject analytics by the entry for the analytic if different from the main entry for the whole book. "

    MASARYK, TOMAS GARRIGUE, PRES. CZECHOSLO-
    VAK REPUBLIC, 1850-1937.
   Masaryk, Jan Garrigue, 1886-1948, p. 337-355:
  Ludwig, Emil, 1881-1948, ed.
    The torch of freedom, edited by Emil Ludwig and Henry B.

Kranz.

> MASARYK, TOMAS GARRIGUE, PRES. CZECHOSLOVAK
>   REPUBLIC, 1850-1937.
> Selver, Paul, 1888-
>   Masaryk, a biography . . . .

Articles (ALA 2d ed. abr. 4)

"A. Disregard an initial article in all languages and
file by the word following it. In English the articles are 'A, '
'An, ' and 'The. ' "

> A apple pie
> Apache
> An April after

> Laski, Harold Joseph
> The last of the Vikings
> LATIN AMERICA

"B. All articles occurring within a title or a heading
are to be regarded, except those that actually are initial articles in an inverted position or at the beginning of a subdivision. "

> Powder River
> Power, Richard Anderson
> POWER (MECHANICS)
> The power of a lie
> Powers, Francis Fountain

> STATE, THE
> STATE AND CHURCH

> AGRICULTURE - U. S.
> AGRICULTURE - THE WEST
> AGRICULTURE - WYOMING

Author entry arrangement (ALA 2d ed. abr. 26)

"B. Works by the author

"1. Alphabet the titles according to the basic rules for
alphabetical arrangement. . . .

"2. Interfile all main and added entries under the same
author heading in one file. Subarrange alphabetically by the

titles of the books.

"3. In both main and added entry headings disregard designations that show the relationship of the heading to one particular work, as 'comp.,' 'ed.,' 'illus.,' 'tr.,' 'joint author' ['editor,' etc.] . . . . "

> Pennell, Joseph, 1857-1926
> The adventures of an illustrator.
>
> Pennell, Joseph, 1857-1926, illus.
> Van Rennselaer, Mariana Griswold
> English cathedrals . . . .
>
> Pennell, Joseph, 1857-1926
> Etchers and etching . . . .
>
> Pennell, Joseph, 1857-1926, joint author
> Pennell, Elizabeth Robins
> The life of James McNeill Whistler.
>
> Pennell, Joseph, 1857-1926
> Our journey to the Hebrides

"4. Arrange different titles that begin with the same words by the title proper, the shorter title before the longer, disregarding any subtitle, alternative title, 'by' phrase, etc. that may follow the shorter title. "

> Auslander, Joseph
> The winged horse; the story of the poets and their poetry.
> The winged horse anthology.

"5. At the beginning of a title the author's name, even in the possessive case, should be disregarded if it is simply an author statement transcribed from the work. However, if the name in the possessive case is the author's pseudonym, or if an author's name is an integral part of the title, do not disregard it in filing. Do not disregard a name other than the author's. "

> Barlow, Peter
> An essay on magnetic attraction
> [Barlow's] tables of squares, cubes, square roots. . . .
> A treatise on the strength of timber . . . .
>
> Shakespeare, William

Selections from Shakespeare.
The Shakespeare apocrypha.
Shakespeare's wit and humor.

✳ "C. Works about the author

"Arrange the subject entries for works about the author
after all entries for works by the author, in two groups" as
follows:

"1. Subjects without subdivision, subarranged by their
main entries, or if an analytic, by the entry for the analytic.

"Exception: An author-title subject entry files in the
author file in its alphabetical place by the title in the heading,
immediately after the author entries for the same title if
there are any.

"2. Subjects with subdivisions, arranged alphabetically
by the subdivisions."

Shakespeare, William, 1564-1616
    The winter's tale.

SHAKESPEARE, WILLIAM, 1564-1616
Alexander, Peter
Shakespeare.

SHAKESPEARE, WILLIAM, 1564-1616
Brandes, Georg Morris Cohen
    William Shakespeare, a critical study.

SHAKESPEARE, WILLIAM, 1564-1616 - BIBLIOG-
    RAPHY
SHAKESPEARE, WILLIAM, 1564-1616 - CHARACTERS
SHAKESPEARE, WILLIAM, 1564-1616, IN FICTION,
    DRAMA, POETRY, ETC.
SHAKESPEARE, WILLIAM, 1564-1616 - NATURAL
    HISTORY

Bible (ALA 2d ed. abr. 29)

✳ "A. Entries for Bible, the sacred book, follow entries
for the single surname Bible."

"B. Arrange Bible entries in straight alphabetical order
word by word, disregarding kind of entry, form of heading, and
punctuation. Under the same author heading subarrange alpha-

betically by titles.

"C. Arrange headings which include a date alphabetically up to the date, then arrange the same heading with different dates chronologically by date. . . .

"D. Arrange different kinds of entries under the same heading in groups in the following order:

"1. Author (main and/or added entry), subarranged alphabetically by titles. . . .

"2. Subject, subarranged alphabetically by main entries."

"F. Numbered books of the Bible follow in numerical order the same name used collectively without number."

```
Bible, Dana Xenophon
Bible
BIBLE. ACTS. see BIBLE. NEW TESTAMENT. ACTS
BIBLE AND SCIENCE
BIBLE - ANTIQUITIES
The Bible in art
Bible.  New Testament.  Corinthians
Bible.  New Testament.  1 Corinthians
Bible.  New Testament.  Matthew
Bible.  Old Testament.  Daniel
Bible.  Old Testament.  Genesis
BIBLE  STORIES
```

Compiler See Author entry arrangement.

Compound proper names (ALA 2d ed. abr. 13)

"Arrange . . . names consisting of two or more separate words, with or without a hyphen . . . as separate words. Alphabet with regard to all words in the name, including articles, conjunctions, and prepositions. . . ."

```
New Jersey
A new way of life
New York
Newark
```

Compound surname entries (ALA 2d ed. abr. 21)

"Interfile compound surname entries alphabetically with the group of titles, etc., following entries for the first part of the name alone as a single surname. "

> Smith, Woodrow
> Smith College
> Smith Hughes, Jack
> Smith-Masters, Margaret Melville
>
> Saint among the Hurons
> Saint-Gaudens,
> St. Petersburg
> Saint Vincent
> San Antonio
> Sanborn
>
> Congresses. See Numerical and chronological arrangement.

Corporate name entries beginning with a surname (ALA 2d ed. abr. 23)

"A. Arrange a corporate name consisting of a surname followed by forenames, etc., in its alphabetical place among the personal names in the surname group. "

> Rand, Edward Kennard
> Rand, Winifred
> Rand McNally and Company (McNally is the surname of
>   a member of the company)
> Randall, John Herman
> Randall-MacIver, David
>
> Wilson, Forrest
> Wilson (The H. W.) Company
> Wilson, James Calmar
> Wilson, Margery

"B. Arrange a corporate name consisting of a surname only, followed by a designation, and compound and phrase names in their alphabetical place in the group of titles, etc., following all surname entries under the same name. "

> Prentice, William Reed
> The prentice
> Prentice-Hall book about inventions
> Prentice-Hall, inc.
> Prentice-Hall world atlas

Editor. See Author entry arrangement

Elisions (ALA 2d ed. abr. 7)

"Arrange elisions, contractions, . . . as written. Do not supply missing letters. Disregard the apostrophe and treat as one word any word or contraction of two words that contains an apostrophe, unless the apostrophe is followed by a space. "

> Who owns America?
> Who reads what?
> Who'd shoot a genius?
> Who's who in American art?
> Whose constitution

Figures. See Numerals.

Forename entries (ALA 2d ed. abr. 25)

"A1. Disregard a numeral following a given name except when necessary to distinguish between given names with the same designation. Arrange first alphabetically by the designation, then when there is more than one numeral, numerically by the numeral. "

"B1. Arrange all given name entries, both single and compound, after the single surname entries of the same name, interfiling alphabetically in the group of titles, etc., beginning with the same word. Alphabet with regard to all designations and words, articles and prepositions included, and disregard punctuation.

"2. When an ordinal numeral follows a given name in a title entry, arrange it as spoken. . . . "

> Charles, William
> Charles Auchester (title)
> Charles Edward, the Young Pretender
> CHARLES FAMILY
> Charles III, King of France
> Charles I, King of Great Britain
> Charles II, King of Great Britain
> Charles the Bold,   see Charles, Duke of Burgundy
> Charles II and his court (Charles the second)
> CHARLES W. MORGAN (SHIP)

Hyphened words (ALA 2d ed. abr. 11)

"A1. Arrange hyphened words as separate words when the parts are complete words. . . ."

Happy home.
Happy-thought hall.
Happy thoughts.

"B. In the case of compound words that appear in the catalog written both as two separate words (or hyphened) and as a single word, interfile all entries, including corporate names, under the one-word form."

Campfire adventure stories
Camp-fire and cotton-field
Camp Fire Girls
The Campfire girls flying around the globe
CAMPFIRE PROGRAMS
CAMPING

Illustrator. See Author arrangement.

Initial articles. See Articles.

Initials (ALA 2d ed. abr. 5)

"A. Arrange initials, single or in combination, as one-letter words, before longer words beginning with the same initial letter, wherever they occur in an entry. Interfile entries consisting of initials plus words with entries consisting of initials only.

"B. Arrange initials standing for names of organizations as initials, not as abbreviations. . . .

"C. Arrange inverted initials standing for authors' names alphabetically with other initials, disregarding the inversion and the punctuation."

A.
A. A.
AAA A
AAA Foundation for Traffic Safety
AAAS Conference on Science Teaching . . . .
A. , A. J. G.
AAUN news

Joint author. See Author arrangement.

Names with a prefix (ALA 2d ed. abr. 14)

"A name with a prefix is one that begins with a separately written particle consisting of an article (e. g., La Crosse), a preposition (e. g., De Morgan), a combination of a preposition and an article (e. g., Del Mar, Van der Veer), or a term which originally expressed relationship (e. g., O'Brien), with or without a space, hyphen, or apostrophe between the prefix and the name.

"A. Arrange proper names with a prefix as one word."

Defoe,
De la Roche,
Delaware
Del Mar, Eugene

El Dorado, Ark.
Eldorado, Neb.

Vanderbilt,
Vanderwalker
Vander Zanden

"B. Arrange names beginning with the prefixes M' and Mc as if written Mac."

McHenry
Machinery
MacHugh
Maclaren, Ian
MacLaren, J
M'Laren, J   Wilson
MacLaren, James

Numerical and chronological arrangement (ALA 2d ed. abr. 36)

"A. A numerical or a chronological arrangement, rather than an alphabetical, should be followed when numbers or dates distinguish between entries, or headings, otherwise identical, with lowest number or earliest date first.

"In relation to other entries in the catalog disregard a numeral or date that indicates a sequence. . . . If the number precedes the item it modifies it must be mentally transposed

to follow the item (i. e., file U. S. Army. 1st Cavalry as
U. S. Army. Cavalry, 1st).

"B. Numerical designations following or at end of titles
that are otherwise identical up to that point."

    More, Paul Elmer
      Shelburne essays. 1st series.
    More, Paul Elmer
      Shelburne essays. Second series.

"C. Corporate headings"

"Dates only"

    Massachusetts. Constitutional Convention, 1779-1780
    Massachusetts. Constitutional Convention, 1853

"Number only"

    U. S. Circuit Court (1st Circuit)
    U. S. Circuit Court (5th Circuit)

"Number and date. Disregard a place name when it follows
a number."

    American Peace Congress, 1st, New York, 1907
    American Peace Congress, 3d, Baltimore, 1911
    American Peace Congress, 4th, St. Louis, 1913

"Place and date. If there is no numeral to indicate a sequence,
the heading being followed only by a place and date in that order, arrange alphabetically by the place, disregarding the date
at the end."

    OLYMPIC GAMES
    Olympic games, Los Angeles, 1932
    Olympic games, Rome, 1960-

"D. Same heading with and without distinguishing numerals or dates."

Arrange as follows: 1. No numerals, no subheadings; 2.
No numerals, interfile all corporate and subject subdivisions
and "longer entries beginning with the same name." 3. With
numerals, but no subheadings. 4. "With numerals, with all
its corporate and subject subdivisions."

    Explorer
    EXPLORER (ARTIFICIAL SATELLITE)

EXPLORER (BALLOON)
EXPLORER II (BALLOON)
An explorer comes home

Ku Klux Klan in American politics
KU KLUX KLAN (1915-   )

United Nations agreements
UNITED NATIONS - BUILDINGS
United Nations Conference on Trade and Employment . . . .
United Nations. Economic Affairs Dept.
UNITED NATIONS - YEARBOOKS
United Nations (1942-1945)

"E. Numerals or dates designating parts of a whole or
inclusive heading. When a series of numerals or dates desig-
nates parts of a whole and there are also alphabetical extensions of the inclusive heading, arrange the alphabetical group
. . ." first.

"Chiefs of state. Disregard the name in parentheses
that follows the dates."

U. S. President, 1801-1809 (Jefferson)
U. S. President, 1953-1961 (Eisenhower)

"Constitutions, charters, etc."

U. S. CONSTITUTION - AMENDMENTS
U. S. Constitution. 1st-10th amendments
U. S. Constitution. 1st amendment
U. S. CONSTITUTION - SIGNERS

"Legislatures"

U. S. CONGRESS - BIOGRAPHY
U. S. Congress. House. Committee on . . . .
U. S. CONGRESS - RULES AND PRACTICE
U. S. Congress. Senate
U. S. 63d Congress, 2d session, 1913-1914. House
U. S. 86th Congress, 1st session, 1959

"Military units."

Military units with distinctive names are arranged alphabetically by their names. Units beginning with a number . . .
are arranged alphabetically by the word following the number,
then numerically by the number. Regard the full name of the

unit but disregard subdivisions or modifications of a unit except in relation to other headings under the unit with the same number.

U. S. Army. A. E. F., 1917-1920
U. S. Army Air Forces. 8th Air Force
U. S. Army Air Forces. Air Service Command
U. S. ARMY - BIOGRAPHY
U. S. Army. 1st Cavalry
U. S. Army. II Corps
U. S. Army. Corps of Engineers

Numerals (ALA 2d ed. abr. 9)

"A. Arrange numerals in the titles of books, corporate names, cross references, etc., as if spelled out in the language of the entry. Spell numerals and dates as they are spoken, placing 'and' before the last element in compound numbers in English, except in a decimal fraction where the 'and' must be omitted."

EGYPT.
1848: chapters of German history.
Ekblaw, Sidney E.
ELECTRIC BATTERIES

Nilson, Arthur Reinhold.
1940: our finest hour.
1939: how the war began.
99 stanzas European.
Norcross, Carl.

On borrowed time.
ONE-ACT PLAYS
100, 000, 000 allies--if we choose.
One hundred non-royalty one-act plays
One man caravan.
1001 mechanical facts made easy.
1000 questions and answers on T. B.
O'Neill, Eugene Gladstone.
OPERA.

⁕   "B. Arrange a numeral following a given name in a title as if spelled out in the language of . . . the title, as spoken. In English the numeral is read as an ordinal preceded by 'the.' " See also Forename entries.

The Henry James reader
Henry V, King of England, 1387-1422   (Henry King of
                                                England, 5)
Henry VIII, King of England, 1491-1547 (Henry King of
                                                England, 8)

    Henry VIII   (Henry the Eighth)
    Shakespeare, William

    Henry V   (Henry the Fifth)
    Shakespeare, William

"C. Arrange the names of classes of aircraft, boats,
etc., in which a numeral is an integral part of the heading
alphabetically as spoken. "

    B. F. V.
    B-58 BOMBER
    B. G.
    B-17 BOMBER
    Baab, August

✕ Order of entries (ALA 2d ed. abr. 19)

"A. When the same word or combination of words, is
used as the heading of different kinds of entry, arrange the
entries in two main groups. . . .

"Single surname entries, arranged alphabetically by
forenames.

"All other entries, arranged alphabetically word by
word, disregarding kind of entry, form of heading, and punctuation.

"B. Arrange subject entries under a personal or corporate name immediately after the author entries for the
same name.

✕ "C. Interfile title added entries and subject entries that
are identical and subarrange alphabetically by their main entries. "

    Love, John L.
    LOVE, JOHN L.
    Love, William

Love
Bowen, Elizabeth

LOVE
Magoun, F. Alexander

Love and beauty
LOVE POETRY
LOVE - QUOTATIONS, MAXIMS, ETC.
LOVE (THEOLOGY)
Love your neighbor

Place arrangement (ALA 2d ed. abr. 31)

"A. Entries beginning with a geographical name follow
the same name used as a single surname.

"B. Arrange all entries beginning with the same geographical name in one straight alphabetical file, word by word,
disregarding punctuation. . . .

"C. Arrange different kinds of entries under the same
geographical name heading in groups . . . " as follows:

"1. Author (main and/or added entry) without subheading, subarranged by titles. . . .

"2. Subject without subdivision, and identical title added
entries, interfiled and subarranged alphabetically by their main
entries.

"3. Heading with corporate and/or subject subdivisions
. . . interfiled alphabetically with each other and with titles,
etc., disregarding punctuation; each corporate author heading
followed by its own subject entries.

"D. Arrange headings for the official governmental divisions of a place (i. e., bureaus, committees, departments,
etc.) by the first [distinctive] word of the subheading. . . . "

U. S.   Dept. of Agriculture
U. S.   Bureau of Education

"E. Different places, jurisdictions, and governments of
the same name are alphabeted by the geographical or parenthetical designations following the names. Arrangement is first
by the complete designation, then under each different heading

according to the general rules . . . above."

United States
UNITED STATES
U. S. Adjutant-General's Office
U. S. - ADJUTANT-GENERAL'S OFFICE
U. S. Agricultural Adjustment Administration
The United States among the nations
United States Steel Corporation
U. S. - TERRITORIAL EXPANSION

New York Academy of Medicine
New York and the Seabury investigation
New York (City) Health Dept.
NEW YORK (CITY) - HEALTH DEPT.
New York (City) Police Dept.
NEW YORK (CITY) - POOR
New York (Colony)
New York (County) Court House Board
New York (State)
NEW YORK (STATE) - GEOLOGY
New York Edison Company
New York tribune.

Lincoln, William Sever
Lincoln and Ann Rutledge
LINCOLN CO., KY.
Lincoln, Eng.
LINCOLN HIGHWAY
Lincoln, Neb.
Lincoln plays

London, Jack
LONDON - DESCRIPTION
London, Ky.
London, Ont. Council

California as I saw it
California, Mo.
CALIFORNIA, SOUTHERN
California State Chamber of Commerce
California. University. Library
California. University. School of law
California. University. University at Los Angeles

GERMANY - BIBLIOGRAPHY
Germany. Constitution

Germany (Democratic Republic)
GERMANY (DEMOCRATIC REPUBLIC) - ECONOMIC CON-
   DITIONS
GERMANY - DESCRIPTION AND TRAVEL
Germany divided
GERMANY, EASTERN
Germany (Territory under Allied occupation, 1945-1955)

Possessive case. See Punctuation marks.

Prefixes. See Names with a prefix.

Publisher. See Corporate name entries.

Punctuation marks (ALA 2d ed. abr. 3)

"Disregard punctuation marks that are part of a title
or corporate name."

"For punctuation in relation to order of entries under
the same word, see Order of entries, Rule 19, and the specific rules for name entries, author and subject arrangement,
etc."

Boys' book of photography
Boys' life of Will Rogers
Boys' Odyssey
Boys of 1812
Boys will be boys

Life
Life--a bowl of rice
"Life after death"
Life, its true genesis
Life! physical and spiritual

References (ALA 2d ed. abr. 35)

"A. A reference or explanatory note precedes all other
entries under the same word or words. In relation to other
entries in the catalog consider only the heading on a . . .
reference or explanatory note; disregard the words [see] and
[see also] the heading or headings referred to, and the
note."

"B2. If a see reference is the same as an actual entry, arrange the see reference first, except that a surname

entry always precedes a reference. "

    Corea, Lois Fleming
    COREA,   see KOREA

✳ "C. File a see also reference before the first entry under the same word or words. "

    CHILDREN,   see also . . . .
    CHILDREN
    CHILDREN - CARE AND HYGIENE,   see also
    CHILDREN - CARE AND HYGIENE
    CHILDREN - CARE AND HYGIENE - BIBLIOGRAPHY

Subject arrangement (ALA 2d ed. abr. 32)

"A. Subject entries follow the same word used as a single surname.

"B. Arrange entries with the same subject heading alphabetically by their main entries, then by title. Arrange subject analytics by the entry for the analytic if different from the main entry for the whole book. "

    BISON, AMERICAN
    Allen, Joel Asaph
        The American bisons, living and extinct.

        BISON, AMERICAN
        Anderson, George S.
    Roosevelt, Theodore
        American big-game hunting

"C. Arrange a subject, its subdivisions, etc., in groups . . . " as follows:

"Subject without subdivision, interfiled . . . alphabetically by their main entries.

"Period divisions, arranged chronologically. . . .

"Alphabetical extensions of the main subject heading: form, subject, and geographical subdivisions, inverted subject headings, subject followed by a parenthetical term, and phrase subject headings, interfiled word by word in one alphabet with titles and other headings beginning with the same word, disregarding punctuation. "

    MASS (MUSIC)

Mass of the Roman rite
MASS (PHYSICS)
MASS - STUDY AND TEACHING

U. S. - HISTORY - REVOLUTION
U. S. - HISTORY - 1783-1865[2]
U. S. - HISTORY - 1783-1809
U. S. - HISTORY - WAR OF 1812
U. S. - HISTORY - CIVIL WAR
U. S. - HISTORY - BIBLIOGRAPHY
U. S. history bonus book
U. S. - HISTORY - SOURCES
U. S. - IMMIGRATION AND EMIGRATION

Title entry arrangement (Pittsburgh, modified)[3]

Title entries are arranged alphabetically, considering each word in turn; the initial article is disregarded, but all other articles and prepositions are to be regarded.

In an unknown land.
In and out of the old missions of California.
In and under Mexico.
In the Amazon jungle.
In the days of the giants.
In the days of the guilds.
In this our life.
In tidewater Virginia.

Why Europe fights.
Why I believe in religion.
Why the chimes rang.
Why the weather.

Translator. See Author entry arrangement.

Umlaut (ALA 2d ed. abr. 2)

"Disregard . . . umlauts. "

Muellen, Abraham
Mullen, Allen
Müllen, Gustav
Mullen, Pat

United States. See Place arrangement; Subject arrangement.

Words spelled in different ways (ALA 2d ed. abr. 10)

"When different entries, including corporate names, begin with or contain the same word spelled in different ways (e. g. , Color and Colour) choose one spelling, according to the criteria given . . . [below] and file all entries under that spelling. "

1. Generally "choose the most commonly accepted current usage. "

2. "When there is a choice between the American and English spellings, choose the American. "

LABOR CONTRACT
Labor in America.
LABOR LAWS AND LEGISLATION
Labour production of the cotton textile industry.
Labor supply.

Refer from the other spellings.

Words written in different ways (ALA 2d ed. abr. 11)

"A. Arrange hyphened words as separate words when the parts are complete words. . . . "

An epoch in life insurance
Epoch-making papers in United States history
The epoch of reform

"Arrange as two words compound words that are written as two separate words.

"Arrange as one word compound words that are written as one.

"B. In the case of compound words that appear in the catalog written both as two separate words (or hyphened) and as a single word, interfile all entries, including corporate names, under the one-word form. "

SEA-POWER
Sea power in the machine age
Seapower in the nuclear age
Sea-power in the Pacific
Search

References

1. A L A Rules for Filing Catalog Cards. Prepared by the A L A Editorial Committee's Subcommittee on the A L A Rules for Filing Catalog Cards, Pauline A. Seely, Chairman and Editor. (2d ed. abr. Chicago, American Library Association, 1968), cited in this chapter as ALA 2d ed. abr. with the number of the rule.

2. Inclusive periods file before subordinate periods.

3. Pittsburgh, Carnegie Library, Rules for Filing Cards (5th ed. ; Pittsburgh, Carnegie Library, 1932), p. 31.

Chapter XII
Related Topics and Miscellaneous Information

Introduction. For the librarian of the small library who has not yet found it feasible to participate in a centralized processing and cataloging center there are a few closely related matters about which some information may be helpful. With a staff of one or possibly two, ordering, accessioning, classifying, cataloging, and preparing books for circulation are so closely associated that they are thought of almost as one process. This chapter contains some practical hints regarding these processes.

Acquisition of the books. The books are usually selected and ordered by the librarian, although a committee of the board of a public library may make suggestions. In most schools the librarian prepares the order but it is sent out by the principal, superintendent, or school purchasing office. When the books and the bill are received, the bill is checked with the books to be sure that the titles and editions received are those which were ordered. Some librarians write the name of the dealer from whom the book is purchased, the date it is received, and the cost in the inner margin of the book on the right-hand page following the title page, writing it parallel to the sewing of the book. This information is useful when one is examining a book with reference to having it rebound, or to seeing how long it has been in the library when one is checking its use with the time it has been available for circulation.

Weeding the book collection. Before beginning to classify and catalog an old library, weed the collection, removing books that are out of date, worn out, unsuitable for that particular library, have very poor print, or have been superseded by a better book. In doing this it is well for the inexperienced librarian to seek the guidance of a trained and experienced librarian, or to check with the best printed book selection aids in the field represented in that library. Books that need mending or rebinding should be put in good physical condition before being cataloged.

Mechanical processes. After checking the bill for a new book, one should cut the pages and open the book correctly,

i. e., take a few pages at the front and at the back alternate-
ly and press them down gently against the covers, until the
middle of the book is reached. This makes it easier to open
and read the book and minimizes the danger of breaking its
back.

The next step is to put in the mark of ownership, which
usually means stamping certain pages of the book with an em-
bossing, perforating, or rubber stamp that gives the name of
the library. Stamp the page following the title page and a certain arbitrary right-hand page, e. g., page 89. If book plates
are used, they are pasted on the inside of the front cover and
no stamp is necessary.

Accessioning. The A. L. A. Glossary of Library Terms[1]
defines the term, accession, as "To record books and other
similar material added to the library in the order of acquisition." The accession number is a serial number given to
each bound volume as it is added to the library. The lines
in an accession record are numbered consecutively, beginning
with one. A brief description of the book follows and the number on this line is written in the book, on the shelf-list card,
book card, and book pocket. Some libraries have no accession
book, but do have an accession number. They use a numbering machine and number each book as it is added to the library. The source of the book, its date of acquisition, and
its cost are the only information which the accession book
gives that the shelf list ordinarily does not, hence these three
items may be added to the shelf-list cards instead of keeping
an accession book. An accession number is useful in identifying books, e. g., number 1312 means a particular book, even
a certain copy or volume. The accession number shows the
number of books which have been added to the library, either
within a given period or the total number, keeping in mind
that some books have been withdrawn from the library. A
count of the shelf-list cards before filing, however, enables
the librarian to keep any necessary record of the number of
books or other materials added to the library, without the
duplication of records involved in an accession book, and
these statistics will appear in the monthly or annual reports.
Even if the library has always kept an accession record it
may be discontinued at any given date and the accession numbers on books, shelf-list cards, etc., ignored. The two reasons most commonly given for keeping an accession record
are (1) that a card, i. e., a shelf-list card, may be more
easily lost than a book; and (2) that if the library receives
books from different funds, the accession record is a conven-

ient record of this.

Most libraries have abandoned the accession book and many, the accession number as well. M. B. Wiese, [2] Director of Library Services, Baltimore Public Schools, states that accession numbers are no longer used, copy numbers are sufficient identification. But V. J. Aceto[3] in his survey of central processing in New York State found that seventeen centers assigned accession numbers and fourteen of these centers used the accession book. Esther Piercy[4] reminds librarians considering not having an accession book to check its possible requirement by law or established policy.

If an accession record is to be used write in the accession book under the proper column heading: (1) the date of the bill of the book, or if there is no bill, the date on which the book is being accessioned; (2) the author heading as found on the title page; (3) the brief title of the book; (4) the publisher's name in abbreviated form as on the catalog card; (5) the date from the title page, or, if none, the copyright date; (6) the volume number; (7) the name of the dealer through whom the book was purchased; and (8) the cost of the book to the library. These are the essential items for an accession record. Follow rules for cataloging in giving the title, capitalizing, etc. If the book is a gift, give the donor's name instead of the dealer's, and use the word gift instead of cost. Use ditto marks--one ditto mark to a column--where items for successive books are the same. Give the date of accessioning (month, day, and year) on the top line of each page of the accession book. If a page is not filled during one day, give the new date on the line for the first entry made later. This accession number is written in each volume or copy of the book on the first right-hand page after the title page, in the center of the lower margin about one inch from the bottom, or as nearly in this place as possible considering the printing on the page. The accession number should also be written on one other page, e. g., the page which is stamped with the name of the library. By means of the accession number one can turn at once to the description of the book in the accession record.

Cataloging routine. The first step in the cataloging process is to order the cards if the printed cards of the Library of Congress or of the H. W. Wilson Company are used. If printed cards are not used, the first step is to classify and assign subject headings, processes described in Chapters I and II. In either case, as soon as the classification number is de-

termined, it should be written in pencil on the page following
the title page, about one inch from the top of the page and
one inch from the hinge of the book. If the number is placed
too close to the top or the hinge, it may be cut off if the
book is rebound.

The next step is to decide on the form of the heading
for the main entry and for other added entries besides subject entries. Check with the name authority file or the catalog to insure consistency in headings and search the aids if
the name is new to the catalog and there is no printed card
for the book. If book numbers, which are discussed in Chapter I, are used, they are assigned as soon as the heading
for the main entry is determined. The book number is written below the classification number on the page following the
title page. If there are printed cards, they are checked with
the book to be sure they match; and if there are no printed
cards, the items to be included on the cards are decided upon.

The third step is to type the main card, or a cataloger's slip, including the tracing for the added cards; or, to
add the headings and call number and make any changes
which may be necessary on the printed cards. If there are
no printed cards, the added entry cards and the shelf-list
card are typed or otherwise reproduced and revised. Duplicating machines for making added entry catalog cards, etc., release time for other work of the library, but they are expensive for the small library. If the library cannot afford a duplicating machine for its exclusive use, possibly it can use one
belonging to another department of the city or state government, or to another department of the organization in the case
of special libraries of associations, commercial firms, etc.
When cards are typed each card has to be revised for accuracy, but mechanically reproduced cards are exactly like
the master card or copy. Consult your state library or state
department of education regarding duplicating machines or
commercial card reproduction centers who may be able to
reproduce your catalog cards correctly, quickly, and less
expensively than having them typed in your library. The
small library as well as the large library should constantly
be on the alert for new technological methods.

The book card and the book pocket are made at the
same time as the catalog and shelf-list cards. The book card
should have the call number in the upper left-hand corner, the
accession number (if one is used) in the upper right-hand cor-

ner; the surname of the author or full heading, if a corporate
author, on the line below the call number, and the title below
that. Indent the first letter of the title to the third space to
the right, to make both author and title more prominent.

When an added copy is acquired by the library, it is
only necessary to remove the shelf-list card from the tray
and add the accession number (or the source, date, and cost
of the new copy) and refile the card, since no change is made
on the catalog cards. On the other hand, when another volume is added to the library, notation of the new volume must
be added to the catalog cards as well as to the shelf-list card.
When a new edition is added, it is necessary to catalog it as
a new book, except that the same classification number and,
as a rule, the same subject headings will be used for the new
edition as for the old one.

After each new book order is cataloged, or once a week
in a library buying books continuously, the catalog and shelf-
list cards should be sorted, counted, and recorded for the annual report. They are then filed above the rod in the catalog
and shelf list respectively, the filing is revised, the rod pulled
out, and the cards dropped and locked in the trays.

Marking the spines of books. Books of nonfiction should
have their call numbers written on the backs for greater convenience in locating a given book or in returning it to the
shelf. If the library participates in the service of a centralized processing and cataloging center the books may come to
the library with the call number already on the spine of the
book or spine labels may be provided for the individual library to apply to the book. Otherwise the library should adopt
a simple, inexpensive system for marking books on the spine,
such as the one described below.

The call number should be placed at the same distance
from the bottom of all books for the sake of ease in locating
books and the appearance of the shelves. A stiff card with
this distance marked on it should be used as a guide. One
and a half inches from the bottom of the book usually avoids
any printing and is a convenient height. The process of marking may be outlined as follows:

1. Mark the place to be occupied by the call number,
   noting the exact place where each line begins if the
   call number consists of two lines.

2. Remove the sizing by painting over the spot with ace-

tone or book lacquer.

3. Write the call number in white ink or with an electric stylus and transfer paper at the place marked. For light colored books use black ink or dark transfer paper.

4. Cover the lettering with a thin coat of book lacquer. Some libraries prefer to cover the entire book with lacquer as it also serves as an insecticide.

Make the figures of the call number vertical and round not angular, so that they may be easily read and so that there may be less variation when the lettering is done by different workers.

Check list of preparation process if the work is done locally.

Librarian:	1. Check books with the bill.
Clerical assistant:	2. Write in each book the name of the dealer, date received in the library, and cost. (This step may be omitted.)
	3. Cut pages.
	4. Open correctly.
	5. Stamp with mark of ownership unless book plate is used.
	6. Accession. (This process may be omitted.)
Librarian:	7. Order printed cards. (Many libraries order the printed cards, especially for new books known to be in print, when they order the book.)
	8. Classify and assign subject headings, making note of them on a slip. (If printed cards are available, compare suggested classification number and headings with the shelf list and library's record of subject headings.)
	9. Decide upon the added entries other than subject entries.
	10. Determine heading for author and such added entries as editor, translator, illustrator. (If printed cards are used,

compare forms of names with those
in catalog or name authority list.)

11. Adapt printed cards or type main
card and shelf-list card.

12. Revise these typed cards.

Clerical assistant: 13. Type added cards, book card, and
items on book pocket.

Librarian: 14. Revise typed cards and book pocket.

Clerical assistant: 15. Paste in book pocket, date slip, and
book plate (if used).

16. Mark book on spine, put book card in
pocket, and put book out for use.

Librarian: 17. Sort cards and count for annual report.

Clerical assistant: 18. File cards in shelf-list and catalog
trays above rod.

Librarian: 19. Revise filing and lock cards in trays.

Withdrawals. When a book is added to the library it is
noted in various records; when it is withdrawn from the library, those records must be changed. This is not done, however, for a year as the book may return. If, for instance, a
book wears out and is to be replaced by a new copy, note is
made on the shelf-list card that the particular copy has been
withdrawn from the library, and note is made of the addition
of the new copy. Since the catalog cards do not show how
many copies of a given title are in the library, withdrawing a
book does not affect the catalog so long as other copies remain. If, however, there is only one copy of the book and it
is not to be replaced, the catalog cards must be taken out of
the catalog, and the shelf-list card (after having the withdrawal note, the abbreviation W and the date, written on it, e. g.,
"W 5-17-67") must also be removed from the shelf list. Some
libraries give the cause, e. g., "W 5-17-67 Worn out. " If one
wishes to make a study of the number of books being lost by
borrowers, being worn out, etc., with reference to a possible
change in policy, it is worthwhile to include in the note the
cause of the withdrawal. This note may be made only as long
as it is needed to show the chief cause or causes of withdrawals. It is unnecessary to continue this additional information indefinitely.

If it is a volume which is being withdrawn, note should

be made, usually in pencil, on the catalog card that such and such a volume is lacking. If it is to be replaced as soon as it can be secured, this penciled note can be easily erased when the new copy of the missing volume is added to the library.

Occasionally it will happen that the book being withdrawn is the only one entered under that name, under that subject, etc. If that is the case, not only should the catalog cards and the shelf-list card be removed, but the name or subject cross references to and from these headings and the corresponding cards in the name and subject authority files should be withdrawn. If a book is to be replaced as soon as funds are available or if it is lost but there is the possibility of its being found, the cards may be withdrawn from the files, properly labeled, and put aside to be used later.

If there are more copies or volumes in the library, after making the proper withdrawal note on the shelf-list card, refile the card in the shelf list.

If the book withdrawn is the only copy or volume, the shelf-list card for that book, with the withdrawal note on it, should be filed alphabetically by author in a special file called a withdrawal file. This file will be found a great convenience when some question comes up as to what has become of a book, whether or not the library ever had a copy, etc. The cards do not need to be kept indefinitely, but might well be kept for five years.

A count of books withdrawn is to be made, just as the count of books added is made. The annual report should show the number of books in the library at the beginning of the year for which the report is being made, the number added during that period, the number withdrawn, and the number in the library at the end of the year.

All library marks of ownership should be removed or "Withdrawn by--(name of library)" should be written or stamped in the book before selling it for old paper or giving it away. Some libraries are governed by definite laws affecting disposal of books.

The first time that a book is withdrawn, the policy should be carefully worked out, note made of the procedure to be followed, and a withdrawal file set up.

Where to catalog. The smallest library should have a
place in which to catalog, even though it is only a desk or
a table in a corner. Have shelves nearby on which may be
kept the necessary cataloging tools and aids and the books
to be cataloged. Label these shelves, so that it will be possible to tell at a glance what stage of preparation the books
are in. Leave any unfinished work clearly marked so that it
may be resumed with a minimum loss of time. A quarter of
an hour or half an hour may be used advantageously to mark
ten books on the back, to order printed cards, or the like.
The longer periods may be used for determining the form
of the author's name, classifying and assigning subject headings, or typing the main cards. The added cards can be typed by any good typist if he is given adequate instruction and
supervision at first.

Cataloging supplies. A few suggestions as to the supplies which will be found necessary in cataloging a collection
as described in this manual may prove useful.

Accession record book. Any of the simplified accession
record books which are sold by Demco, [5] Gaylord, [6] Library
Bureau[7] to mention only three of the older, well-known firms,
will be found satisfactory. A loose-leaf accession book, which
may be used on a typewriter, is preferable. Accession books
are listed according to the number of lines they contain. As
each volume in the library requires one line, the number of
lines desired depends upon the number of volumes on hand
and the approximate number that will be added in the next two
or three years.

Catalog cards. Cards of the same quality may be used
for the shelf list and for the catalog. Medium-weight cards
are best as they are strong enough to stand the wear, without
taking up unnecessary room or adding unnecessary weight to
the card cabinets. The medium weight is similar to that of
the printed cards, and for that reason is much more satisfactory if the library uses printed cards in addition to its own.
It pays to buy the best catalog cards, and it is important to
use only one kind so that all the cards in the catalog will be
of the same size and thickness and, therefore, can be handled
more quickly in the trays. For fiction at least three cards
for each book, namely, author, title, and shelf list, will be
necessary. For nonfiction, if many analytical entries are made,
an average of five cards for each book is the minimum number to count on. Catalog cards come in boxes of 500 or 1000
and cost less if bought in this or larger numbers.

Medium-weight cards, number 263-2, unruled, from Demco; medium-weight cards, number 311, unruled, from Gaylord; and medium-weight cards, number 33020CM, unruled, from the Library Bureau are the most suitable cards.

Catalog guide cards. Guide cards should be inserted at intervals of about an inch. Satisfactory plain buff guide cards, punched for a catalog tray rod, cut in thirds or halves (i. e., the tab is one-third or one-half the width of the cards) may be purchased in packages of one hundred, five hundred, or one thousand.

Demco's angle tab guides, cut in halves, catalog numbers 644-L, left hand position; 644-R right hand position; 644-C center position which may be ordered in quantities of twenty-five, one hundred, five hundred or one thousand are good. In ordering specify the number of each position desired. Black Snap-out Labels are furnished with guides number 669-G or printed headings may be ordered, e. g., number 661-G, 383 headings suitable for a school library catalog, number 662-G, 683 headings suitable for a public library; number 663-G, 2060 headings suitable for a public or a college library. Eight hundred and six supplementary headings suitable for a Catholic school or college library are also available.

Gaylord's tilted tab catalog guides, number 305, have left, right, and center position tabs and the purchaser should specify the quantity of each desired. Blank labels for typing headings are included for each guide. Gaylord also has printed headings for these guides: 425-S, 250 headings for a school library; 425-L, 550 headings for a public library; and 425-P, 2, 000 headings for a public or a college library.

The Library Bureau has angle tab visible name guides, number 45529. 1CM. Strips of scored inserts are supplied with the guides. The Library Bureau also has pre-printed guide inserts for these guides in sets. The catalog numbers are: 187L-1000; 187L-5000; and 187L-11, 000. The blank inserts come in sheets, 187B.

Demco, Gaylord, and the Library Bureau have sets of shelf-list guide cards for libraries using the Dewey Decimal Classification. Demco has number 638 "Long Life" white fibre, number 640 of gray pressboard and 640-C buff with celluloid tabs giving the ten main guide headings; sets of one hundred, number 639 "Long Life" white fibre and number 641 gray pressboard with plain tabs. Gaylord has number 91 of

pressboard, a set of ten guides; or number 91.1 a set of one
hundred guides. Catalog number 491.1 are one hundred headings to be used with their shelf-list guides. When ordering
specify ten center, fifty left, and forty right position tabs. The
Library Bureau has number 431-10 SL, a set of ten guides on
buff stock printed with the ten main Decimal classification
numbers and headings. All tabs are center position and cel-
luloided. The Library Bureau also has a set of 100 guides on
buff stock one-half cut tabs in left and right positions, cellu-
loided, number 431-100SL.

Miscellaneous supplies. If extension cards for the catalog are to be tied to the first card, use heavy linen thread,
which may be purchased at any department store.

The special supplies needed for marking call numbers
on the spine of the books are an electric pencil or an electric stylus and transfer paper, which may be obtained from
Demco, Gaylord, or the Library Bureau. Transfer paper may
be secured in white, black, or dark blue. Use the white on
dark colored books, the dark paper on light colored books.
Call numbers may also be put on the spine with white ink;
black ink is used on the light colored books. Demco has
"Radiant White Ink" and Higgins India Ink; Gaylord has white
ink and Higgins' Black Engrossing Ink. A bottle of acetone is
needed to remove the sizing from the back of the book before
applying the ink; and a bottle of book lacquer to put over the
ink when it is dry. Demco, Gaylord and Library Bureau have
book lacquer. Any good pen point, the type depending upon
the choice of the person doing the lettering, is satisfactory.
Usually a bowl pointed pen is preferred.

A good steel eraser or a razor blade with a bar top
with which to erase words, or more especially letters, is a
necessity. Gaylord, Library Bureau, and Demco have steel
erasers. A good bar pencil and ink eraser is also very useful, as well as a typewriter eraser.

A typewriter is a necessity in any library for the typing
of cards for the books and other material for which printed
cards are not available, for typing book orders and business
letters, and for typing book lists, etc. Get a good standard
typewriter, e.g., Royal, having a removable platen with an
immovable steel strip the length of the platen. Buy an additional platen for use in typing letters, lists, etc. If subject
headings are to be in red, bichrome typewriter ribbons will
be necessary. Elite type is best.

Card catalog cabinets. Although there are many firms making card catalog cabinets, it pays to get the best, such as those manufactured by Demco, Gaylord, and the Library Bureau, whose catalog cabinets are especially well adapted for library use. These firms have cabinets varying in size from one to sixty trays, and their catalogs give an estimate of the number of cards which the cabinets of different sizes will hold. Knowing the number of books in the library and the approximate number of new books added each year, one can easily decide by counting five cards to a book the size of cabinet needed.

Card catalog cabinets should have standard trays and should be purchased from the same firm so that they will match exactly and so that the trays will be interchangeable when cards are shifted with the expansion of the catalog. Each tray should have a follower-block to hold the cards erect when the tray is only partially filled, and a rod which runs through the holes in the cards and locks them into the tray. It is also very important to have the cards fit the tray exactly so that they will stand straight, drop in easily, and remain in alignment for the rod. The three firms mentioned have trays which meet these requirements. Catalog trays should be only two-thirds full if the cards are to be consulted easily. The shelf-list cards may be filed in one or more trays of a catalog cabinet.

If the library can afford it, the sectional cabinet is best, as added units are less expensive than the same number of trays in a separate cabinet and the sections fit together and form one cabinet. If as many as eight or nine trays are needed or will be needed relatively soon, it will pay to buy the sectional catalog cabinet, which may be bought in units of five, ten, or fifteen trays from Gaylord or Library Bureau. The same base and top will serve for several units.

References

1. A. L. A. Glossary of Library Terms (Chicago, American Library Association, 1943).

2. The Southeastern Librarian 11:232-241 (Fall, 1961).

3. V. J. Aceto, "Panacea or Pandora's Box? A Look at Central Processing in New York State," Library Journal 89:322-324 (Jan. 15, 1964).

4. Esther J. Piercy, Commonsense Cataloging (New York, Wilson, 1965), p. 14.

5. Demco, Madison, Wis.

6. Gaylord Bros., Inc., Syracuse, N. Y., and Stockton, Calif.

7. Library Bureau, Remington Rand, Inc., New York, N. Y.

Appendix I
Sample Catalog Cards

I. Wilson printed catalog cards

96. Main entry

---

551   Gamow, George
       A planet called earth. Viking 1963
       257p illus maps

       Replaces the author's: Biography of the earth,
first published 1941
       The author discusses "the history of the
earth to its eventual death, the beginning and
evolution of life, and the most recent discover-
ies in the sciences." Bk Buyer's Guide

       1 Earth 2 Geology 3 Universe I Title   551
       63W11, 913   (W) The H. W. Wilson
                                    Company

---

97. Subject card with heading printed on

      GEOLOGY

551   Gamow, George
       A planet called earth. Viking 1963
       257p illus maps

       Replaces the author's: Biography of the
earth, first published 1941
       The author discusses "the history of the
earth to its eventual death, the beginning and
evolution of life, and the most recent dis-
coveries in the sciences." Bk Buyer's Guide

---

98. Added entry for title

         A planet called earth

551   Gamow, George
         A planet called earth. Viking 1963
         257p illus maps

         Replaces the author's: Biography of the
       earth, first published 1941
         The author discusses "the history of the
       earth to its eventual death, the beginning and
       evolution of life, and the most recent discov-
       eries in the sciences. " Bk Buyer's Guide

---

99. Shelf-list card

---

551   Gamow, George
         A planet called earth. Viking 1963
         257p illus maps

         1 Earth 2 Geology 3 Universe I Title   551

         63W11, 913   (W) The H. W. Wilson
                                            Company

II. Library of Congress printed catalog cards

100. Main entry

---

309. 22
W62   Whittlesey, Susan.
           U. S. Peace Corps, the challenge of good
       will. New York, Coward-McCann [1963]
           120 p. illus., ports. 22 cm. (Challenge
       books; eye witness reports)
           Bibliography: p. 116-117.

                    1. U. S. Peace Corps.

       HC60. 5. W47   309. 2206173 63—10181
           Library of Congress   [67q7]

---

101. Added entry for subject

---

309. 22   U. S. - PEACE CORPS
W62   Whittlesey, Susan.
            U. S. Peace Corps, the challenge of good
        will. New York, Coward-McCann [1963]
            120 p. illus., ports. 22 cm. (Challenge
        books; eye witness reports)
            Bibliography: p. 116-117.

                    1. U. S. Peace Corps.

        HC60. 5. W47   309. 2206173   63—10181
            Library of Congress [67q7]

---

102. Shelf-list card

```
309. 22
W62     Whittlesey, Susan.
            U. S. Peace Corps, the challenge of good
        will. New York, Coward-McCann [1963]
            120 p. illus., ports. 22 cm. (Challenge
        books; eye witness reports)
            Bibliography: p. 116-117.
B. & T.    1-30-68    $4. 50
            1. U. S. Peace Corps.
        HC60. 5. W47              309.2206173     63—10181
        Library of Congress     [67q7]
```

III. Main entries

103. Main entry under pseudonym

```
        Scipio, pseud.
            Emergent Africa. With a foreword by
        Philip E. Mosely. Boston, Houghton Mifflin,
        1965.
            191, [1]p. map. 21 cm.
            "The Charter of the Organization of Afri-
        can Unity": p. 181-[192]

            1. Africa, Sub-Saharan--Politics.   I. Or-
        ganization of African Unity. Charter.  II. Title.
        DT352. S354              309. 16          65—15153
        Library of Congress     [3]
```

104. Compound surname without hyphen

García Lorca, Federico, 1898-1936.
    The gypsy ballads; translated by Rolfe
Humphries, with 3 historical ballads.
Bloomington, Indiana University Press, 1953.
    64p. 24 cm. (Indiana University poetry
series)

    I. Title.

PQ6613.A763P72   861.6   53—9826 rev

Library of Congress   [r64h 1/2]

---

105. Married woman's name--maiden name in parentheses

Gilbert, Katharine (Everett) 1886-1952.
    A history of esthetics, by Katharine
Everett Gilbert and Helmut Kuhn. Rev. and
enl. Bloomington, Indiana University Press,
1953.

    xxi, 613 p. 22 cm.

    Includes bibliographies.

    1. Aesthetics--Hist. I. Kuhn, Helmut,
1899-   joint author.

BH81.G5 1953   *101 701.17 53—7022

Library of Congress [65w 1/2]

---

106. Nobleman entered under his title

Chorley, Robert Samuel Theodore Chorley,
    baron, 1895-
        Shipping law, by Lord Chorley and O. C.
    Giles. 5th ed. London, I. Pitman [1963]

        xxiv, 376 p. 23cm.

        1. Maritime law--Gt. Brit. I. Giles,
    Otto Charles Felix William, joint author.
    II. Title.
                                        67—1114

        Library of Congress   [2]

107. Real name as entry with pseudonym in title

Norway, Nevil Shute, 1899-1960.
        Stephen Morris [by] Nevil Shute [pseud.]
    New York, Morrow, 1961.

        303 p. 21 cm.

        I. Title.

    PZ3. N83St   61—12980‡

        Library of Congress   [15]

108. Personal name heading with unused forename

Bate, H   Maclear, 1908-
    South Africa without prejudice. London,
Laurie [1956]
    206 p. illus. 22 cm.

      1. Africa, South--Pol. & govt. --1909-
I Title.

DT779. B34   968   56—3139$^+$
Library of Congress   [2]

109. Government publication--government agency as author

    Gt. Brit. Ministry of Housing and Local
      Government.
      Cars in housing. London, H. M. S. O.,
    1966-

      v. illus., col. plans, tables. 30 cm.
    (Its Design bulletin 10 v. 1: 12/6
                   (v. 1: B 66—23344)
      Bibliography: v. 1, p. 54.

      Contents. —1. Some medium density
    layouts.

110. Government publication--person as author

```
        Haykin, David Judson, 1896-1959.
          Subject headings; a practical guide. Wash-
        ington, U. S. Govt. Print. Off., 1951.
          v, 140 p.  26 cm.
          At head of title: The Library of Congress.


          1. Subject Headings.  I. U. S.  Library of
        Congress.  II. Title.

        Z695. H36            025. 33          52—60002
        Library of Congress      [a60r52y²15]
```

111. Firm as author

```
        Andersen (Arthur) and Company.
          Tax and trade guide, Venezuela. [Chicago?
        1966]
          xii, 135 p.  col. map.  26 cm.  (Tax and
        trade guide series)
          "Subject file AA6900, item 21. "
          Bibliography: p. 123-124.
          1. Taxation--Venezuela--Law.  2. Industrial
        laws and legislation--Venezuela.  I. Title.

                          340              66—16494
        Library of Congress      [5]
```

112. Association as author

> American Economic Association.
> Readings in business cycles; selected by
> a committee of the American Economic As-
> sociation, [edited by Robert A. Gordon and
> Lawrence R. Klein] London, Allen & Unwin,
> 1966.
>
> x, 731 p. tables, diagrs. 22 1/2 cm.
> 48/-
> (B 66—11287)
> Bibliographical footnotes.
>
> 1. Business cycles--Addresses, essays,

113. Name of conference as heading including place and date
held

> National Conference on Law and Poverty, Wash-
> ington, D.C., 1965.
> Conference proceedings. Washington, For
> sale by the Superintendent of Documents,
> U.S. Govt. Print. Off. [1966]
>
> xvi, 200 p. 24 cm.
>
> "Co-sponsored by the Department of
> Justice and the Office of Economic Oppor-
> tunity."
> Bibliography: p. 181-200.

114. Main entry under first author, both authors in title.
     Note tracing

    Floherty, John J
        Skin-diving adventures, by John J. Floherty
    and Mike McGrady. Lippincott 1962
    192p illus
        "Firsthand story of the men and women who
    search beneath the sea--for sport, for excite-
    ment, for treasure, or for knowledge. A Pu-
    get Sound skin diver wrestles the many-armed
    octopus; a Mexican youth stalks a 300-pound
    monster-fish with a spear gun; a photographer
    rubs elbows with a hungry shark, a treasure
    hunter uncovers ancient pirate ships; an ar-
    chaeologist looks for sunken cities, and a
                                (Continued on next card)

---

115. Main entry under first author, both authors in title.
     Note tracing

    Floherty, John J Skin-diving adventures.
        1962. (Card 2)

    SCUBA scientist searches for data. " Publish-
    er's note

    1 Skin and scuba diving I Jt. auth. II Title
                                                627. 7

    62W16, 678   (W) The H. W. Wilson
                                  Company

---

116. Main entry under first author, both authors in title.
Note tracing

> Owen, Wilfred.
>   Wheels, by Wilfred Owen, Ezra Bowen,
> and the editors of Life. New York, Time
> inc. [1967]
>
>   200 p. illus. (part col.) map. 28cm.
> (Life science library)
>   Bibliography: p. 196.
>
>   1. Wheels. I. Bowen, Ezra, joint author.
> II. Life (Chicago)
> TJ181. 5. O9   388   67—14186
>   Library of Congress   [67g^{3}10]

117. Main entry under first author--Person and a corporate
author

> Raymond, Louise, 1907-
>   Good Housekeeping's book of today's eti-
> quette, by Louise Raymond with Good
> Housekeeping Institute. Illus. by Burmah
> Burris. [1st ed.] New York, Harper & Row
> [1965]
>
>   vii, 470 p. illus. 24 cm.
>   1. Etiquette. I. Good Housekeeping Insti-
> tute, New York. II. Title. III. Title: Book of
> today's etiquette.
>
> BJ1853. R33   395   64—18095
>   Library of Congress   [66j4]

118. Main entry for an adaptation

```
398
M16       Macleod, Mary, d. 1914.
              The book of King Arthur and his noble
          knights: stories from Sir Thomas Malory's
          Morte Darthur.        New York, F. A.
          Stokes Co.   [n. d. ]
              370 p.    illus.
```

119. Anonymous classic--main entry

```
          Arabian nights.
              The portable Arabian nights; edited and
          with an introd. , by Joseph Campbell. [John
          Payne, translator] New York, Viking Press,
          1952.
              xiv, 786 p.   17 cm. (The Viking portable
          library)

              I. Campbell, Joseph, 1904-       ed.

          PJ7715.P3 1952     [398.21]  892.73 52—7413
          Library of Congress   [64n1/2]
```

120. Sacred book--main entry

> Bible. English. 1952. Authorized. O. T.
> Psalms.
>   The book of Psalms, from the Authorized
> King James version of the Holy Bible. New
> York, Priv. print., press of A. Colish, 1952.
>
> xii, 195 p. 15 cm.
>
>   "Four hundred and fifty copies ... number
> 94."
>
> BS1422 1952   53—26242
> Library of Congress   [1]

121. Editor in author position

> Forman, Charles W   ed.
>   Christianity in the non-western world,
> edited by Charles W. Forman. Englewood
> Cliffs, N. J., Prentice-Hall [1967]
>
>   viii, 146 p. maps. 21 cm. (The Global
> history series)
>
>   A Spectrum book.
>   Bibliography: p. 143-146.

122. Composite work--main entry under editor--first con-
     tributor mentioned in title

Hoffman, George Walter, 1914-   ed.
   A geography of Europe. Contributors:
Nels A. Bengtson [and others] New York,
Ronald Press Co. [1953]

   ix, 775 p. illus., maps. 24 cm.

   Includes bibliographies.

   1. Europe--Descr. & trav. --1945-
I. Title.

D907. H6   914   53—5719
   Library of Congress [60I^{2}2]

---

123. Composite work--main entry under title--first contrib-
     utor mentioned in title

Note

Grand slam; the secrets of power baseball, by
Jim Bunning [and others] New York, Viking
Press [1965]

   126 p. illus., ports. 23 cm.

   Contents. --My kind of pitching, by J.
Bunning. --Pitching, by W. Ford. --Power
hitting, by M. Mantle. --Hitting and running,
by W. Mays.

   1. Baseball--Addresses, essays, lec-

---

124. Title in author position

The Best American short stories.
    Fifty best American short stories, 1915-
1965. Edited by Martha Foley. Boston,
Houghton Mifflin, 1965.

    x, 814 p. 22 cm.

    1. Short stories, American. I. Foley,
Martha, ed. II. Title.

    PZ1.B446234Fi   65—11538

    Library of Congress   [66p5]

---

125. Periodical title in author position--main entry for book

---

    The Saturday evening post.
        The Post reader of fantasy and science
fiction. Selected by the editors of the Satur-
day evening post. [1st ed.] Garden City,
N. Y., Doubleday, 1964.

    311 p. 22 cm.

    1. Science fiction. I. Title.

    PZ1. S234Pn   64—11293

    Library of Congress   [64f2]

---

126. Periodical title in author position--main entry for book

```
        Life (Periodical)
            The wonders of life on earth, by the editors
        of Life and Lincoln Barnett.  Time, inc.  1960
        300p illus maps
                Companion volume to: The world we live in
                Based on articles which appeared in Life
            from 1957 to 1959 with many new illustra-
            tions added
                Following the route of Darwin's expedi-
            tion and studies, this copiously illustrated
            book tells the story of life: what "it is,
            what has shaped it, and how--through cease-
            less change and proliferation--it has unfolded
```

127. Encyclopedia--main entry under title

```
        The Columbia encyclopedia, edited by William
            Bridgwater and Elizabeth J. Sherwood.  2d
            ed.  New York, Columbia University Press,
            1950.

            2203 p.  31 cm.

            Kept up to date by cumulative supplements.

            1. Encyclopedias and dictionaries.  I.
        Bridgwater, William, ed.  II. Columbia Uni-
        versity.

        AG5.C725   1950        031        50—11218 rev 2

        Library of Congress      [r62f²5]
```

128. Continuation--main entry under title gives date of first
     volume, frequency, etc.

> The Journal of the astronautical sciences.
>   v. 1-   fall 1954-
>   [New York, American Astronautical Society]
>   v. in   illus., ports., diagrs. 24-
>   29 cm. quarterly.
>   Title varies: fall 1954-spring 1955, Astro-
>   nautics.--summer 1955--winter 1957, The
>   Journal of astronautics.
>   1. Astronautics--Period. I. American
>   Astronautical Society.
>
>   TL787.A6A3   62—3158
>   Library of Congress   [5]

IV. Edition statement, imprint, collation, series and
    other notes

129. Edition statement for first edition--unnecessary for
     small general library, but correct so not marked out

> Cassels, Louis.
>   What's the difference? A comparison of
>   the faiths men live by. [1st ed.] Garden
>   City, N.Y., Doubleday, 1965.
>
>   xi, 221 p. 22 cm.
>
>
>   1. Creeds--Comparative studies. 2. Re-
>   ligions.   I. Title.
>
>   BL425.C3   291   65—17248
>   Library of Congress   [5]

130. Imprint bracketed as not on title page

Year.
    Year's pictorial history of the American
Negro. [Maplewood, N. J., C. S. Hammond,
1965]

    144 p. illus., facsims., ports. 20 cm.

    Bibliography: p. 142.

    1. Negroes--Hist. 2. Negroes--Civil
rights. I. Title.

E185. Y4   301. 451   65—18139

Library of Congress   [42-1]

---

131. Name of state omitted in imprint as first word of head-
    ing

New York. State College of Ceramics, <u>Alfred.</u>
    <u>Library.</u>
    Library publication.
Alfred.

    no. in   v. 29 cm.

    Title varies: Publication.

Z881. N675   53—16064 rev ‡

Library of Congress   [r61b1/2]

---

132. Imprint for mimeographed material

Adams, James Frederick, 1927-
  A workbook to occupations. [Spokane]
Mimeographed by the Mimeograph Office of
Whitworth College, c1953.
  1 v. illus. 30 cm.

  To be used with Dictionary of occupation-
al titles, prepared by Division of Occupa-
tional Analysis, U. S. Employment Service.

  1. Occupations--Terminology. 2. Occu-
pations--Classification. I. U. S. Employ-

---

133. Subject series--series note and added entry under ser-
     ies

Dickinson, Emily, 1830-1886.
  Poems; selected and edited with a com-
mentary by Louis Untermeyer, and illustrated with drawings by Helen Sewell. New
York, Heritage Press [1952]

  xxviii, 284 p. illus. 26 cm. (The American poets)

  (Series)

PS1541. A6 1952a   811. 49   53—1806

Library of Congress   [5]

---

134. Publisher's series--unnecessary to include in description, but correct so not marked out

---

Lee, Maureen.
    A house in Paris: a one-act play with seven female characters (and one male voice off stage) by Maggie Northe. London, Deane; Boston (Mass.), Baker [1966]

    25 p. 18 1/2 cm. (Deane's series of plays) 2/6

                    (B 66—6454)

    I. Title.

PR6062. E4H6   822. 914   66—78773
Library of Congress   [2]

---

135. Series note including number of items--tracing

Tyler, Poyntz, ed.
    Securities, exchanges and the SEC. New York, H. W. Wilson Co., 1965.

    201 p. 20 cm. (The Reference shelf, v. 37, no. 3)

    Bibliography: p. 186-193.

    1. Securities--U. S. 2. Stock-exchange--U. S. 3. U. S. Securities and Exchange Commission. I. Title. (Series)

HG4910. T9   332.60973 64—25034

Library of Congress   [65q28]

---

136. Contents for work in two volumes

> Cézanne, Paul, 1839-1906.
> Paul Cézanne sketch book, owned by the
> Art Institute of Chicago. New York, C.
> Valentin, 1951.
> 2 v. illus. 15 x 23 cm.
> Contents. --1. Introductory text, by C. O.
> Schniewind. Contents of the sketchbook. --
> 2. Plates.
>
> I. Chicago. Art Institute.
>
> NC248. C37A47　　741. 91　　　52—1411
> 　　　Library of Congress　　[7]

137. Note for bibliography--first page of bibliography not
numbered in book, hence bracketed

> Hignett, Charles.
> A history of the Athenian Constitution to
> the end of the fifth century B. C. Oxford,
> Clarendon Press, 1952.
> x, 420 p. 23 cm.
> Bibliography: p. [398]-401.
>
> 1. Athens--Constitutional history.
>
> JC79. A8H5　　　　342.3809　　53—1875
> 　　　Library of Congress　　[66d1]

138. Note about changed title and tracing for former title
      added

Wilson, Amy V
    A nurse in the Yukon [by] Amy V. Wil-
son. New York, Dodd, Mead [1966]

    209 p. illus. , map. 21 cm.

    First published in 1965 under title: No man
stands alone.

    I. Title.   II. Title: No man stands
alone.

RT37.W53A3 1966   610.730924   66—27940

Library of Congress   [67h7]

---

139. Appendixes important for small library added on printed
      card

Lincoln, Frederick Charles, 1892-
    Migration of birds. Illustrated by Bob
Hines. Garden City, N.Y. , Doubleday, 1952.

    102 p. illus. 20 cm.

    Bibliography: p. 94-98.

    Appendixes: I. List of birds mentioned in
the text. -II. Bird banding.

    1. Birds--Migration.

QL698.L479   598. 2   52—5234

Library of Congress   [20]

---

140. Tracing--title and catch title

> Hogan, Inez, 1895-
>   Read to me about the littlest cowboy;
> written and illustrated by Inez Hogan. [1st
> ed.] New York, Dutton [1951]
>   45 p. illus. 26 cm.
>
>   Music on lining papers.
>
>   I. Title. II. Title: The littlest cowboy.
>
> PZ7. H683Re   51—9926 rev
>   Library of Congress   [r53k10]

141. Tracing--translator, editor, catch title, series with au-
      thor and title and number of item

> Goethe, Johann Wolfgang von, 1749-1832.
>   George Ticknor's The sorrows of young
> Werter; edited with introd. and critical
> analysis by Frank G. Ryder. Chapel Hill,
> 1952.
>
>   xxxiii, 108 p. 24 cm. (The University of
> North Carolina studies in comparative liter-
> ature, no. 4)
>
>   Bibliographical references: p. [105]-108.
>
>   I. Ticknor, George, 1791-1871, tr. II.
> Ryder, Frank Glessner, 1916-   ed. III.
>   (Continued on next card)

142. Tracing--translator, editor, catch title, series with
      author and title and number of item

```
    Goethe, Johann Wolfgang von, 1749-1832.
      George Ticknor's The sorrows of young
    Werter.  1952.  (Card 2)




      Title: The sorrows of young Werter.  (Ser-
      ies: North Carolina. University.  Studies in
      comparative literature, no. 4)

      PT2027.W3  1952       832.62           52—4994

      Library of Congress     [7]
```

V. Dramatization of a work

143. Main entry for work dramatized, note concerning dra-
      matization

```
    McLean,  Kathryn (Anderson) 1909-
        ... Mama's bank account. New York, Har-
    court,  Brace and company [1943]

        5 p. 1., 3-204 p.  20 cm.

        Author's pseud., Kathryn Forbes, at head
    of title.
        "First edition."

        Dramatized by John Van Druten and pub-
    lished under title: I remember mama.

        I. Title.

    PZ3.M22367 Mam                        43—4313
    Library of Congress      [66r45e³1]
```

144. Main entry for work dramatized, note concerning dramatization

---

Benson, Sally, 1900-
  Junior miss, by Sally Benson ... Garden
City, N. Y. , Doubleday & company, inc.
[1947?]
  4 p. 1. , 11-214 p. 20 1/2 cm. (Young
moderns)
  Dramatized by Jerome Chodorov and published under same title.
  I. Title.

PZ3. B44356Ju 4   47—20097
  Library of Congress [60f1/2]

---

145. Tracing shows added entry for original author

Chodorov, Jerome.
  Junior miss; comedy in three acts, by Jerome Chodorov and Joseph Fields, based on the book by Sally Benson. [New York] Dramatists play service, inc. [1944]
  92 p. front. , diagr. 19cm.
  "Revised. "
  I. Fields, Joseph, 1895- joint author. II.
Benson, Sally, 1900- Junior miss. III. Title.
              44—3222
  Library of Congress PS3505. H812J8 1944
        [3]   812. 5

---

146. Main entry for dramatization--same author for both--
tracing shows added entry for joint author of dramatization

Wright, Richard, 1908-
    Native son (the biography of a young
American) a play in ten scenes by Paul
Green and Richard Wright, from the novel
by Richard Wright. A Mercury production
by Orson Welles, presented by Orson Welles
and John Houseman. New York and London,
Harper & brothers [c1941]

    ix p., 1 l., 148 p. front. 21 cm.

    Includes songs with music.
"First edition."

VI. Audio-visual materials

147. Filmstrip--main entry showing number of frames, color,
width in millimeters

The Glacial valley (Filmstrip) Society for Visual Education, 1966.

    63 fr. color. 35 mm. and phonodisc: 1 s.
12 in., 33 1/2 rpm., 17 min. (Earth science:
the evolution of landscapes)

    With teacher's guide.
    Credits: Authors, Harold R. Hungerford,
John R. Neel.
    Summary: Discusses the development of
glaciers and the role of present-day valley
glaciation in the development of landscape

(Continued on next card)

---

148. Filmstrip--main entry showing number of frames,
      color, width in millimeters

The Glacial valley (Filmstrip) 1966.   (Card 2)

features. Explains how to interpret the landscape of a glacial valley.

1. Glaciers. I. Society for Visual Education, inc., Chicago.   Series: Earth science:
the evolution of landscapes (Filmstrip)

                                    Fi A 66—3135
Society for Visual   Education for
  Library of Congress   [1 1/2]

---

149. Filmstrip with teacher's manual and guide book

Beyond the stars (Filmstrip) Moody Institute
of Science of the Moody Bible Institute,
1952.

54 fr., color, 35 mm. (Sermons from science)

Adapted from the motion pictures God of
Creation and Hidden treasures.
With teacher's manual and guide book.
Summary: Photographs of the heavens are
presented as evidence of the power and glory
of God.

                              (Continued on next card)

150.   Filmstrip with teacher's manual and guide book

Beyond the stars (Filmstrip) 1952.   (Card 2)

   Ansco color.

   1. God--Omnipotence.   I. Moody Bible
Institute of Chicago.   II. God of Creation
(Motion picture)   III. Hidden treasures (Mo-
tion picture)   (Series: Sermons from sci-
ence (Filmstrip))
                                231. 4   Fi 52—1322
   Library of Congress   [9]

---

151.   Phonodisc--main entry--conventional title, title, number of sides, diameter, revolutions per minute, notes

---

Mozart, Johann Chrysostom Wolfgang Amadeus,
   1756-1791.
      [Symphony, K. 551, C major]   Phonodisc.

      Symphony no. 41 in C major, K. 551 (Jupi-
ter). Angel ANG. 35459. [1957]

      1 s.   12 in.   33 1/3 rpm.   microgroove.

      Royal Philharmonic Orchestra; Sir Thomas
Beecham, conductor.
      Program notes by Deryck Cooke on slip-
case.

                                (Continued on next card)

---

152. Phonodisc--main entry--conventional title, title, number of sides, diameter, revolutions per minute, notes

---

Mozart, Johann Chrysostom Wolfgang Amadeus,
Symphony no. 41 [1957] (Card 2)

With the composer's Divertimento, woodwinds, 4 horns & strings, K. 131, D major.

1. Symphonies--To 1800.   I. Royal Philharmonic Orchestra. II. Beecham, Sir Thomas, bart., 1879-1961.

R A 66—170

San Fernando Valley   State Coll. Library
for Library of Congress [1]

---

153. Phonodisc--main entry with contents

Easter at Riverside. [Phonodisc] Westminster
XWN 19125. [1967]
    2 s. 12 in. 33 1/3 rpm. microgroove.
Frederick Swann playing the organ in the Riverside Church, New York; in part with Louise Natale, soprano.
Recorded Dec. 1966.
Program notes on slipcase.

Contents. --Fanfare, by F. Jackson. --Two
· Easter hymns: Come, ye faithful, raise the strain, and Christ, the Lord, is risen today.--The way to Emmaus, solo cantata, by

(Continued on next card)

---

154.   Phonodisc--main entry with contents

Easter at Riverside. [1967] (Card 2)

    J. Weinberger (with Louise Natale)--Easter
chorale preludes from Orgelbüchlein, no.
27-32, by J. S. Bach. --Partita on the Easter
chorale Christ ist erstanden, by R. Purvis.
    1. Organ music. 2. Easter music. 3.
Solo cantatas, Sacred (High voice) I.
Swann, Frederick, 1931-   II. Natale, Louise.

                         R 67—2563

Library of Congress   [2]

Appendix II
Abbreviations

These abbreviations are used anywhere in the entry except that words in the title up to the first mark of punctuation are not to be abbreviated. Abbreviations given on the title page are to be used whether included in this list or not. For a list of abbreviations used in the cataloging of audio-visual materials, see page 221.

abridged	abr.
association	assoc.
augmented	augm.
baronet	bart. [1]
book	bk.
born	b. [1]
Brother, Brothers	Bro., Bros. [2]
bulletin	bull.
colored	col.
Company	Co.
compiled, compiler[1]	comp.
Congress	Cong.
copyright	c
Corporation	Corp.
corrected	corr.
County	Co.
Department	Dept.
died	d. [1]
edited, edition, editor, editors	ed., eds.
engraved, engraver	engr.
enlarged	enl.
et cetera	etc.
His (or Her) Majesty's Stationery Office	H. M. Stationery Off.
illustration, illustrations, illustrator	illus.
incorporated	inc.
introduction, introductory	introd.
Junior	Jr.
limited	ltd. [2]
no date of publication	n. d.
number, numbers	no., nos.
page, pages	p.

part, parts	pt., pts.
portrait, portraits	port., ports.
preface, prefatory	pref.
President	Pres. [3]
press (in publishers' name)	Pr.
printing	print.
privately printed	priv. print.
pseudonym	pseud.
publication, published, publisher, publishers, publishing	pub.
revised	rev.
Saint	St. [4]
second	2d [5]
Senior	Sr.
series	ser.
session	sess.
supplement, supplements, supplemented	suppl.
table	tab.
Territory	Ter.
third	3d[5]
translated, translation, translator[1]	tr.
United States	U. S.
university (as publisher)	Univ.
volume, volumes	v., vol., [6] vols. [6]

Geographical names. Abbreviations for geographical names in headings are to be decided upon and a list made of those to be used in a given catalog. U. S. for United States is customarily used in all headings, but in titles the usage of the title page is followed. The usual abbreviations for states are used when they follow the name of a city. A library may also compile a list of abbreviations for well-known cities to be used whenever they occur on catalog cards, except as the first word of a heading.

Publishers. List of publishers, with their abbreviations, to be used without place: We use the place

Abingdon Press	Abingdon
American Book Company	Am. Bk.
American Library Association	A. L. A.
Appleton-Century-Crofts	Appleton
A. S. Barnes & Company	Barnes, A. S.
Bobbs-Merrill Company, Inc.	Bobbs
R. R. Bowker Company	Bowker
The British Book Centre, Inc.	British Bk. Centre

Coward-McCann, Inc.	Coward-McCann
Thomas Y. Crowell Company	Crowell
Crown Publishers	Crown
The John Day Company	Day
Dodd, Mead & Company, Inc.	Dodd
Doubleday & Company, Inc.	Doubleday
E. P. Dutton & Company, Inc.	Dutton
Farrar, Straus & Giroux, Inc.	Farrar, Straus
Funk & Wagnalls Company, Inc.	Funk
Ginn & Co.	Ginn
Grosset & Dunlap, Inc.	Grosset
Hammond, Inc.	Hammond
Harcourt, Brace & World, Inc.	Harcourt
Harper & Row, Publishers	Harper
D. C. Heath & Company	Heath
Holt, Rinehart, & Winston, Inc.	Holt
Houghton Mifflin Company	Houghton
Alfred A. Knopf, Inc.	Knopf
J. B. Lippincott Company	Lippincott
Little, Brown & Company	Little
Lothrop, Lee & Shepard Company, Inc.	Lothrop
McGraw-Hill Book Company, Inc.	McGraw
The Macmillan Company, Publishers	Macmillan
G. & C. Merriam Company	Merriam
William Morrow & Company, Inc., Publishers	Morrow
Thomas Nelson & Sons	Nelson
W. W. Norton & Company, Inc., Publishers	Norton
L. C. Page & Company, Inc., Publishers	Page
Prentice-Hall, Inc.	Prentice-Hall
G. P. Putnam's Sons, Inc.	Putnam
Rand McNally & Company	Rand McNally
Random House, Inc.	Random House
The Scarecrow Press, Inc.	Scarecrow
Scott, Foresman & Company	Scott
Charles Scribner's Sons	Scribner
Simon and Schuster, Inc., Publishers	Simon & Schuster
Superintendent of Documents, Government Printing Office	Supt. of Doc.
D. Van Nostrand Company, Inc.	Van Nostrand
The Viking Press, Inc.	Viking
Albert Whitman & Company	Whitman, A.

John Wiley & Sons, Inc.   Wiley
The H. W. Wilson Company   Wilson, H. W.
The World Publishing Company   World Pub.

References

1. Used only in headings.

2. Used only in names of firms and other corporate bodies.

3. Used only in a personal name heading.

4. Used only when preceding the name, as St. Paul's Cathedral.

5. All other ordinal numbers are abbreviated as usual, e. g. , 1st, 4th.

6. Used at the beginning of a statement and before a Roman numeral.

Appendix III
Definitions of Technical Terms

Accession. To record books and other similar material added to a library in the order of acquisition. (A. L. A. Glossary)[1]

Accession number. The number given to a volume in the order of its acquisition. (A. L. A. Glossary)

Accession record. The business record of books, etc., added to a library in the order of receipt, giving a condensed description of the book and the essential facts in its library history. (Cutter)[2]

Adaptation. A rewritten form of a literary work modified for a purpose or use other than that for which the original work was intended (A. L. A. Glossary), e.g., Lamb's Tales from Shakespeare.

Added entry. la. An entry, additional to the main entry, under which a bibliographical entity is represented in a catalog; a secondary entry. (A. -A. 1967)[3]

Alternative title. A second title introduced by "or" or its equivalent, e. g., The tempest; or, The enchanted island. (A. -A. 1967)

Analytical entry. An entry for a work or part of a work that is contained in a collection, series, issue of a serial, or other bibliographical unit for which another, comprehensive entry has been made. (A. -A. 1967) An analytical entry may be under the author, subject or title for a "part of a work or of some article contained in a collection (volume of essays, serial, etc.) including a reference to the publication which contains the article or work entered. " (A. L. A. Glossary)

Anonymous. 1. of unknown authorship. (A. -A. 1967)

Anonymous classic. A work of unknown or doubtful authorship, commonly designated by title, which may have appeared in the course of time in many editions, versions, and/or

321

translations. (A. L. A. Glossary)

Author analytical entry. See Analytical entry.

Author entry. An entry of a work in a catalog under its author's name as heading, whether this be a main or an
added heading. The author heading may consist of a
personal or a corporate name or some substitute for it,
e. g., initials, pseudonym, etc. (A. L. A. Glossary)

Author number. See Book number.

Author-title added entry. An added entry consisting of the author and title of a work. (A. -A. 1967)

Authority list or file. An official list of forms selected as
headings in a catalog, giving for author and corporate
names and for the forms of entry of anonymous classics
the sources used for establishing the forms, together
with the variant forms. If the list is a name list, it is
sometimes called Name list and Name file. (A. L. A.
Glossary)

Body of the entry. That portion of a catalog entry that begins
with the title and ends with the imprint. (A. -A. 1967)

Book number. A combination of letters and figures used to
arrange books in the same classification number in alphabetical order. (A. L. A. Glossary)

Call number. See Book number.

Card catalog. A catalog made on separate cards and kept in
trays. (Cutter, adapted)[4]

Catalog. A list of books, maps, etc., arranged according to
some definite plan. As distinguished from a bibliography
it is a list which records, describes, and indexes the
resources of a collection, a library, or a group of libraries.

See also Dictionary catalog. (A. -A. 1967)

Catchword title entry. See Partial title entry.

Classification. "The putting together of like things." Book
classification, as defined by C. A. Cutter, is "the group-

ing of books written on the same or similar subjects. "⁵

Collation. That part of the catalog entry which describes the
work as a material object, enumerating its volumes,
pages . . . and the type and character of its illustrations. (A. L. A. Glossary)

Collection. If by one author: Three or more independent works
or parts of works published together; if by more than
one author: two or more independent works or parts of
works published together and not written for the same
occasion or for the publication in hand. (A. -A. 1967)

Compiler. One who produces a work by collecting and putting
together written or printed matter from the works of
various authors. Also, one who chooses and combines
into one work selections or quotations from one author.
(cf. Editor) (A. -A. 1967)

Composite work. An original work consisting of separate and
distinct parts, by different authors, which constitute
together an integral whole. (A. -A. 1967)

Compound surname. A surname formed from two or more
proper names, often connected by a hyphen, conjunction,
or preposition. (A. -A. 1967)

Contents note. A note in a catalog or a bibliography entry that
lists the contents of a work. (A. L. A. Glossary)

Continuation. 1. A work issued as a supplement to one previously issued. 2. A part issued in continuance of a
book, a serial, or a series.

See also Periodical, Serial. (A. -A. 1967)

Continuation card. See Extension card.

Conventional title. See Uniform title.

Copyright date. The date of copyright as given in the book,
as a rule on the back of the title leaf. (A. L. A. Glossary)

Corporate body. An organization or group of persons that is
identified by a name and that acts or may act as an entity. Corporate bodies cover a broad range of categories

of which the following are typical: associations, institutions, business firms, non-profit enterprises, governments, specific agencies of government, conferences.
(A. -A. 1967)

Cover title. The title printed on the original covers of a book
or pamphlet, or lettered or stamped on the publisher's
binding, as distinguished from the title lettered on the
cover of a particular copy by a binder. (A. -A. 1967)

Cross reference. See Reference, "See also" reference, "See"
reference.

Cutter number. See Book number.

Dictionary catalog. A catalog in which all the entries (author,
title, subject, series, etc.) and their related references
are arranged together in one general alphabet. The subarrangement frequently varies from the strictly alphabetical. (A. -A. 1967)

Discard. A book officially withdrawn from a library collection
because it is unfit for further use or is no longer needed.
(A. L. A. Glossary)

Edition. 1. All the impressions of a work printed at any time
or times from one setting of type, including those printed from stereotype or electrotype plates from that setting (provided, however, that there is no substantial
change in or addition to the text, or no change in make-
up, format, or character of the resulting book). A fac-
simile reproduction constitutes a different edition. 2.
One of the successive forms in which a literary text is
issued either by the author or by a subsequent editor.
3. One of the various printings of a newspaper for the
same day, an issue published less often, as a weekly
edition, or a special issue devoted to a particular subject, as an anniversary number. 4. In edition binding,
all of the copies of a book or other publication produced
and issued in uniform style . . . . (A. L. A. Glossary)

Editor. One who prepares for publication a work or collection
of works or articles not his own. The editorial labor
may be limited to the preparation of the matter for the
printer, or it may include supervision of the printing,
revision (restitution) or elucidation of the text, and the
addition of introduction, notes, and other critical matter.

For certain works it may include the technical direction of a staff of persons engaged in writing or compiling the text. Cf. Compiler. (A. -A. 1967)

Entry. 1. A record of a bibliographical entity in a catalog or list. 2. A heading under which a record of a bibliographical entity is represented in a catalog or list; also, in the case of a work entered under title, the title. . . . See also Heading. (A. -A. 1967)

Entry word. The word by which the entry is arranged in the catalog, usually the first word (other than an article) of the heading. (Cf. Heading) (A. -A. 1967)

Extension card. A catalog card that continues an entry from a preceding card. Sometimes known as Continuation card [or Second card]. (A. L. A. Glossary)

Filing medium. The word, phrase, name, or symbol on a card or material to be filed that determines its place in a systematic arrangement. Sometimes called Filing term or Filing word. (A. L. A. Glossary)

Filing title. See Uniform title.

"First" indention. The distance from the left edge of a catalog card at which, according to predetermined rules, the author heading begins; . . . Also called . . . Author indention. (A. L. A. Glossary)

Form division. A division of a classification schedule or of a subject heading based on form or arrangement of subject matter in books, as for dictionaries or periodicals. (A. L. A. Glossary) The 17th edition of the Dewey Decimal Classification calls these divisions "Standard subdivisions. "

Form heading. A heading used for a form entry in a catalog, e. g. , Encyclopedias and dictionaries, Periodicals, Short stories. Sometimes known as Form Subject Heading. (A. L. A. Glossary)

Guide. A card . . . having a projecting . . . tab higher than the material with which it is used, inserted in a file to indicate arrangement and aid in locating material in the file. For a card the term Guide card is also used. (A. L. A. Glossary)

Half title. 1. A brief title . . . without imprint and usually
    without the author's name, printed on a separate leaf
    preceding the main title page . . . the text or introduc-
    ing the sections of a work. . . . (A. L. A. Glossary)

Hanging indention. Specifically, a form of indention in cata-
    loging in which the first line begins at author indention,
    and succeeding lines at title indention. (A. L. A. Glos-
    sary)

Heading. 2. In cataloging the word, name, or phrase at the
    head of an entry to indicate some special aspect of the
    book (authorship, subject content, series, title, etc.)
    and thereby to bring together in the catalog associated
    and allied material. (A. L. A. Glossary)

Holdings. 1. The books, periodicals, and other material in
    the possession of a library. 2. Specifically, the vol-
    umes or parts of a serial in the possession of a library.
    (A. L. A. Glossary)

Illustration. A pictorial or other representation in or belong-
    ing to a book or other publication, as issued; usually de-
    signed to elucidate the text. In the narrow sense the
    term stands for illustrations within the text (i. e. , those
    which form part of the text page . . .). (A. L. A. Glos-
    sary)

Imprint. 1. The place and date of publication, and the name
    of the publisher or the printer (or sometimes both); or-
    dinarily printed at the foot of the title page. . . . (A. L. A.
    Glossary)

Imprint date. The year of publication or printing as specified
    on the title page. (A. L. A. Glossary)

Indention. Specifically, the distance from the left edge of a
    catalog card at which, according to predetermined rules,
    the various parts of the description and their subsequent
    lines begin. (A. L. A. Glossary)

Introduction date. The date of a book as given at the begin-
    ning or at the end of the introduction. (A. L. A. Glossary)

Joint author. A person who collaborates with one or more as-
    sociates to produce a work in which the contribution of
    each is usually not separable from that of the others.

(A. -A. 1967)

Location mark. A letter, word, group of words, or some distinguishing character added to catalog records, often in
conjunction with the call number, to indicate that a book
is shelved in a certain place, as in a special collection.
Also called Location symbol. (A. L. A. Glossary)

Main entry. 1. The complete catalog record of a bibliographical entity, presented in the form by which the entity is
to be uniformly identified and cited. The main entry
normally includes the tracing of all other headings under which the record is to be represented in the catalog. . . . See also Added entry, Unit card. (A. -A. 1967)

Monograph. A work, collection, or other writing that is not
a serial. (A. -A. 1967)

Monographic series. (Monograph series). See Series 1. (A. -A.
1967)

Name authority file. See Authority list or file.

Notation. A system of symbols, generally letters and figures,
used separately or in combination, to represent the division of a classification scheme. (A. L. A. Glossary)

Open entry. A catalog entry which provides for the addition
of information concerning a work of which the library
does not have a complete set, or about which complete
information is lacking. (A. L. A. Glossary)

Partial title entry. An added entry made for a secondary part
of the title as given on the title page, e. g., a catchword title, subtitle, or alternative title. (A. -A. 1967)

Periodical. A serial appearing or intended to appear indefinitely at regular or stated intervals, generally more
frequently than annually, each issue of which normally
contains separate articles, stories, or other writings.
Newspapers disseminating general news, and the proceedings, papers, or other publications of corporate bodies primarily related to their meetings are not included
in this term. (A. -A. 1967)

Phonodisc, -tape. A recording of sound on the subject named
at the end of each of these terms. (A. -A. 1967)

Phonorecord. Any object on which sound has been recorded.
(A. -A. 1967)

Preface date. The date given at the beginning or end of the
preface. (A. L. A. Glossary)

Pseudonym. A name assumed by an author to conceal or ob-
scure his identity. (A. -A. 1967)

Publisher. The person, firm, or corporate body undertaking
the responsibility for the issue of a book or other printed matter to the public. . . . (A. L. A. Glossary)

Reference. A direction from one heading or entry to another.
(A. -A. 1967)

Second card. See Extension card.

"Second" indention. The distance from the left edge of a
catalog card at which, according to predetermined rules,
the title normally begins; . . . Also called . . . Title
indention and Paragraph indention. (A. L. A. Glossary)

Secondary entry. See Added entry. (A. -A. 1967)

"See also" reference. A direction in a catalog from a term
or name under which entries are listed to another term
or name under which additional or allied information
may be found. (A. L. A. Glossary)

"See" reference. A direction in a catalog from a term or
name under which no entries are listed to a term or
name under which entries are listed. . . . (A. L. A. Glossary)

Sequel. A work, complete in itself, that continues a narrative
from an earlier work. (A. L. A. Glossary)

Serial. A publication issued in successive parts bearing numerical or chronological designations and intended to be continued indefinitely. Serials include periodicals, newspapers, annuals (reports, yearbooks, etc.), the journals,
memoirs, proceedings, transactions, etc. of societies,
and numbered monographic series.

See also Periodical, Series 1. (A.-A. 1967)

Series. 1. A number of separate works issued in succession and related to one another by the fact that each bears a collective title generally appearing at the head of the title page, on the half title, or on the cover; normally issued by the same publisher in a uniform style, frequently in a numerical sequence. Often termed "monographic series,". . . 2. Each of two or more volumes of essays, lectures, articles, or other writings, similar in character and issued in sequence, e. g., Lowell's Among my books, second series. 3. A separately numbered sequence of volumes within a series or serial, e. g., Notes and queries, 1st series, 2d series, etc. (A. -A. 1967)

Series entry. In a catalog, an entry, usually brief, of the several works in the library which belong to a series under the name of the series as a heading. . . . (A. L. A. Glossary)

Series note. In a catalog or a bibliography, a note stating the name of a series to which a book belongs. The series note ordinarily follows the collation. (A. L. A. Glossary)

Shelf list. A record of the books in a library arranged in the order in which they stand on the shelves. (A. L. A. Glossary)

Spine. That part of the cover or binding which conceals the sewed or bound edge of a book, usually bearing the title, and frequently the author. . . . (A. L. A. Glossary)

Subject analytical entry. See Analytical entry.

Subject authority list or file. An official list of subject headings used in a given catalog and the references made to them.

Subject heading. A word or a group of words indicating a subject under which all material dealing with the same theme is entered in a catalog. . . . (A. L. A. Glossary)

Subtitle. The explanatory part of the title following the main title; e. g., The creative adult; self-education in the art of living. (A. L. A. Glossary)

"Third" indention. The distance from the left edge of a catalog card at which, according to predetermined rules, certain parts of the description begin or continue; generally as far to the right of the second indention as the second indention is to the right of the first indention. (A. L. A. Glossary)

Title. 1. In the broad sense, the name of a work, including any alternative title, subtitle, or other associated descriptive matter preceding the author, edition, or imprint statement on the title page. 2. In the narrow sense, the name of a work, exclusive of any alternative title, subtitle, or other associated descriptive matter on the title page. (A. -A. 1967)

Title analytical entry. See Analytical entry.

Title entry. The record of a work in a catalog or a bibliography under the title, generally beginning with the first word not an article. In a card catalog a title entry may be a main entry or an added entry. (A. L. A. Glossary)

Title page. A page at the beginning of a publication, bearing its full title and usually, though not necessarily, the author's (editor's, etc.) name and the imprint. . . . (A. -A. 1967)

Tracing. 1. In the broad sense, any record of entries or references that have been made in connection with the cataloging of a particular work or publication, or with establishing a particular heading. 2. In the narrow sense, the record on the main entry of the additional headings under which the publication is represented in the catalog. (A. -A. 1967)

Uniform title. The particular title by which a work that has appeared under varying titles is to be identified for cataloging purposes. (A. -A. 1967)

Unit card. A basic catalog card, in the form of a main entry, which when duplicated may be used as a unit for all other entries for that work in the catalog by the addition of the appropriate headings. (A. -A. 1967)

Withdrawal. The process of removing from library records all entries for a book no longer in the library. (A. L. A. Glossary)

References

1. A. L. A. Glossary (Chicago, American Library Association, 1943).

2. C. A. Cutter, Rules for a Dictionary Catalog (4th ed. rewritten; Washington, Govt. Print. Off., 1904), p. 13.

3. Definitions with the source indicated in this way are from Anglo-American Cataloging Rules. North American Text (Chicago, American Library Association, 1967), p. 343-48.

4. Cutter, op. cit., p. 14.

5. Corinne Bacor, Classification (rev. ed.; Chicago, American Library Association, 1925), p. 1.

Appendix IV
Aids in the Cataloging of a Small Library

The following list was selected with reference to the availability of the material and its probable usefulness to the librarian of the small library.

A. L. A. Rules for Filing Catalog Cards, 2d ed. abr. Chicago, American Library Association, 1968. 104 p.

Anglo-American Cataloging Rules. North American Text. Chicago, American Library Association, 1967. 400 p.

Barden, Bertha R. Book Numbers; a Manual for Students with a Basic Code of Rules. Chicago, American Library Association, 1937. 31 p.

The Booklist and Subscription Books Bulletin: a Guide to Current Books. Chicago, American Library Association, 1905-
Gives the Dewey Decimal Classification number, subject headings, and the number for Library of Congress printed catalog cards for all books listed.

Cutter, Charles A. Alphabetic Order Table, Altered and Fitted with Three Figures by Kate E. Sanborn. (For sale by The H. R. Huntting Company, Inc., 300 Burnett Rd., Chicopee, Mass. 01020.)

Dewey, Melvil Dewey Decimal Classification and Relative Index. Ed. 17, Lake Placid Club, N. Y., Forest Press, Inc. of Lake Placid Club Education Foundation, 1965. 2 v.

Dewey, Melvil Dewey Decimal Classification and Relative Index. 9th abr. ed. Lake Placid Club, N. Y., Forest Press, Inc., 1965. 594 p.

Douglas, Mary P. The Teacher-Librarian's Handbook. 2d ed. Chicago, American Library Association, 1949. 166 p.

Eaton, Thelma Cataloging and Classification; an Introductory Manual. 3d ed. Champaign, Ill., Distributed by The

332

Illini Union Bookstore [1963]. 199 p.

Haykin, David J. Subject Headings: a Practical Guide. Washington, D. C., Govt. Print. Off., 1951. 140 p.

Herdman, Margaret M. Classification; an Introductory Manual. 2d ed. Chicago, American Library Association, 1947. 50 p.

Kunitz, Stanley J. and Haycraft, Howard. The Junior Book of Authors. 2d ed. rev. New York, Wilson, 1951. 309 p.

Kunitz, Stanley J. and Haycraft, Howard. Twentieth Century Authors, a Biographical Dictionary. New York, Wilson, 1942. 1577 p.

Kunitz, Stanley J. Twentieth Century Authors. First Supplement. A Biographical Dictionary of Modern Literature. New York, Wilson, 1955. 1123 p.

Lake Placid Club Education Foundation. Guide to the Use of Dewey Decimal Classification; Based on the Practice of the Decimal Classification Office at the L. C. Lake Placid Club, Essex Co., N. Y., Forest Press of Lake Placid Club Education Foundation, 1962. 133 p.

Pearson, Mary D. Recordings in the Public Library. Chicago, American Library Association, 1963. 153 p.

Piercy, Esther J. Commonsense Cataloging: a Manual for the Organization of Books and Other Materials in School and Small Public Libraries. New York, Wilson, 1965. 223 p.

Rue, Eloise and LaPlante, Effie. Subject Headings for Children's Materials. Chicago, American Library Association, 1952. 149 p.

Rufsvold, Margaret I. Audio-Visual School Library Service: a Handbook for Libraries. Chicago, American Library Association, 1949. 116 p.

Sayers, William C. B. An Introduction to Library Classification. 9th ed. rev. London, Grafton, 1954. 320 p.

Slocum, Robert B. Sample Catalog Cards Illustrating Solutions to Problems in Descriptive Cataloging. New York, Scarecrow, 1962, 190 p.

Webster's Biographical Dictionary. Springfield, Mass., Mer-
     riam, 1943. 1697 p.

Westby, Barbara M. , ed. Sears List of Subject Headings.
     9th ed. New York, Wilson, 1965. 641 p.

Wilson (H. W.) Company. Children's Catalog. 11th ed. New
     York, Wilson, 1966. 1024 p.

Wilson (H. W.) Company. Standard Catalog for High School
     Libraries. 8th ed. New York, Wilson, 1962. 1257 p.
     Has Supplements.

Wilson (H. W.) Company. Standard Catalog for Public Libra-
     ries, 1959-1963. New York, Wilson, 1964. 526 p.

     The Readers' Guide to Periodical Literature, The
Abridged Readers' Guide, and periodical indexes in particular
fields, e. g., the Education Index, the Industrial Arts Index
are useful in establishing name headings and suggesting subject headings for new subjects. The Special Libraries Association, 31 E. 10th Street, New York, N. Y., 10003, maintains
a file of special classification schemes. Lists of subject headings for special subjects will be found in books, periodicals,
and as printed, photo-offset, etc., lists issued by governmental and other organizations.

Corporate bodies, 111-12; created or controlled by a government, 99-100; government bodies, 99-100
Corporate body, defined, 323
Corporate body or subordinate unit, 84-85
Corporate entry, see Names of organizations
Corporate headings, arrangement in catalog, 263-64
Corporate name entries beginning with a surname, 259
Corporate names, 89-90; additions to, 91-92; changes of names, 92-93; conventional form of name, 90; language, 91; modifications of, 92
Court rules, 87
Courts, 103
Cover title, defined, 324
Cross references, see References
Cutter, C. A., quoted, 43, 57 (reference)
Cutter numbers, see Book numbers
Cutter-Sanborn table, 33-36

Dana, J. C., quoted, 11
Dates: choice of, 133-34; different in different volumes, 134; see also Copyright date; Imprint date; Introduction date; Preface data
Decimal Classification, see Dewey Decimal Classification; Dewey Decimal Classification scheme
Delegations, 105
Demco, address, 286 (reference)
Description of publications: organization, 124; source, 124
Dewey Decimal Classification: Abridged Edition, 35 (reference); changes in, 27-28; different editions, reproduction of parts: of indexes, 19, of tables, 11-14, 16-17; Edition Seventeen, 35 (reference); Relative index, 18
Dewey Decimal Classification scheme, 11-19; choices in numbers, 28
Dictionary catalog, defined, 324
Discard, defined, 324
Distinctive word in subdivision under name of country, underscored, 118 (reference)
"Divide like", 15
Double-spread title page, 122
Double title page, 122
Douglas, M. P., 41, 57 (reference)
Dramatization, sample cards, 310-12

Edition, defined, 324
Edition statement, 130; sample cards, 291, 302-03
Editor, see Author entry, arrangement in catalog
Editor, defined, 324
Editor as author, sample card, 299

Editor of a series, reference card, 166
Editorial direction, works produced under, 80 (reference)
Elisions, arrangement, 260
Embassies, 105
Encyclopedias, 185; sample card, 302
Entry, defined, 325
Entry word, defined, 325
Epics, see Anonymous classics
Explanatory references, 114-15
Extension card: defined, 325; for added entries, 167; items on, 144; rules, 144; sample cards, 45, 143

Fatka, Veda, 236
Fiction, 146-48; items on cards, 147; printed cards, 147; rules, 147; sample cards, 148; title card, 148
Figures, see Numerals
Filing, 250-73
Filing medium, 325
Filmstrips, 208-12; accompanying material, 210; added entries, 212; continuations, 212; credits, 210, 222 (reference); identification number, 208-09; imprint, 210; items in description, 209; Library of Congress printed catalog cards, 209, 211, 312-14; main entry, 209; more than one on a strip, 209; notes, 210; physical description, 210; summary, 212
Firm as author, sample card, 294
"First" indention, 123; defined, 325
Forename entries, 66; arrangement in catalog, 260; with byname, 66
Form division, see Standard subdivisions
Form division, defined, 325
Form headings, 43; defined, 325

Gaylord Bros., address, 286 (reference)
General index, sample card, 143
General reference card, 51; sample card, 51
General subject entry, sample card, 44
Geographical names, 96; abbreviations, 318; additions, 96-97; omissions and alterations, 97
Given name, see Forename
Government officials, 101, 102
Government publications, sample card, 293; with personal author, sample card, 294
Governments, 97-101
Governors, 102
Guide, defined, 325
Guide cards, 250, 283-84

Occupying powers, 98, 102
Old Testament, see Bible
Open entry, defined, 149 (reference), 327
Order of entries, 266-67
Organizations, see Names of organizations

Paging, 135
Partial title, 153; examples, 154; tracing, sample card, 309
Partial title entry, defined, 327
Period divisions, arranged chronologically, 270
Periodical title in author position, sample cards, 301-02
Periodicals, 184; change in title, 187; defined, 327; entry,
     79; rules, 186-88; sample cards, 185-87
Personal author or corporate author, 82-83
Personal names, 58-73; basic rule, 59; choice among dif-
     ferent names, 59; see also Forename entries; Married
     women's names; Noblemen; Pseudonyms
Phonodisc, defined, 327; see also Records
Phonorecord, defined, 201, 328; see also Records
Phonotape, 204; defined, 327
Piercy, E. J., 276
Place (country, state, city), arrangement, 267-68
Popes, 109
Possessive case, see Punctuation marks
Preface date, defined, 328
Prefixes: arrangement in catalog, 262; surnames with, 63-
     65
Presidents, see Chiefs of state, etc.
Presidents as personal authors, 83-84
Printed catalog cards, 223-48; adapting for catalog, 238-40;
     see also Library of Congress cards, Wilson cards
Privately printed book, sample card, 299
Pseudonym included in title, sample card, 292
Pseudonyms: defined, 328; joint, 83; rules for entry, 60-
     61; sample card, 290
Publisher, defined, 328
Publishers used without place, 318-20
Punctuation marks, arrangement in catalog, 269

Radio and television stations, 109
Records: added entries, 207; arrangement, 202; cataloging,
     202-04; collation, 204; contents, 205; conventional title,
     203; identification number, 202; imprint, 203-04; items
     in description, 202; Library of Congress printed catalog
     card, 208; notes, 204-05; separate works on each side,
     206; serials, 206; series notes, 204; sample cards,
     314-16; shelf-list cards, 208; tracing, 207
Reduction of numbers, 18

Shared authorship: added entries, 127-29; rules for entry, 127-29

Shelf arrangement of books within a class, 31

Shelf list, 171-74; accession numbers, 172; arrangement, 172-74; defined, 57 (reference), 171, 329; printed cards, 174, 288, 290; rules, 171-72; sample cards, 173, 193; serials, 192-93; uses of, 171; when to make, 174

Skeleton card showing location of items, 122

Slides, 219-20; added entries, 219; identification number, 219; items in description, 219; sample card, 220

Sovereigns, 101-02

Spacing on cards, 122-23

Spine, defined, 329

Standard subdivisions: defined, 12; examples, 12; see also Form division

Subject analytical entries, 39, 162; arrangement in catalog, 254; sample card, 162

Subject authority file, 53; defined, 329; sample cards, 54-56

Subject authority file on cards, advantages, 57

Subject cross references, see Subject references

Subject entries, 154-55; arrangement in catalog, 270-71; referring to a group of books, 41-42; rules, 155; sample cards, 155, 287-89

Subject headings, 37-57; aids for assigning, 52-53; defined, 329; determining the subject, 38; fiction, 37; number of, 38, 40; organizations, 46; persons, 46; selection 39-40

Subject headings lists, 45-48; checking, 52-53; examples of checking, 47; use, 46

Subject references, 48, 168

Subject subdivisions, 42-43; arrangement in catalog, 270-71

Subordinate agencies and units (Government bodies), 100-01

Subordinate bodies, 93-94; additions to names, 94

Subtitle, defined, 329

Supplements, rules, 143

Surnames, 61-62; see also Personal names

Synthesizing the notation, 13

Technical terms, defined, 321-31

Television stations, 109

"Third" indention, 123; defined, 329

Title: additions, 126; alternative, 126; defined, 330

Title abridgment, 126

Title analytical entries, 159-61; arrangement in catalog, 254; sample card, 161

Title entry: arrangement in catalog, 271; defined, 330